# Why Women Are Poorer Than Men

Annabelle Williams is a journalist and editor who specialises in investing, economics and consumer affairs. Previously a columnist at *The Times*, Williams has appeared on live TV, radio and panel debates talking about her passion for the finance inequality between genders.

*Why Women Are Poorer Than Men And What We Can Do About It* is her first book.

D1388878

# Why Women Are Poorer Than Men

## ...And What We Can Do About It

ANNABELLE WILLIAMS

MICHAEL JOSEPH

MICHAEL JOSEPH

UK | USA | Canada | Ireland | Australia
India | New Zealand | South Africa

Michael Joseph is part of the Penguin Random House group of companies
whose addresses can be found at global.penguinrandomhouse.com

First published by Michael Joseph 2021
001

Typeset by Jouve (UK), Milton Keynes
Printed and bound in Great Britain by Clays Ltd, Elcograf S.p.A.

The authorized representative in the EEA is Penguin Random House Ireland,
Morrison Chambers, 32 Nassau Street, Dublin D02 YH68

A CIP catalogue record for this book is available from the British Library

HB ISBN: 978–0–241–43316–4
OM ISBN: 978–0–241–43833–6

www.greenpenguin.co.uk

To Elisa

# Contents

# Introduction: Finance Is a Feminist Issue

Money gives you freedom. It will never buy you happiness, but having enough money allows you to have choices: over where you live, what you do for work and how you spend your free time.

Money is vital for women's independence. Over the past 150 years, women have fought for the right to own property, to inherit, to borrow and to earn. In 1918 in the UK, wealthy property-owning women over the age of thirty were given the right to vote. Poorer women had to wait until 1928. Access to money determined what women could do a hundred years ago, and it still does today.

The societal implications of how wealth is distributed are hugely important. Who has money today and how much of it they have has a bearing on the future of individuals, communities and society as a whole. Actuaries can look at the levels of money-saving by different demographics and use it to predict what society will look like in thirty years' time. How wealth is shared across a nation speaks volumes about that culture's values. It reflects who policymakers care about and whose concerns they choose to ignore.

In every part of our lives that touches on money women are financially disadvantaged, from work to state benefits, from savings to childcare and entrepreneurship. Essentially, it's accepted as natural that women are poorer than men.

When I started out in financial journalism over a decade ago I became aware of a phrase that's often used in finance:

women 'don't like risk'. It's repeated in press releases and research reports put out by banks, financial advisers and asset managers and is used to explain why women are far less likely to have investments than men. It's also used to say something about female leaders and the way they manage companies. I found this notion that risk aversion is an inherent part of womanhood very odd. Moreover, none of the people I interviewed was able to explain exactly why this might be the case. It seemed clear to me that fewer women invest because they lack the money, the knowledge and exposure to the finance industry. Men vastly outnumber women at professional and managerial levels in investment and banking,[1] so many women don't have mothers, sisters or female friends they can talk to about investments. As for female leaders and risk appetite, we can count on two fingers the number of women prime ministers there have been in the UK and, today, there are just six female CEOs in the FTSE 100 list of leading companies. They are the exception and under extra scrutiny because of their gender, and this combination of exceptionalism and exposure makes their position precarious. If they are more cautious than their male peers, it is no surprise why.

I began reading in my spare time about women and finance, the female relationship to money and women's economic position. It was fascinating, but also deeply complex. The idea that women 'don't like risk' is overly simplistic and fails to take account of the socio-economic circumstances that many find themselves in.

So far, most of the conversation about women and financial equality has focused on the gender pay gap. Most people don't realize that women are poorer than men throughout their lives. Women save less, bear the brunt of cuts to social services and make up the majority of the elderly poor. Women hold fewer of the highest-paying jobs, are less likely to invest their money and are held back financially by providing literally thousands of hours of free labour during their lives. Even among the super-rich, wealth isn't distributed equally. In 2020 the media celebrated a record number of women making it onto The Sunday Times Rich List of Britain's 1,000 wealthiest people. There were just 150 women. Only a single Black woman made the list: Valerie Moran, a technology entrepreneur.

Female economic inequality goes back hundreds of years and, despite decades of legislation, women today are facing the same issues that their grandmothers did. The seeds are sown when girls are of school age, when their choices about what to study are often shaped by gender norms rather than by thoughts about their future financial security. Once in the workplace, unconscious bias proves a barrier to progression and women in many industries struggle to increase their seniority. Globally, women hold only 34 per cent of managerial roles.[2] Only in Colombia, Jamaica and St Lucia do women hold at least half of management positions in the workplace, according to the United Nations Population Fund.[3]

There is no country where women in work collectively earn as much as men for their labour. Across Europe and Australia, women earn an average of 18–19 per cent less than men and the pace of change is so slow that, according to the World Economic Forum, it will take 257 years for the gap to close. During her working life, the typical British woman will earn £223,000 less than the average man, while for an American woman the figure is half a million dollars. Pay gaps are worse for women of colour, with Pakistani and

3

Bangladeshi women earning an average of 26 per cent less than white British men.[4] The gender pay gap is a big problem, but by looking at salaries through the prism of gender we see only one aspect of female wealth inequality.

Sometimes economic inequality is blatantly obvious. Flip through the pages of a newspaper and see how many female experts are quoted talking about business, finance or tax. The absence of women's voices in these areas speaks volumes about our economic position. At other times, it's harder to spot, such as the 'pink premium' added to anything from toiletries to stationery and toys marketed at women and girls, while identical products branded for men and boys cost much less. A man's dollar has greater buying power.

Economic inequality is present in the small things, such as the tax on tampons that has been charged by countries as diverse as India, Australia and Spain. It's also in the big things: female entrepreneurs face sexist scrutiny in the boardroom, and only one penny in every pound of venture capital funding goes to start-ups run by women.

This inequality is exacerbated by male-dominated governments who make decisions about tax and welfare policy without considering the gendered effects of their actions. One of the clearest examples is when governments decide to cut budgets for healthcare and state support – cuts that largely affect women because they are more involved in caring roles and are more reliant on state support. In the UK, the slashing of budgets for social services and social security since 2010 has cost women £79 billion, compared to £13 billion for men.[5]

In the past few years, a new breed of work and money guru feminists has emerged. These are typically high-earning women with corporate careers who are laser-focused on conquering their corner of the business world, and they advise other women on how to thrive in it too. The advice is generally centred around asking for a pay rise, advocating for oneself in the office and, to use a phrase that's now become a cliché, to 'lean in' to their careers.

This line of thinking suggests that women can achieve equality with men in the workplace and financially if only they go about it in the right way. So what happens if a woman asks for a pay rise and doesn't get it? With this philosophy, the explanation would be that she didn't approach it in the correct way. This narrative ignores the systemic, legal and cultural factors that hold women back. By all means, be your own best friend, but economic inequality runs much deeper than how much women get paid, and no amount of self-advocacy at work will change a system that is structured to keep women poorer. This 'lean in' approach is also based on a fallacy: research has found that women ask for pay rises as frequently as men but are 25 per cent less likely to be given them.[6] It's structural sexism and assumptions about women's worth that keep us down.

Of course, women who help others follow in their footsteps are doing so with the best intentions. But there is little point in exhorting women to spend less in the supermarket and open a savings account paying 1.3 per cent interest instead of 1.1 per cent without acknowledging that the bigger problem is changing the reasons why women are poorer than men in the first place. Moreover, the solutions that many work-and-money gurus are spreading are highly influenced by the principles of neoliberalism, a form of free-market capitalism. This has become so widespread that scholars now refer to 'neoliberal feminists'.

Neoliberal feminism is a mash-up of women's rights feminism and neoliberalism, the dominant ideology of our time, which says that to create flourishing societies governments must maximize wealth creation. Neoliberalism is ignorant of social justice. It's behind the trend for limited government spending, deregulation and fierce individualism, and it promotes the idea that welfare is best delivered informally (and for free) in communities rather than through the state. Who will end up providing that welfare? Who keeps the healthcare system and social services running in spite of government cuts, by working harder? Women. Neoliberalism is an ideology that has been responsible for increasing inequality and creating hardship through the decimation of state healthcare and social services.[7] Given that women are suffering disproportionately from the injustices created by neoliberalism, the emergence of neoliberal feminism is a worrying trend.

The last century of capitalism and free-market economics has raised living standards for many, but there are limits to what the current economic model can achieve. Yet it's not too late to temper this philosophy to create a fairer world for women.

This isn't a book about smashing the glass ceiling. With its focus on high-earners seeking the most prestigious jobs, the glass ceiling is a concept that resonates with a minority of women. It obscures the widespread nature of economic inequality that affects women of all income levels and at every stage of our lives.

No individual can fight economic inequality on their own. Any narrative that suggests people should ignore the context and focus solely on what they can do to change their lives is foolish. If the rules of the game are unfair, we need to change them. Many of the problems outlined above are deeply rooted, and it will take institutional, political and legislative change to ensure that both genders have equal access to wealth.

Throughout my career I've been passionate about fighting economic inequality and championing women's issues. I wrote this book to start some much-needed conversations about gender, money and fairness. It would be impossible for me to have all the answers to a problem that sprawls generations and has seeped into every area of our lives, but there are many things we can try. I've outlined areas for change throughout this book.

While overarching change requires collective action, on a personal level everyone could benefit from adopting the mindset that taking care of your money is a vital part of self-care. Saving money today shows you care about your future self as much as yourself today. So I've included sections on how to understand pensions and investing.

This book is about how we can address female economic inequality, but there is no suggestion that every man is wealthier than every woman, or that poverty and economic injustice do not affect men. Men are twice as likely as women to struggle with drug and alcohol disorders, which can be risk factors for poverty and homelessness.[8] Unrestrained neoliberal capitalism has created social injustices that affect everybody, for example, the expansion of insecure, low-paid employment. The terms 'mancession' and 'he-cession' were coined to describe the economic downturn of 2007–9, when men were particularly badly affected by the demise of manufacturing and heavy industry in the West. A man can't sell his strength as he once could. The economic shift towards service-led and information industries that's been underway for the past thirty years may suggest that the workplace of the future favours stereotypically feminine qualities – communication, cooperation and social intelligence. Machines can't replicate these qualities, or not yet, anyway. Over time, changes in the type and availability of work have profound effects on communities and no doubt there will be more conversations to be had in this area. So, while the intersection of masculinity with poverty is a serious problem that deserves more attention, it is beyond the scope of this book.

It's also vital to emphasize that gender equality isn't a zero-sum game. Men don't lose out when women are able to spend more time in paid work, do the jobs that match their skills and experience, or have bigger retirement funds. The exact reverse is true. Societies are held back when half the population is frustrated in their ambitions, whatever form this takes. Spread the good news: prosperity for women means prosperity for all.

The ramifications are local, as wealth inequality places greater burdens on men and makes life harder for anyone involved in a caring role. They are generational, as inequality limits opportunities for the next generation. Wealthier people benefit the wider economy as they pay more taxes, lift their households out of poverty, spend more, invest in education, and exercise more control over their lives.[9] Improved participation in the workforce among ethnic minorities (where fewer women work and face larger pay gaps when they do) could add £24 billion to the UK economy.[10] Gender parity is, to an extent, dependent on personal choices, such as participation in the workforce. It isn't necessarily a normative ideal. But in capitalist societies, a person's independence, power and opportunities for self-determination are largely reliant on access to wealth. This has historically been denied to women, and there are still structural barriers limiting our access. Money is the last area of gender inequality that has yet to be seriously tackled – and I believe it's the most important. I don't believe you can be a feminist and not care about money. You cannot be in favour of gender equality and over-look the foundation from which inequality grows: money.

This book is written from a Western European perspec-tive with a focus on Western European culture. My focus is on the West because in these countries people tend to believe that the equality battle is over. It's not. Hidden inequality persists in the realms of money and wealth.

Clearly, women living in economically developing nations also face monetary inequality and deprivation – and often far worse than women in the West – but these problems tend to have different causes and require different solutions. Development economics is a field that has been transformed over the past twenty years thanks to the work of Abhijit Banerjee, Esther Duflo and Michael Kremer, who won the Nobel Prize in Economics in 2019. There will hopefully be more transformative work to eradicate poverty in the future.

A note about gender categorization. When I use the term 'women' I am typically referring to cisgender people, and this is because there is little research about the relationship between financial exclusion and its interaction with gender diversity (or sexual identity), although, where possible, I have tried to include this. For example, larger companies in Britain have to report their gender pay gap as the difference between male and female employees' earnings, but it is unclear how employers should categorize transgender and non-binary staff who don't fit neatly into either 'male' or 'female'.[11] We don't know how not conforming to the gender binary model affects wealth and wages, and this data gap needs to be addressed.

For the same reason, in some sections I've used pronouns that refer to heterosexual relationships. The data gap means that the effect of marriage and divorce on the personal finances and pension savings of LGBTQ+ people is largely unrecorded. There is also the fact that women and men in long-term relationships often shift towards traditional gender roles once there is a child in the picture or someone in the family needs looking after.

I'm also aware that it's impossible to discuss a subject, to represent anything, without showing a particular interpretation of the subject. There is no one way to 'be' a woman, but any book, film, advert or other creative work which includes women will have to depict them in a certain way.

When women are repeatedly portrayed in one light, it can inadvertently reinforce those gender norms. In this book, whenever I discuss the male breadwinner and female homemaker stereotypes, be aware that I'm using these tropes because they are what the data is based upon. My point is that this old dynamic persists because it's facilitated by the structure of the societies in which we live. Undoubtedly the characterization of women as 'caregivers' will sit uncomfortably with many women who haven't assumed those roles. But, unfortunately, subtle discrimination on the basis of sex persists regardless of whether we're involved in caring roles or not.

As this book was finalized at the start of 2020, the Covid-19 pandemic broke out. The pandemic brought female economic inequality into the spotlight. While the world went into lockdown, women headed straight into the path of the virus as cooks, cleaners and care workers in essential services. Half of frontline care workers earn less than the living wage and they are four times as likely to be on insecure zero-hours contracts.[12]

While these women were suddenly being referred to as 'key workers' by politicians, there was no legislative change to ensure they earned enough to pay their bills and feed their families. Their working conditions didn't improve, they weren't given contracts that guaranteed them paid work each week, and as the nation 'Clapped for Carers' from their windows every week I wondered if this was the best we could do.

The response to the pandemic from governments across the world was to rewrite the rules of acceptable economics. After more than a decade of Britain's ruling Conservative party cutting public spending to the absolute minimum, being content to let female poverty and homelessness rise while schools and hospitals were on the cusp of bankruptcy, the narrative changed. By June 2020 the government had spent an extra £190 billion – that's more than the entire year's budget for the health service[13] – a level of spending which had previously been considered either totally unacceptable or outright immoral.

Meanwhile, the world's twenty biggest economies were kept afloat with government support worth $9 trillion by the end of May.[14] Decisions to borrow and spend jaw-dropping sums were seemingly made at the drop of a hat. Very rarely is there such an upheaval in economic orthodoxy.

If there's one lesson we can take from the Covid-19 pandemic, it's that we're constantly told the economic status quo cannot change, that social reform is impossible – until the day it suddenly isn't. Throughout this book I touch on issues which at their core are the result of sexist and discriminatory government spending decisions, and other problems unique to women that could benefit from revisions to policy.

We are living through a period of once-in-a-generation change and it is vital that feminists capitalize on this moment to ensure that women's needs are at the top of the policy agenda while societies rebuild from the rubble of corona-ruin.

Let's unite to end female financial inequality – let's make money equal.

# 1. Where We Are Today

Despite everything that's been achieved for women, some of the richest countries in the world are blighted by gendered inequality in wealth. We all know about the gender pay gap, but what isn't discussed enough is the wealth gap this creates. 'Wealth' doesn't mean riches and CEO-level pay but the savings that working women can accumulate during their careers when they earn less, on average, than men.

There's already a wealth gap between men and women under the age of forty-five in Britain, but it widens with age, so that the average British woman aged between forty-five and sixty-four has wealth of £293,700, while men in that age bracket have, on average, wealth of £376,500.[1] And the wealth gap in the US is huge: the median single American man aged between eighteen and sixty-four has wealth of $31,150, while his female counterpart has $15,120 – less than half of the man's amount.[2]

To illustrate the extent of female economic inequality in the UK, consider this.

What would you say was the number-one reason women are prosecuted for breaking the law? Shoplifting? Public intoxication? Driving offences?

It's for being too poor to pay for a television licence.[3]

By law, every household watching live television through a TV set or online has to pay £157.50 annually towards funding the BBC, the country's public service broadcaster. Not buying a licence is a criminal offence and people can be prosecuted, fined up to £1,000 and may even go to prison for not paying. Nearly three-quarters of those prosecuted for this crime of poverty are women – over 96,000 of them in 2017.[4] The licence is controversial and there are people who refuse to pay out of principle. But women are more likely to answer the door to the enforcement officers when they visit, more willing to engage with them, and they form the majority of those on a scheme to manage the payments – all of which suggests that women aren't paying because they can't afford to, not because of opposition to the system.

This pay-or-be-prosecuted system is gender blind. It's a government-mandated cost which requires an equal contribution from every household, every year, irrespective of income, and it makes criminals of those who cannot afford to pay – mostly women. But this is just the tip of the iceberg of the systemic disadvantages that women face.

## Feminized poverty

The TV-licence situation is a small example of a problem that social scientists call 'the feminization of poverty'. The term was first coined in 1978 by Professor Diana Pearce, but it hasn't gone away. Around the world, on every measure used to assess wealth and poverty, from cradle to grave, women fare worse than men. Women make up the majority of the poor in both developed and developing countries[5] and they are more likely than men to be unemployed or vulnerably employed.[6] Globally, men are nearly twice as likely as women to have 'good jobs' – that is, be in full-time paid work for an employer; in South Asia, they are more than three times as likely.[7]

There's a regular pattern to the statistics across the developed world. In Japan, 31 per cent of working-age women who live alone are in poverty, compared to 25 per cent of men.[8] Across the US, 14 per cent of females survive on incomes below the poverty line, compared to 11 per cent of males.[9]

While these nuggets of data give a glimpse into feminized poverty, the intricacies of women and wealth inequality remain an area that has been badly under-researched, especially in rich countries. No problem can be addressed without proper data about its causes and consequences. In 2019 the UK government announced plans to formulate more accurate measures of deprivation, but the project was put on hold by the Covid-19 pandemic. When the gendered facts of economic inequality remain under-researched and little discussed, women lose out.

The most widely used benchmark for poverty in Europe is a person or household having less than 60 per cent of the income of the median household in that country. This means that statisticians take the salaries of every household, arrange them in a list from lowest to highest, and calculate the middle figure – this would be the amount that the typical person lives off. Not every person can have the average income but everybody can have at least 60 per cent of what the typical person has.

In pounds and pence, Britain's Joseph Rowntree Foundation estimates that the average median income for UK households after housing costs was £425 a week (£22,100 a year) in 2016–17, so an income of 60 per cent of this would be below £13,260. Based on this 5.1 million women are in poverty, alongside 4.6 million children and 4.5 million men, according to the Social Metrics Commission.[10] That equates to 20 per cent of women, 34 per cent of children and 18 per cent of men.

One of the main drivers of feminized poverty in the UK and US has been the increase in lone parents since the 1980s, of whom 90 per cent are women. Figures for the US show that in 1960, single-mother families made up 28 per cent of those in poverty, but by 1987 this had more than doubled to 60 per cent.[11] In Britain today, 45 per cent of single parents live in poverty – which means their children are living in poverty, too. Although the government introduced legally binding targets for reducing rates of child poverty in 2010, it removed them in 2016 and has no plans for reinstatement.

Single women overall – including older women who have been widowed and younger women without partners – have higher poverty rates than men in Britain, and over the past few years the proportion of single men who are poor has fallen.[12] Disability is also a factor that jumps out of the data. Some 3.7 million people living in poverty are disabled, and there are more disabled women (54.4 per cent) than men.[13] Who do you think is looking after them? Nearly three-quarters of family carers (read: 'unpaid carers') are women – and let's not forget that women make up almost 80 per cent of the paid workers in the care sector, which is also among the lowest-paid fields.

The governments of wealthy countries can strongly influence incomes through specific policies – through employer regulations such as the minimum wage and sick pay, through the tax system and through redistribution of wealth via the welfare state. These mechanisms give the state sway over the levels of poverty and wealth inequality within society, and it can choose which social groups to support and which are left to flounder (in Chapter 6 we'll look more closely at how the welfare state is failing women).

Poverty among women can also be rendered invisible under a cloak of 'protection' from men. This is because women almost always appear richer when they are living in households with others, usually their male partners. Statisticians focus on household wealth when examining relative wealth, a method which is straightforward in single-person households when the person who earns the money is also the one who decides where it's spent. But in couple households, often one person is designated the 'financial reporter' and they share details of the family's assets. The assumption is that household wealth is split equally between the adults in each home, so women on lower salaries living with higher-earning partners are pulled up into the wealthier household demographics.

This distorts the data and makes it hard to gauge the true level of female economic inequality, especially since research consistently finds that money isn't shared equally between men and women in a household. One study of seven rich nations found that, on average, women controlled less than a third of the household's wealth. Half of the women in Italy had no income of their own, even from the state, while more than a quarter of women in France, Germany and the UK had no income other than state welfare.[14] These are households that may look middle class or wealthy on paper, but if the man disappeared and took his earnings with him, in many cases the woman would be left with next-to-nothing to live on. Not all statisticians use this single financial reporter approach, and some long-running surveys of household wealth ask both the adults in a marriage to report their income. This doesn't change the fact that large numbers of women remain financially dependent on men in the UK and other rich countries in the twenty-first century. When a woman stays out of paid work to look after house and home, she effectively subsidizes her partner's ability to build wealth, including his earning capacity for today and the future, his savings, credit score and retirement fund. It has been suggested that to accurately measure female inequality, women in this position should be classed as 'in poverty' because, as individuals, they are.[15]

There is limited research on the intersection of race, disability, sexuality and other identities with poverty, although studies from India, the US and Brazil suggest that same-sex couples and LGBTQ+ people are more likely to be poor than the general population.[16] In the US, lesbian couples are twice as likely to receive food stamps as mixed-sex couples.[17] A separate study suggests female same-sex couples have a higher risk of poverty than male couples 'because the gender wage gap keeps earnings in households without male earners relatively low'.[18] As mentioned, female poverty is worse among ethnic minority groups compared to white women. Pakistani and Bangladeshi women tend to have the highest rates of poverty at 50 per cent and also higher rates of unemployment at around 80 per cent.[19]

Poverty is such a gendered issue it defies belief that it is rarely framed as such. Ideally the poverty data gaps would be addressed at government level with an annual report that takes a gendered lens to deprivation, alongside legally binding targets for alleviating female poverty. Academic Jane Millar suggests that a gender-sensitive approach to data collection would include asking adults about their contribution to household resources and also their level of financial reliance on others in the household.[20] In addition, rather than looking at salaries alone, the definition of 'income' needs to be extended to include the other sources of wealth that people own such as second homes, investments, land or savings. Including these assets in the data would likely make men appear even wealthier, on average, than women – as globally women are far less likely to have sources of income outside of their job. This is really important because the financial gains from owning property or stock market investments can be far higher than what an individual can make through employment.[21]

## Wealth inequality

At the other end of the scale, the gender skew is an inescapable feature of wealth distribution among the rich. There's a clear male dominance among the highest-earning business leaders, with more men called Steve running the UK's top 100 companies than there are women with any name. In America there are more men called John working as CEO of the country's 1,500 largest companies than there are female CEOs. In fact, there are four men named James, John, Robert or William working as CEO among the top 1,500 companies for every woman CEO.[22]

Globally the divisions between the super-rich, the middle classes and the just-about-managing have widened to the extreme. People at the top of the corporate pyramid have done exceptionally well for themselves. In 2017, a CEO at one of America's largest companies earned, on average, $15.6 million, or 271 times the annual pay of the typical worker; in 1989, chief executives earned 59 times the average salary.[23] But even when women make it to the top, they are paid a fraction of what their male peers earn; the six women lead-ing FTSE 100 companies earned 4.2 per cent of the total pay awarded to all the FTSE 100 CEOs.[24] Among the top twenty-five highest-paid CEOs in Britain, there is one woman, Emma Walmsley of pharmaceuticals giant Glaxo-SmithKline, with a pay package of nearly £6 million in 2018. By contrast, the highest-paid man that year was Jeff Fair-burn, who took home just under £39 million as the boss of housebuilder Persimmon.[25]

Extreme wealth inequality is partly an inevitable out-come of the capitalist system where people who have capital (money or assets) can 'capitalize' on it (make the most out of it) to earn more capital, which gives them a bigger amount to capitalize on, and so forth. But it's also the result of eco-nomic policy from governments and central banks since 2009.

Until Covid-19 struck, the 2007–9 global financial crisis was the biggest economic disaster since the 1920s. Among the political responses was the introduction of record-low interest rates, which encouraged people with savings to take their money out of the bank (where it would not earn much interest) and invest it in stock markets, property or bonds in the hopes of receiving a higher return. Meanwhile central banks around the world, including in Britain, the US and the eurozone, embarked on 'quantitative easing' or 'asset purchases' – jargon which, in very simple terms, means they created billions in digital currency, which was passed over to banks and big financial institutions. The idea was that these organizations would use the money to invest, preventing economies from grinding to a halt.

Money flooded into all kinds of investments, and from 2010 to 2019 stock markets around the world rose to a series of record highs. The same thing happened with property prices in global hotspots such as London, Paris and New York, where prices of houses and apartments have become inflated vastly above local salaries. The people wealthy enough to already have portfolios of company shares or second homes – or the money to buy them – could sit back and watch as the value of their investments rose. Britain's 600 aristocratic families have doubled their fortunes over the last ten years, the number of millionaires has trebled since 2000 and the number of billionaires has doubled.[26]

And so wealth creation has been driven by participation in business and by asset ownership; in other words, investment in company shares, properties or other 'assets' that rise in value. The Bank of England acknowledged this in 2012 and stated that only 15 per cent of people in Britain have invested their savings in the stock markets (this doesn't include people's pension savings) – and, as mentioned, women are far less likely to own investments.[27] Only 13 per cent of ultra-high net worths (people with assets of more than $30 million) are women.[28] Women are three times more likely to have inherited their wealth than men. Unless more women are able to be successful entrepreneurs or investors, or reach the upper echelons of the corporate world and be remunerated equally, the proportion of super-wealthy women to men will not change.

Western societies have been profoundly changed by another of the political responses to the financial crisis: so-called austerity measures, a euphemism for severe cuts to government spending combined with tax rises. Politicians of all stripes had flirted with ideas of the retrenchment, restriction and rolling back of the welfare state since the 1980s, but it is only in the post-crisis era that austerity has been presented as an inevitable, logical progression that ought to be embraced for its benefits.

The rationale for austerity is scarcity, or the idea that financial resources are so limited in the richest countries in the world that state support should be as meagre as possible and only offered to the worthiest. Austerity is among the reasons why an ethos of self-serving individualism is becoming more deeply embedded. Rich or poor, it's every woman for herself, every patient, parent and worker fighting for her share of the permanently shrunken welfare budget.

Such inequality raises questions about the purpose of government and democracy. Against this backdrop, the period from 2009 to 2020 was also a time when feminism emerged from the shadows.

## The Fourth Wave

Historians talk about feminism happening in successive 'waves', periods when gender issues have bubbled up and received widespread political and media attention. Each wave has had a different emphasis, depending on the concerns of women at the time.

The Fourth Wave emerged around 2010–12, as feminists began harnessing the power of social media to challenge ideas about what it means to be a woman.[29] In Britain, the new wave of feminism was spurred on by revelations in 2012 that well-known TV presenter Jimmy Savile had been a prolific sexual abuser and paedophile. In December of that year, the horrific gang rape and murder of Jyoti Singh on a bus in Delhi, India, shocked the world. It exposed the continued need for human rights campaigning in the twenty-first century and proved to be a global catalyst for the women's rights movement.

Broadly, Fourth Wave feminism has focused on issues of justice, representation and the sexualization of women and girls. The sexual abuse and exploitation of women has also come into the spotlight and investigations into historic abuse have taken place. The #MeToo Twitter hashtag was tweeted more than a million times as women shared their experiences of sexual harassment and local language equivalents appeared: #YoTambien in Spain; in Arab countries, #وأنا_كمان; while in France the more pointed hashtag of #balancetonporc (denounce your pig) went viral.[30] Sexual harassment, and physical scrutiny generally, has been – and still is – a huge obstacle to women's advancement professionally.

Unrealistic depictions of women have been challenged through the body-positivity movements, and there has been a backlash against the ubiquitous airbrushing of women's bodies in adverts and magazines. Campaigns to increase the positive representation of women led to nineteenth-century author Jane Austen featuring on the reverse of the new £10 note in 2017, following a hard-fought campaign where feminists received death threats.

The Fourth Wave has taken 'feminism' from the margins to the mainstream and has enfranchised a generation of women. So far the most high-profile issues have all been cultural concerns as opposed to issues of structural inequality – the set-up of society, the way institutions are organized (school hours don't fit with office hours), the laws and hangovers from history that give men a head start economically (such as the ineffectual Equal Pay Act from 1970, which hasn't guaranteed women equal pay). Structural inequality is woven into the fabric of society, but campaigners fighting this kind of gender oppression are yet to experience the same kind of success. This is not the fault of activists – patriarchy persists because societies are built around male dominance, which includes men having more financial and economic power than women.

Female economic inequality is both a cultural issue (it's reflected in the lack of representation of women in the highest-paid jobs and as experts in the media, for example) and a structural one (a lack of decent childcare nationwide prevents women from earning as much as men). Only by challenging both will women become economically equal with men. This is difficult when campaigning in the digital age. Although the likes of Twitter, Facebook and Instagram have been vital in spreading Fourth Wave feminism and have increased the reach of campaigns, they are also mediums that favour image-led causes and simple concepts. Complex issues around government policy and old-age poverty do not make for great photo opportunities or retweetable memes.

Economic inequality is rarely reducible to a hashtag, although some campaigners have tried. #periodpoverty has been spread on Twitter to raise awareness of women and girls who have to go without proper sanitary protection during their time of the month. The slogan 'poverty is sexist' has been adopted by One, a charity fighting extreme poverty, while more recently Feminism of the 99% has organized women's strikes.[31]

The impact of social media and the digitization of the press mean that, politically, we are immersed in the age of the quick fix and the hot take. As traditional media outlets from London to San Francisco have suffered from declining revenues and the trend towards clickbait continues, reporting has become more superficial. The media struggles to cover effectively the kind of long-term social issues that, by their nature, don't lend themselves to snappy headlines or make for great pictures – feminized poverty, discrimination, race. Much of Britain's regional media has disappeared and the remainder is predominantly London-based, making it more inclined to cover matters of importance to the urban elite. Reversing gendered economic inequality has no quick-fix solution that an online petition could address.

## Neoliberal feminism

Neoliberals see the world as a place that's made up of individuals in constant competition with one another, working for their own self-interest. It sees people primarily as consumers who can be made happier – and live better lives – if they are offered the maximum number of possible free choices in 'the market', which is anywhere people buy goods or services. The role of government, to neoliberals, is to leave businesses as unregulated as possible.

So neoliberal feminism is women's rights activism – 'women should fight for equality' – merged with the neoliberal philosophy of 'every individual in competition'. The outcome of this strange alliance is that female empowerment gurus encourage women to fight for gender equality by themselves. The onus is on the individual to improve their lot in life, with a notable absence of any demands placed on employers or government – and there is no talk of collective action.

This attitude inadvertently places the blame for female

inequality on the shoulders of the individual (she needs to make better choices, negotiate her pay, and so forth). It's a perspective which fails to acknowledge the structural inequalities that disadvantage women, such as gender-based pay inequality across entire industries, the disproportionate burden of domestic responsibilities on women or the limitations of maternity pay. The feeble response of neoliberal feminism to economic inequality is, I believe, one of the reasons why it will take 257 years for women to reach economic parity with men.[32]

I should point out that the term 'neoliberalism' is most often used today as a pejorative. There is an argument to say that the liberalization of the free market has benefited women both socially and economically. That's true to an extent, but there are limits to what the current model can achieve in terms of gender equality. Neoliberal feminism has also been called 'corporate feminism' or 'consumer feminism' but I prefer to use the term neoliberal, partly because not all of those who promulgate these ideas are in what you would call 'corporate' roles.

The people who share neoliberal feminist ideas often do so because it's become such a dominant message, not because they are staunch free-market capitalists. Neoliberal feminist thinking began spreading widely after the publication in 2013 of *Lean In* by Sheryl Sandberg, chief operating officer at Facebook. Sandberg pinpoints female reticence to engage with corporate life as one of the reasons why women lag behind men in earnings and status at work. She begins with the anecdote that when she became pregnant she realized the company had no women-friendly parking spaces near the entrance to the building. Sandberg raised the issue and more convenient parking spaces were allocated for pregnant ladies. Her point was, why hadn't women raised this before? Perhaps expectant mothers at Facebook had raised the issue and been ignored. Or perhaps the culture was such that no woman wanted to draw attention to discomfort with her pregnancy, lest she might be perceived as less capable at work. (The US has no formal paid maternity leave policy.)

Sandberg's book was criticized for its relentlessly can-do, 'go get 'em girl' philosophy, which was reduced in the popular imagination to the message 'If you work hard enough you can have the career, the man and a great family.' *Lean In* was more nuanced than that and, to her credit, Sandberg later spoke out publicly after the death of her husband and admitted she didn't know how hard it was to be a single parent. Some writers have argued that a small but significant demographic of highly paid, highly educated women now form an elite breakaway group, for whom typical 'women's concerns' about childcare are irrelevant. The theory is that lower- and middle-income women may be left to fend for themselves, as the divide between their needs and what the most powerful women are willing to advocate for grows ever wider. Books that feature some of these ideas include *The End of Men* by Hanna Rosin and *The XX Factor* by Alison Wolf.

The problem isn't the women leaders and mentors so much as the collective failure to recognize the message of neoliberal feminism for what it is: a clever way for the powerful to glibly commandeer the language of gender equality and female empowerment while simultaneously denying that socio-economic and cultural structures shape our lives.

So how do you spot neoliberal feminism? These are some of the core messages:

## 1: Women should play by the rules, not change them

Neoliberal feminism calls on women to alter their behaviour and mindsets to be more amenable to the corporate workplace. It doesn't challenge employers to improve working culture but instead urges women to make themselves fit around their work, whatever it demands. The workplace has become a designated neutral space into which anyone can slot if they have the right attitude and exhibit the correct behaviour. When a space is assumed to be neutral, when a problem does arise it's considered an aberration and something specific to one woman, rather than something to do with the workplace. How could work be the problem when everyone else fits in just fine? The onus is then on the woman to overcome discrimination.[33] This is quietism, not feminism.

Instead of altering our behaviour, we should question why presenteeism is demanded in so many workplaces. What benefit do employers get from staff sitting it out into the evening? Are these people even being productive? In *The Year of Living Danishly*, journalist and former editor of *Marie Claire* magazine Helen Russell chronicles her experience of living in Denmark, dubbed 'the world's happiest country', after moving for her husband's job.[34] She writes that Danish workers leave the office on time and look askance at people who stay late, assuming that they have productivity issues and can't get their work done in the allotted time. Since when did sitting at your desk until 10 p.m. become the marker of competency? A culture of presenteeism in the office disadvantages women who have other responsibilities outside of work that they need to leave the office for. The men who do this usually have the privilege of someone else to pick up their kids from school and make the dinner. Presenteeism is sexist. (More on this in Chapter 10.)

## 2: Women need to be more assertive/forthright/self-confident

Neoliberal feminism urges women to adopt the traits that men supposedly use to help them advance professionally, such as behaving more assertively, having greater self-belief, and thinking more strategically. It's sometimes said that women are so unused to being competitive that they have internal barriers to achievement, which they need to overcome.

The problem is that the behavioural and psychological demands of corporate life are often opposed to the needs of people. 'Hard-Won Lessons from Trailblazing Women at the Top of the Business World' is the subtitle of *Earning It* by Joann Lublin, which frames success on the 'corporate battle-field' as a feminist ideal and promises a 'compelling career compass that will help you reach your highest potential'.[35] The language used here is illuminating: the modern workplace is similar to a war zone, yet conquering it will lead to personal fulfilment. But the real-life experiences of the women described in the book also reveal what this corporate career path is really like: 'Two women suffered strokes at relatively young ages while heading sizeable businesses', reads one anecdote.[36] Nevertheless, they still 'exuded grit, resilience and a determined unwillingness to admit defeat when they confronted career obstacles'. Solidarity with other women is intrinsic to feminism. This is a dispassionate description of female suffering caused by the stress of work – and it's in a book that advocates that women pursue careers in the same vein.

## 3: Find work–life 'balance'

Men are never asked how they manage work–life balance, but neoliberal feminism lauds 'exceptional women' who have managed to 'have it all' by combining a well-paid, fulfilling job with a partner and children. They continually suggest ways of achieving 'balance' without ever demanding institutional change that would make it easier to have careers and kids at the same time. There's a strong emphasis on the future: keep trying to juggle work and children, try different approaches and, eventually, you will find equilibrium. Neoliberalism promises great things in the future – just not now.

By reifying women who have beaten the system, neoliberal feminism repudiates the idea that women are systematically discriminated against and reinforces the acceptability of the existing system.

Before the influence of neoliberalism, traditional feminism would encourage women to galvanize their energy towards creating a system that helps parents manage work and motherhood – free childcare, anyone? The reality is that work–life–family balance is incredibly difficult for those without substantial financial resources or a very supportive family. This is reflected in changing birth rates; the trend now is for the wealthiest and most highly educated women in America to have more children than their peers – when historically people in lower socio-economic classes tended to have larger families.[37] A third of families earning over $500,000 have three or more children, while fewer than a third of women aged 40–45 from every income bracket under $500,000 have three children.[38] Under neoliberal capitalism, increasingly it's only the highest earners who can afford the larger homes, the help to manage raising children, and can give them the best opportunities. One theory suggests that the partners of highly educated women are more inclined to share parenting too.

Away from the super-rich, studies have shown that the more children a woman has, the less likely she is to receive the same salary as men the same age.[39] This isn't because the individual choices of these women were not optimal, because they missed some trick or other. It's the archaic set-up of society; employers don't offer sufficient holiday to cover school holidays, childcare costs are extortionate and so forth.

These are issues that should be at the top of the agenda for feminists who care about economic inequality. While it can be inspirational to hear from women who have succeeded against the odds (and these people often have fascinating backstories), the emphasis on 'having it all' isn't just divorced from reality, it reinforces a social set-up that disadvantages women.

## 4: Wealth as worth

'Know your worth' has become a catchphrase used by female mentors advising other women on furthering their careers and personal finances. I checked three such guides aimed at women and each of them advised some variant of 'Ask for what you truly believe you are worth', while there are frequent events called 'Know Your Worth for Equal Pay' and 'How to Know Your Worth and Negotiate'. Tickets to one five-hour 'money makeover' event which takes place regularly in London cost up to £169.

A person earning £10 an hour does not have any less worth than someone who has a job paying £500 a day.

Millions of people do jobs that are vital to society but are not highly paid. The wage that someone earns at any given time is a reflection of society's attitude to different kinds of work, and on a personal level it is the result of hundreds of different circumstances that accumulate over a lifetime.

Having more money makes life more materially comfortable and increases the opportunities for the individual and their family. It removes the stress of want and the pain of seeing loved ones go without. For those reasons, trying to earn more money is a good idea. But on the whole this 'know your worth through your salary' message speaks only to a certain kind of woman, those working in large private companies awash with cash (where there's scope for negotiating bonuses and perks) or women who already have a large amount of freedom and choice in their working lives. Many women are not in a position to negotiate their salary or move freely between jobs. In many organizations change is slow, budgets are tightly constrained and there is much less scope for changing job descriptions, haggling over perks and being rewarded for assertiveness.

Equating your salary with your worth is foolish. You will never earn 'what you are worth' because your salary is just the amount you are earning at a certain point in time and is unrelated to your worth. Even if you settle on a figure that you think reflects your capabilities or experience, you still need to find someone willing to pay it. The daily rate for a lawyer, surgeon or psychotherapist is ultimately set by how many such specialists are working in a particular area and the demand for their skills. There may be times when an employer or client thinks you're marvellous and decides to pay you a high sum. Don't let it go to your head; conversely, if you receive a lower salary for your next job, it does not mean your worth has declined – and neither does an employer's decision to make you redundant.

## Depoliticizing feminism

Ultimately, neoliberal feminism is depoliticized; it doesn't speak of mass action or corral people together to change the world. It has little association with the principles of the women's rights movements that have sustained it over centuries: social justice, fairness and emancipation.

Compare neoliberal feminism to feminist ideology in the past. The First Wave galvanized support for women's suffrage in the late nineteenth and early twentieth centuries. It led to the passing of the Representation of the People Act in 1918, which gave all men the right to vote. It also enfranchised women for the first time, but only those aged over thirty who lived in property worth more than £5: middle- and upper-class women. Many women qualified through their husband's property, rather than their own.

The Second Wave was from roughly 1960 to 1980 and used the slogan 'the personal is political'. Campaigners cast light on previously ignored problems within the domestic sphere, such as marital abuse, childcare and the frustrations of women confined to the home. Until then, gender divisions at home and at work were not considered politically important. If the differing economic status of men and women was discussed at all, it would have only been in the context of what's 'natural', according to biology.[40] The publication in 1963 of *The Feminine Mystique* by Betty Friedan struck a chord with millions of women with its focus on the boredom and unhappiness that women experience as housewives. Friedan called it 'the problem with no name', and during the Second Wave, feminists argued that gender inequality at home was part of a broader system of female oppression. For the first time, the differences between men's and women's lives began to be taken seriously at government level.

The Third Wave began in the 1990s, as feminism was taken up by a younger generation of women who sought to resolve some of the divisions that had emerged within the movement. In this period, feminists emphasized the fluidity of gender and sexuality. They critiqued the norms of beauty and femininity, and the concepts of 'girl power' and 'female empowerment' became part of popular culture, encapsulating the ambition, individualism and assertiveness that supposedly defined women's liberation.[41] Arguably, this was the time when capitalism started to merge with feminism, as it became more important for women to express their freedom through the clothes and make-up they bought and the image they projected.

None of these 'waves' were perfect and, like every ideology, feminism has encompassed a range of beliefs and taken on different social and political aims over the centuries. Neoliberal feminism concentrates on individual personal growth, making it more of a self-help programme than a political movement. The language used reflects this: a good corporate feminist ought to delve inside herself, discern the mental barriers she has put up which prevent her from being successful at work – such as fear of promotion or public speaking – and work on her confidence. This is so far away from feminism's core as a political philosophy that galvanized collective action and called on women to support each other in the fight for economic and legal rights. As feminism has evolved, so it can continue to change again. It's time to leave the neoliberal influence as a relic of the past.

## Choice feminism

Aren't women poorer than men because they make choices such as going part-time at work after having children? Or because they choose to stay at a lower level of seniority when they could change employer for a promotion?

Whenever there is a discussion about female economic inequality the same question is always raised: whether women have chosen to be in a weaker financial position, either consciously or unconsciously. This is partly because over the past decade it has become widely believed that the aim of feminism is to increase the range of choices for women. 'Choice feminism' rests on the logic that the choices a woman makes are inherently empowering, because she exercises her autonomy when making them, therefore her choices are feminist.

It's true that in the past women were restricted in exercising their autonomy and that increasing the choices available to women – being able to go to university, practise medicine and open a bank account – has helped boost gender equality. It's also true that women in some parts of the world are *still* restricted in exercising their autonomy, and in these places greater freedom of choice will be a vital part of emancipating them from male control. (A good example is Saudi Arabia, where a ban on women driving was lifted only in 2018. The freedom that Saudi women have now to drive where they want without a male chaperone is greatly empowering and this was a vital win for gender equality campaigners in the country.)

However, it is a mistake to think that feminism is solely or predominantly about enhancing choice, and here's why: choices are not made in a vacuum. Like everyone, women make choices based on the options available and the constraints they face. Framing a woman's actions or her personal situation as a result of her choices ignores her lived experience. This is clear when we apply the logic of choice feminism to female economic inequality. What we have is women cutting their hours after they have children purely out of choice, or women putting their money into childcare rather than their pensions out of choice. This kind of feminism disregards the power structure within which these choices are necessarily made. As a consequence, there is no space for a critique of the structure itself. Chalking the pay gap or any other feature of female experience up to choice does nothing to further gender equality.

Women's rights became so passé in the 1990s and early 2000s that few women were willing to associate themselves with feminism publicly. This changed radically after 2012 and since then celebrities, politicians and business leaders have been publicly 'coming out' as feminists. 'Many of the feminists I know didn't even refer to themselves as feminists until recently,' writes business journalist Adriana Lopez.[42] 'They aren't parading the streets with signs or charred bras, perhaps because they are too busy building their careers,' she adds, rolling out the derogatory cliché that equality advocates are angry people who set underwear alight.

I contend that feminism would never have become a badge of honour that it is for women in business and pop culture if it hadn't been for the influence of neoliberal and choice feminism. These strands of feminism can be used to brand literally any situation or action as 'feminist', provided someone is getting 'empowered' or has made a choice.

Neoliberal ideas have tied themselves neatly to feminism and the two go hand in hand, at least when it comes to 'helping' women with economic inequality. But they're not such cosy bedfellows.

Ending female economic inequality means disentangling the goals of women's rights movements from the influence of neoliberalism and choice feminism. It's time to look beyond the social world as a series of individuals battling in their own corner and shift to a perspective of feminism as a collective movement, one that calls for societal action to create gender equality.

# 2. How We Got Here

Until 1950, in England the definition of a person too incapacitated to deal with income tax was: 'Any infant, married woman, lunatic, idiot or insane person.'[1] Throughout history, there have been times when ranking women alongside children and the mentally ill was considered totally normal, especially when it came to thinking about who is entitled to money. Even when women were granted certain freedoms – to work or to vote, for example – there are countless instances of societies infantilizing and incapacitating women by restricting their access to money, property, bank accounts and loans. We think this stuff is ancient history, but much of the economic independence we enjoy today has been won during our lifetimes, and our mothers'. It wasn't until 1980 that the law changed in the UK to allow women to take out a bank loan without a male guarantor – even if she earned more than him. Before then, banks could refuse a woman credit if she didn't have a man promising that he would step in to pay the money back if she couldn't. A woman's word wasn't good enough – and you know what? That patronizing myth that women can't be trusted with money persists forty years later – just take a look at Chapter 3.

Until 1990, a married woman's money belonged to her husband, in the eyes of the law at least. The UK tax system retained the 180-year-old practice that required the man of the house to add his wife's income to his own, and they were taxed as a couple under his tax code. The law was changed to give women the same privacy and independence in their tax affairs that men had. It also ended the situation where lower-earning wives were paying tax at their higher-earning husband's rate.[2] In Jersey, married women only won the right to pay their own taxes in 2020.

This is the history of the disenfranchisement of women. Not just in terms of our rights to vote or participate in politics but in the way our ability to do the paid work we want to, to have money and assets – things which could give us a sense of identity, agency and security – was taken from us on the assumption that we couldn't handle it. And the effect of this belittlement remains today, in the barriers that exist to women achieving financial equality.

If you didn't live with these restrictive and patronizing laws, then your female relations, bosses and teachers did. The consequences of treating generations of women as economically illiterate are that women have been unable to educate their daughters about money, women have been shut out from one of the main sources of power in capitalist societies (money), and few girls have grown up believing that finance is a career for them.

## Women as property

For hundreds of years, women were not able to have property because they *were* property; first, they belonged to their fathers; then to their husbands. We were assets, judged on our age, looks and our usefulness to men who wanted someone to cook and clean, raise children and warm their beds. We were traded through marriage, with parents and siblings complicit in the exchange of women for dowries, their inheritance or status. Women were often powerless over the choice of their future spouse and were generally not in a strong enough position financially to say no to a marriage if they didn't want it – and this is still the case for some women around the world today.[3]

The concept of virginity has been used to commodify women. In the marketplace for wives, female bodies were the product, virginity was the most desirable condition and a girl's value rose or fell depending on beliefs about her supposed purity. A preoccupation with female virginity still pervades Western societies today (think of the instances of young women selling their virginity online, or the purity balls attended by teens and their fathers in the US). Meanwhile, patriarchal societies have encouraged men to draw their value from their ability to control women. Masculinity has been linked to a man's ability to formalize a relationship with a (typically younger) woman through marriage and to support her financially.

Medieval English law, which was later exported to the American colonies, considered women 'chattels', just like any moveable possession, such as a packhorse. Upon marriage, the law cemented a woman's lack of rights through a concept called 'coverture', which meant that a wife became indivisible from her husband in legal terms and all rights went to him. Married women couldn't keep their wages, enter into contracts, or own property; nor could they write a will. Any possessions a wife inherited became her husband's and he could sell them without her permission. Even if he wanted to, a husband couldn't give his wife property or make a legal agreement with her; it would have been equivalent to making an agreement with himself. Husbands controlled the ideas that women came into contact with through education, and wives couldn't better themselves intellectually without their permission.

Ownership is intrinsic to power. Wealthy women were attractive to potential suitors as a source of power but, once married, without the ability to own anything, they were stripped of agency and dignity.

Women didn't have legal rights over their children. They belonged to their husband and, if he knew he was going to die, he could appoint an unrelated guardian to look after them, a person who would take precedence over their mother.[4] This sounds outrageously medieval, but it wasn't until 1925 that women had equal rights with such a guardian in the event of their husband's death. And until the law changed again, in 1973, mothers in married couples couldn't authorize medical treatment for their children or apply for passports in their name.[5]

By the same logic, a child born of unmarried parents was a *nullius filius*, or 'son of nobody'. The father didn't have ownership over the mother so he couldn't own her children. Tremendous stigma was attached to single mothers; they were seen as an economic problem and a drain on society's resources. There was no concept that society should be structured so that women could support themselves and their children, or that communities could benefit from population growth.

There are echoes of this in social policy today. In 2019, bosses at NHS South East London, which oversees public healthcare for 2 million people, issued a statement that it would no longer offer single women IVF treatment because 'they are a greater burden on society'.[6] The organization invoked the logic of ancient Greek philosopher Aristotle in its official guidelines to back this up: 'Aristotle's principle of equality says treat equals equally, so a couple compared to a couple is equal. A woman or man compared to a couple is not equal, and attempting to think of them as such has no ground or support.' Aristotle died more than 2,300 years ago and believed that women are by nature 'inferior', 'a deformity' and 'incomplete', compared to men.[7]

So-called bastardy laws began to be introduced from 1576, which aimed to punish people who had children they could not afford out of wedlock and to determine paternity as a means to get child-support payments out of fathers. The laws were enforced by local parishes (churches), which usually had to support destitute mothers. These were grim times for women. An English law of 1609 sent 'lewd' women to jail for up to a year if they had a baby whom the parish had to care for, while a law of 1743 punished unwed mothers with public whipping. Illegitimacy was an issue that transcended class. Bastard babies were born into rich and poor families alike,[8] following affairs, sexual exploitation, or after the man in a couple intending to marry went into the army, was sent to prison or died.

Until 1834, women were legally entitled to receive a modest maintenance from the father of their child, but it was difficult for an unwed woman to get this money.[9] The authorities sought to encourage moral virtue and a strong work ethic, amid fears that a class of 'idle poor' was choosing social support over paid work. They also believed that poor men were at the mercy of devious women who fell pregnant out of wedlock and that parish support was too readily available for these wanton females.

In a departure from hundreds of years of law, in 1834 a new Poor Law and bastardy clause removed the obligation for fathers to provide child support for women they hadn't married. Illegitimate children were now the sole responsibility of women until the age of sixteen.

There was an outcry over this change in the law, as it made women solely financially responsible for an illegitimate child who had two parents. However, rather than discouraging premarital sex, in parts of the country the number of illegitimate babies increased because men no longer had to bear any responsibility for the women whom they made pregnant.[10] There were also concerns about a rise in infanticide and abortion.[11] (These concerns can still be found in Britain today, as the number of abortions has reached a record high, driven by older women, nearly 60 per cent of whom have already had at least one child. Charities say that limits to government child-support payments have been a factor.)[12] Mothers with no way to support themselves were forced to move into workhouses alongside their children. Victorian workhouses were state-run, prison-like institutions that provided shelter for those at the margins of society – the disabled, the elderly, the sick, orphans and unmarried mothers – in return for their labour. The cost was supposed to be met by the work done by the occupants. Workhouses were designed to be harsh in order to deter all but the most desperate from relying on this form of state support, and conditions were worse than those the lowliest labourers in the world outside endured.

This practice of now almost 200 years ago of sending the poor to workhouses shares striking similarities with the welfare policies of Britain's Conservative government throughout the past decade. The Conservatives have created a deliberately punitive system of state support – Universal Credit – which has caused true hardship to those reliant upon it – mostly women with children. (See Chapter 6 for more on this.) The logic is that reducing state benefits to the bare minimum will act as a deterrent to claiming state support. The reality, however, is the same as it was when the Poor Law was introduced. Many mothers find themselves in an impossible situation of having to care for young children 24/7 while simultaneously earning the money to feed and house themselves. How are women supposed to do both, unless they have either affordable childcare during their working hours or a partner who can financially support them?

While laws treating women as property were abolished in England in 1857, incredibly they remained on the statute books in Ireland until 1981. In 1972 a German businessman called Werner Braun took advantage of this archaic law to sue the lover of his wife Heide. The Brauns were living in Cork, southern Ireland, and had a turbulent marriage which led Heide to have an affair with Stanley Roche, a wealthy local businessman. Ireland was a deeply Catholic country where extramarital sex was considered scandalous enough to bring shame on the entire family. Braun's fury at discovering their affair led him to pursue a court claim that his 'possession' (Heide) had been 'debauched' and 'corrupted' by Roche.

As the jury retired to consider their verdict, the judge in the case advised them that 'A wife in this country is regarded as a chattel, just as a thoroughbred mare or a cow' and that if they considered Heide a 'loose' woman who was 'hardly worth losing' then Braun shouldn't succeed in his claim.[13] Heide must have been perceived as a valuable possession, as for the 'loss' of his wife Braun was awarded £12,000 – enough to buy a substantial family home at the time.[14] Heide and

Roche married and spent their lives together. Irish parliamentary debates raised the question of why women were still legally considered male property, but Desmond O'Malley, the then-Justice Minister, reportedly said there was no need for urgent change.[15]

## Winning financial rights

Gaining the right to ownership was vital for women. Not only were women without property left dependent on others for a roof over their head, they did not have any stake in an asset that could store wealth for the long term.

The US had adopted Britain's coverture system but its vast geography helped with the expansion of women's rights. Men could be away for months or even years at a time exploring America's frontiers, and women needed to be able to manage household finances to survive. Massachusetts, for example, passed a law in 1787 allowing married women to act as 'femme sole traders' in some circumstances, which meant they could do business on their own if their husbands were at sea or away from home for a long period.

In terms of property, a law was passed in 1664 in Maryland stating that when a man wanted to sell his wife's property a judge had to speak privately with her to confirm that she gave her assent. In 1771, similar legislation was passed in New York requiring a man who wanted to sell or transfer his wife's property to have her signature on the deed giving her approval, alongside a private meeting with a judge.[16] A wife could still be coerced into selling her property, but this was progress nonetheless. Yet the general attitude was that women needed to remain under men's control for their own protection. To give a flavour of the mindset of the time, in 1776, John Adams, who would later become America's second president, was among the leaders who wanted to lay the foundations for a freer, fairer society after the young nation threw off the shackles of the British.

His wife, Abigail Adams, was an unusually well-educated woman and became one of her husband's closest advisers. She documented her views on government and politics extensively through letters to her husband who was hundreds of miles away, while managing the family home during the American Revolutionary War in an area battling a smallpox epidemic. In one letter she implored that women could be freed from the coverture, to live without the unrestrained and arbitrary power that men had over them. 'Remember the ladies, and be more generous and favourable to them than your ancestors,' she wrote. Her despair at the way men abused their authority comes through as she writes: 'That your sex are naturally tyrannical is a truth so thoroughly established as to admit of no dispute.'[17]

John's response? 'I cannot but laugh,' he wrote, dismissing her concerns with patronizing humour.[18]

Abigail's attempts failed because people believed women had no interests or needs that ought to be represented politically. But although they were forced into dependency, women did not lack ambition. In Britain, engineer Sarah Guppy was the first woman to design and patent a bridge in 1811, although it was never built. She mentored the prolific engineer Isambard Kingdom Brunel and was likely influential behind the design of his iconic Clifton Suspension Bridge, which spans the Avon Gorge in Bristol, England.[19]

Sybilla Masters is considered by some to be the first woman inventor in America: in 1712 she designed a new corn mill, but the invention was patented in London under her husband's name in 1715. The first woman to be awarded an American patent was Connecticut inventor Mary Dixon Kies in 1809; she came up with a method of weaving straw with silk or thread to make attractive hats. Her innovation came during something of a fashion emergency in America. With the Napoleonic Wars in full swing in Europe, American ships were being harassed, and in retaliation President Thomas Jefferson banned imports from Britain. To make up for the lack of goods coming in, women had to become creative and a hat-making industry blossomed in New England, allowing women the chance to receive an income and express themselves through fashion.

In 1870, Victoria Woodhull and her sister Tennessee became the first women to open a stockbroker business on Wall Street. 'I went on to Wall Street not particularly because I wanted to be a stockbroker, but because I wanted to plant the flag of women's rebellion in the center of the continent,' Victoria said.[20] She was also the first woman to run for president – and at a time when women didn't even have the right to vote, or to enter a shop or restaurant without a male chaperone. 'I am quite well aware that in assuming this position I shall evoke more ridicule than enthusiasm at the outset. But this is an epoch of sudden changes and startling surprises. What may appear absurd today will assume a serious aspect to-morrow,' she wrote in a column in the *New York Herald*, announcing her candidacy.[21]

Newspaper cartoons depicted Victoria as the devil; the notoriety led to her being evicted from her home and her daughter was withdrawn from school, as other parents didn't want their children to associate with her. She continually had to fend off claims that she was unnatural and wicked. Imagine her dismay if she knew that, 150 years later, the most powerful position in American politics has still not been held by a woman, even though more than 200 women have now run for president.[22]

## Marriage of equals

With growing financial freedom, women were able to express their independence in other ways.

Lucy Stone became famous for refusing to take her husband's surname after marriage in Massachusetts in 1855, a decision which led her to have considerable difficulties with public authorities. 'A wife should no more take her husband's name than he take hers. My name is my identity and must not be lost,' she wrote in a letter to her spouse.[23]

Her husband was Henry B. Blackwell, an open-minded chap whose sister was one of the first women in America to receive a medical degree.[24] Prior to getting married, the couple agreed on a kind of prenuptial contract, and Lucy believed women should support themselves financially. 'Money is power,' she said in a speech arguing that securing access to money-making opportunities should be a goal of the women's rights movement. She told an audience of women in Cincinnati that their priorities should be getting an education, saving some money and investing it in land.[25]

Regarding parenthood, Lucy and Henry were influenced by ideas about women's sexual autonomy and argued that husbands should not force their wives to yield to their passions. Since women were the ones who had to deal with the consequences of sex (that is, children), Henry wrote to Lucy promising that 'you shall choose when, where and how often you shall become a mother'.[26] (In Chapter 11, I will look at how the control of fertility has been crucial for women in gaining economic power.)

## Rights to work

During the first and second industrial revolutions Western nations changed from agrarian to urban societies fuelled by manufacturing and industry. The revolutions were partly spurred on by women, as economic necessity lured them into factories, houses, shops and coal mines where they worked as textile producers, domestic servants and launderers. By 1851 only a quarter of women were not in paid work.[27]

There are two sides to the story of women and the Industrial Revolution. The positives were that standards of living rose for some women through the wages they earned. Their lives away from home gave them independence and they were in frequent contact with the wider community. Slowly women began to assume new identities as citizens and economic agents. The negatives were considerable: for the majority, the early years of the nineteenth century brought an additional form of hardship into women's lives on top of their existing burdens. No one took over wives' and mothers' responsibilities for child-rearing or housework, and women continued to labour hard while pregnant. The wages a wife earned were legally her husband's, and male wages were often insufficient to support a family. Relationships at home were put under stress. It remained legal for a man to beat his wife until 1879.

The hardship of the Industrial Revolution stimulated the women's rights movement. Feminists rose up over the years following 1891, when the Factory and Workshop Act prohibited employers from knowingly employing new mothers within four weeks of giving birth. There was no mention of where else their income would come from. Two years later it was extended to keep new mothers off work for eleven weeks after birth.

The balance shifted during the First World War when women went to work en masse, filling roles that had traditionally been held by men, including bus conductors, police officers and munitions workers. Typically, women were paid lower salaries than the men had been for doing the same job. Women's contribution to the war effort challenged the notion that they were intellectually and physically inferior, and it became harder to justify denying them the vote and keeping them out of the workplace. War had shaken the conservatism from society; social and political change had begun to seem less threatening.[28] Women developed the confidence to fight for their rights and the feminist movement became more organized, which led to 8.5 million women winning the right to vote in 1918 (as we saw earlier, it was those aged over thirty who owned property worth more than a certain value, or were married to a man who did). Voting rights were extended to all women in 1928.

Attitudes towards women's roles had softened, but there was still opposition to their advancing into paid employment. There were fears that giving women rights somehow diminished men – a theme that crops up repeatedly.

The First Wave of feminists who fought for women to get

the vote believed that once this was achieved, other forms of gender-based oppression would fall away.[29] The reality was disappointing. From the 1920s onwards male earnings eventually rose to a level where a man could support his family on one wage and what we call the 'traditional' family was born, with breadwinner husbands and stay-at-home wives. Women retreated from the factory to the home, which laid the foundations for the gendered economic inequality that we see today.

Across the Atlantic there was a similar story as so-called 'protective laws' placing restrictions on how, when and where women could work began to appear. In Michigan, women were banned from jobs that could be bad for their health or could corrupt their morals[30] – such as bartending – and in some states women were not allowed to work at night, when these jobs often had higher wages.[31] Men had the flexibility to work wherever they could find employment.

In Ohio, women were banned from jobs including baggage handling, shoe shining and working in pool halls and bowling alleys, while New York prevented women from working in restaurants at night to protect their 'health'.[32] This was probably because these were places where women would come into contact with a lot of men, often rough men, and there was a fear that they would 'negatively influence women's behavior'.[33]

States including California, Ohio and Oregon also limited women's working hours.[34] This was problematic for women who didn't have a man providing for them, had ambitions they wanted to save towards or who were struggling to make ends meet. In a court case the decision to restrict working hours was upheld, with the court citing women's 'physical structure and the performance of maternal functions'.[35]

# The marriage bar

Until as late as the 1970s in the UK, the US, the Netherlands and Ireland, it was common practice for women to lose their jobs when they got married. This was known as the 'marriage bar': women who worked in teaching, government, banks or administration were either forced to retire upon marriage or were refused jobs once they were married. The belief was that allowing married women to stay on in their jobs 'takes employment from those who need it more' – meaning men – and that 'girls who work for a few years and then retire provide necessary turnover'. A *Spectator* article of 1946 states that married women are 'less reliable and less mobile than unmarried women'[36] – an attitude that's still unconsciously present in many modern workplaces.

Forced retirement after marriage persisted despite the fact that employers would have invested time and money in training women, and even though staff turnover creates disruption and increased costs in hiring new people. A government report from 1944 noted that 'it is apparent that there is an appreciable amount of unwilling retirement among educated and trained women'.[37] Again, little consideration was given to the woman's financial situation. On the contrary, sacking less wealthy married women was justified on the grounds that 'for lack of the means to employ domestic help, [women] would in most cases withdraw on marriage anyhow' to fulfil their cleaning and housekeeping duties.[38]

The marriage bar was also a justification to pay women lower salaries, as since they would retire earlier, their 'career value' was lower.[39] In Britain in 1944, the marriage bar was lifted at the BBC and for teachers – when the authorities realized that married women were suitable for educating children – but it remained in the civil service and the post office until 1954. Some union offices retained the practice into the sixties.[40]

## *The professions*

To improve their financial fortunes and achieve a more equal status with the opposite sex, women had to be able to earn as much as men. Yet there was staunch resistance to the presence of women at universities, and even after they were pushed into admitting female students to study and pass exams, women were not allowed to hold degrees and couldn't go on to practise in their field. The fight for women's rights to work in the most lucrative professions such as medicine went on for decades and in the case of the legal profession, British women remained shut out long after Canadian and American women had won the right to practise law.

Doors were closed to women in fields considered more intellectually challenging because of male beliefs about the intrinsic inferiority of women, who were considered too feeble-minded to manage mathematical, scientific or logical ideas. The persistence of this prejudice is summed up by this anecdote: when the typewriter was invented in 1867 it was considered too complex for a woman to handle, but 100 years later, in a now infamous advert for an Olivetti typewriter from the late 1960s, a beautiful blonde-haired woman sits in front of the machine with the caption: 'A typewriter so smart, she doesn't have to be.'

Ironically, the woman pictured was anything but stupid. Her name was Shere Hite and she had taken up modelling to help pay for her PhD studies in history at the prestigious Columbia University. Hite was under the impression that she had been chosen for the Olivetti job because of her impressive typing skills, and didn't realize how her image would be used until later. She had the last laugh. Hite went on to sell 50 million copies of her book *The Hite Report: A Nationwide Study of Female Sexuality*, which revolutionized the way that women thought about their bodies.

Women's supposed intellectual inferiority was thought to be a biological fact, but even after this belief had begun to wane, female biology was used against us. It was thought that sitting through university lectures might somehow affect the womb or dry up the mammary glands.

Eliza Orme was the first woman in England to receive a law degree, in 1888, from University College London. She believed that women needed more advocacy and such a well-paid, worthwhile profession ought to be open to women, but she had to wait thirty-one years before she was legally allowed to practise as a solicitor. A case was brought to court in 1913 by four women, including Gwyneth Bebb, who had studied jurisprudence (law) at Oxford University and achieved first-class marks in her exams but didn't formally graduate.

Bebb applied to the Law Society to take the exams to practise as a solicitor, but they returned her fee, saying that if women arrived for the examination they would not be admitted because they couldn't be lawyers. Bebb took the Law Society to court, arguing that legislation referring to 'persons' being lawyers included women. The court found that the entire female gender was outside the definition of 'persons': 'A woman is not a person within the meaning of the Solicitors Act 1843 . . . and on that ground is properly refused admission to the preliminary examination held by the Law Society,' reads the ruling from the Court of Appeal.[41] The judgment relied on a medieval treatise that stated: 'The law will not suffer women, nor infants or serfs, to the legal profession.'[42]

Often it was the case that the more prestigious the institution, the longer it held out before giving women equivalent status to men – a fact that's echoed today in women's lack of equal representation at the pinnacles of government, in the judiciary, academia, finance and medicine. Britain's elite Oxford and Cambridge were the last of the country's universities to treat women equally; Oxford University only began awarding women degrees in October 1920, even though women had been studying and passing exams at its four dedicated women's colleges for nearly fifty years.[43] Cambridge University held out until 1948. This progress came with caveats, as Oxford limited the number of female students from 1927 onwards to a maximum of 840 women or one-sixth of all undergraduates, lest the floodgates open. Twenty-one years later the limit was raised to allow ninety more women, but the quota wasn't removed until 1957.

This was a significant barrier to economic equality, since having a more prestigious education could lead to higher earnings. Women were considered a distraction. The head of one women's college at the University of Oxford wrote of 'a very tiresome complaint that the men examinees are disturbed by the way our students sit in their tight skirts and show their legs'.[44] It's not women's fault if some men can't concentrate on what they're supposed to be doing.

Women faced the same setbacks in the medical profession. Margaret Ann Bulkley, born in County Cork, Ireland, in 1789, assumed the disguise of a man in order to study medicine at Edinburgh University, and became the UK's first female doctor. With the help of some wealthy patrons, they styled themselves as Dr James Barry, and became a skilled military surgeon who practised in South Africa, St Helena, and Trinidad and Tobago, and performed the first successful Caesarean section in the British empire.[45] It was only when Dr Barry died that the woman preparing the body for burial realized that Barry was female, a revelation that scandalized Victorian Britain. This was more than fifty years before women were allowed to practise medicine. If it were up to me, Dr Barry's face would be on the £10 note.

Although Barry was slight of build and effeminate-looking, no one guessed that the surgeon had been born a woman. Instead, 'Whispers began to circulate among the students about the peculiar, unsociable Barry. It was put about that "Mr" James Barry was not a man at all – he was very obviously a young boy . . . a child, not even past puberty. The evidence was abundant and unambiguous: his short stature, his slightness of build, his unbroken voice, his delicate features and smooth skin.'[46]

The absurdity of this situation says a lot about the expectations of male and female intellect at the time. The small, girlish medical student could only have been a precociously talented boy.

When women weren't explicitly barred from a workplace, there were other forms of discrimination to hold them back. Until 1982, pubs could refuse to serve women; it was up to the landlord whether women should be allowed to spend their money in these 'male establishments'. This changed in November of that year when solicitor Tess Gill and journalist Anna Coote complained that a lively pub on Fleet Street, El Vino, banned women from buying a drink at the bar and standing nearby. Women were confined to a back room where there was table service, something that El Vino claimed was about upholding chivalry. El Vino was a City institution, beloved of journalists, barristers and solicitors as a place to gather and gossip, and even though in 1970 a group of female journalists had stormed the bar demanding to be served, management had stuck with their policy.[47]

While one court said the women were not being discriminated against, the Court of Appeal acknowledged that women could be disadvantaged in their jobs if they could mingle only in a certain part of the bar. The judge said: 'If a man wishes to take a drink in El Vino's, he can drink, if he wishes, by joining the throng which crowds round the bar and there he can join his friends and pick up, no doubt, many an interesting piece of gossip, particularly if he is a journalist . . . If male journalists are permitted to do it, why shouldn't she?'[48]

## Toilets

Lack of toilet facilities was often a reason why women were disadvantaged in the workplace or prevented from bettering themselves. Harvard University was one of the US colleges that held out the longest, using the lack of toilets as a reason not to admit female students to medicine until 1945 – almost 100 years after the first woman had applied. Harvard Law School opened its doors to women in 1950, a mere seventy-nine years after the first female applicant. Yale Medical School admitted women in 1916, but only after economics professor Henry Farnam paid for women's toilets to be installed because his daughter was intent on studying there.[49] Virginia Military Institute, the country's most prestigious military academy, used this excuse as recently as 1996.

The problem of insufficient toilets for women is known in the US as 'potty parity'. The absence of women's bathrooms in certain professions and halls of power is a marker of female exclusion.

Incredibly, the US House of Representatives didn't have women's toilets located nearby until 2011.[50] Male toilets were a few steps away from the House chambers and had amenities including a shoe-shining stand, fireplace and televisions to show the House proceedings live so the men didn't miss a moment of what was going on. The first women came to Congress in 1917, and by 2011 there were seventy-eight female members, but they had to walk such a distance to the ladies' bathroom that it often took longer than the scheduled break times in House sessions to get there and back, which meant they would miss some of the debate. Reportedly, installing women's toilets closer to the chambers was considered in 2007, but 'with the nature of a historic building and adding plumbing, it was just too expensive'.[51]

## Pregnancy

The fact that a woman could potentially become a mother was a consistent barrier to women finding and keeping paid jobs up until the 1980s and it allowed for systemic discrimination.

In the US, it was written into federal policy between 1935 and 1968 that pregnant women were unemployable – so when a woman is at her most vulnerable, the law stated that it was acceptable, even preferable, for (male) employers to cut off her income. On both sides of the Atlantic pregnant women were routinely sacked long before their due date until this was outlawed in 1978 in the US, and in 1975 in the

UK through the Sex Discrimination Act. In spite of this legal change, women continued to be sacked from jobs for reasons related to pregnancy, and the courts that deal with workplace disputes didn't see that this constituted a violation of the Sex Discrimination Act.[52]

A key case that challenged the law in Britain was in 1980, when a Mrs Turley took her employer, Allders department store, to court, arguing that she had been dismissed because she fell pregnant less than a year after joining the company. The store denied this. The tribunal considered that something could be discriminatory if a man would not be treated in the same way. And so it found that Mrs Turley had not been discriminated against because men couldn't get pregnant; therefore there was no way to gauge whether a man would have been sacked if he had been in Mrs Turley's shoes.[53] The case went to the European Court of Justice where the decision was overturned.[54]

Even today, the Equality and Human Rights Commission believes that 50,000 pregnant women each year are fired illegally in the UK, a figure that has doubled since 2005. Global sports brand Nike recently made the headlines after it was revealed that the company financially penalizes athletes when they become pregnant. In sports such as track and field, much of an athlete's income comes from sponsorship deals rather than through association with a club or league, as in other sports. However, the contracts offered by Nike and many other sponsors reserve the right for the company to reduce or pause pay if an athlete fails to meet performance guidelines. There is no exception made for periods of pregnancy, childbirth or post-partum recovery – all times when a female athlete may not be performing at her best. The discrimination was revealed in 2019 when American runner

Alysia Montaño said that her former sponsor, Nike, told her that if she wanted to have a baby, it would be 'simple, we'll just pause your contract and stop paying you'.[55] She said, 'The sports industry allows men to have a full career. And when a woman decides to have a baby, it pushes her out at her prime', adding that confidentiality clauses have prevented athletes from speaking out. Determined to prove that women can have athletic careers while pregnant, Alysia competed while eight months pregnant.

Later, Allyson Felix, an American track and field athlete and six-time Olympic gold medallist, said that Nike had told her it would reduce her pay to 70 per cent of the usual rate while she was pregnant. Allyson said she felt pressured to return to the sport soon after she had her child, even though she had needed a Caesarean because of life-threatening pre-eclampsia. Nike has since changed its contracts to ensure that women will not suffer any financial penalty related to pregnancy for eighteen months, starting from eight months before the due date.

It was a long, hard slog but women have escaped the shackles of the lowest legal and social status. Today we rank alongside men as fully autonomous adults with powers of ownership and decision-making over our children, money, property and future. However, while we have been assimilated into the workforce, the shadow cast by historical discrimination means that women don't have an equal share of the highest-paying and most prestigious jobs.

# 3. What We Believe about Money

Women are frivolous; men are discerning. Women are spenders; men are earners. When it comes to money, there's an everyday sexism in the way the media talks to us about money.

A linguistic study of 300 articles found that the genders are split definitively into two categories – the 'thrifty-splurger' female and the 'adept-financier' male. The study, by Starling Bank, found that the language used portrays women as heavy spenders prone to 'splurging' on non-essentials and in need of help to restrict their outgoings. Articles aimed at women that discuss money tend to focus on household finances and thrift or encourage seeking help from others. This is in direct contrast to the uplifting message aimed at men: money and wealth are attainable, aspirational and part of a masculine ideal. The language employed in articles geared towards men includes terms associated with strength, power and competition. Finance is something to be 'conquered' by those 'daring enough' to try.

This is how the media reinforces negative attitudes towards women and our capabilities regarding money, often inadvertently. Yet what's interesting is that banks report that there is little difference in the way that men and women spend. The stereotype that females spend frivolously and men don't is sexism, pure and simple.

We absorb these messages about each gender's apparent ability to manage money. When researchers analysed 1.7 million words used in communications between retirement savers and the UK's Pension Advisory Service, a public organization that tries to help people understand retirement savings, they found that women used more negative language than men when describing their problems with pension savings, with frequent use of words such as 'worried', 'concerned' and 'confused'.[1] It's as though women have internalized the message that they are inept with money and approach financial matters already convinced they have got it all wrong.

These are the main myths about women and money:

## Myth 1: Women are risk averse

Myths about female aptitude with money have combined with wage inequality to create a little-discussed problem: women are far less likely to invest their savings, instead keeping them in cash. This 'gender investment gap' hinders women's ability to expand their wealth over time and exacerbates the gender wealth gap. Investing can make your money grow; it can turn one pound into two, or five. It may feel safe to have cash savings but, over time, inflation erodes the value of money. With good investments, your savings will grow much more quickly than they will if you rely on interest from cash deposit accounts. I will explain how to do this in Chapter 15.

The lack of female investment is often seen as a consequence of our supposed dislike of risk. That women are extra-cautious is one of the most patronizing, persistent myths about women – and it's especially pernicious when it comes to looking at women and their financial security. It's simply not true for many women but, like any trope, it has the potential to become self-reinforcing. One study asked women which gender they thought was better at investing – only 9 per cent thought women would make better investors than men.[2]

Women are often chided for risk aversion; it's perceived as a fault and the gender gap in pension savings is often blamed on a female lack of appetite to invest more aggressively. The difference between risky and rash behaviour is slim: being keen on risk isn't intrinsically good. At work and on the stock market, prudence is a virtue we could do with seeing more of.

Alongside the pay, wealth and pensions gaps, women are counted on to carry out the bulk of childminding and housekeeping duties, focused on short-term outgoings of food and housekeeping products; more women than men work part-time, so they have lower earnings. A review of two dozen papers on female attitudes to risk found that most studies blew small discrepancies out of proportion, using a lot of hot air to reinforce deep-rooted beliefs about women and men. 'The results are considerably more mixed than might be expected . . . [The belief] merits reconsideration,' it said.[3] A separate study of American professors and their investment portfolios found that there was no gender difference in risk tolerance among people with the same level of education. Where gendered risk aversion does exist, it's down to income, marital status and how many children there are in a household.

When economic status is separated from risk appetite, a different picture emerges. Contrary to the stereotypes, women are no more risk averse financially than men, according to the UK's Pension Advisory Service, which found that the main differences in attitude were down to how much money people had.[4] Wealthier women and those expecting an inheritance are happy to play the stock market. Another study found that LGBTQ+ people, African Americans and women who have experienced discrimination in the workplace are less willing to invest their savings. This suggests that the sense of precarity caused by experiencing discrimination has a direct effect on people's financial decisions.[5]

Several studies have found that when women do invest, they're better at it than men.[6] Men appear to be more sensitive to news about stock markets, as they trade (buy and sell shares) on average thirteen times per year, compared to nine times for women, according to a study from Warwick Business School.[7] The difference may sound small, but owning shares over a longer period of time (rather than buying and selling them frequently) can be a far better investment tactic. One of the reasons is that every time you trade, a charge is incurred, and this eats into profits. It looks as though what is perceived as female caution is actually financial sense.[8]

The Warwick Business School researchers also found differences in the kinds of stocks that the genders picked, with men preferring 'lottery style' investments in speculative, lower-priced shares that might increase in value substantially. They also tended to keep shares that show a loss while selling off their winners – the ones that have increased in value. One of the key learnings from history's legendary investors is that accepting you were wrong about an investment and selling it when it's falling, rather than holding on and hoping you will be proved right and it will rise in value again, is absolutely vital. Some people find admitting they were wrong about a money decision incredibly difficult, and this can cost them dearly with investment.

Professor of Behavioural Science Neil Stewart, who carried out the study, explained: 'If you have ever watched a bad movie to the end, you are having trouble letting go of a loss. If you have ever bought a lottery ticket, you have been attracted to big wins, but wins that are very unlikely. Men are just a little more likely to be drawn to more speculative stocks, whereas women are more likely to focus on shares that already have a good track record. This possibly means women are investing more to support their financial goals, whereas men are attracted to what they see as the thrill of investing.'

In the study, women investors beat male investors substantially, by making 1.94 per cent more than the FTSE 100 index each year. Male investors achieved returns 0.14 per cent above the index annually. This is hugely significant statistically because of how women's extra investment performance adds up over decades. The *Guardian* newspaper crunched the numbers and found that if the FTSE grew by 5 per cent a year, with £100 invested a month, we'd expect the men to see their savings grow by £18,000 over twenty years, while the women would make £28,000.[9]

The myth of the risk-averse woman affects how we are treated when we seek financial advice. One study by researchers at King's College London found that financial advisers given fictitious client profiles rated the 'females' as having less financial knowledge and lower tolerance for risk. Clients thought to be female were recommended to invest in lower-risk portfolios, which are less likely to lose money but are also expected to achieve lower returns. It was the opposite for 'male' clients: they were advised to take on more adventurous, higher-risk portfolios that had the potential for higher returns. What's interesting is that female financial advisers made the same recommendations as their male counterparts, which suggests that they have preconceived notions about what other women can handle.[10]

The big issue here is that women tend to earn less than men throughout their careers and need to counteract the pay gap by maximizing the amount of money made through investments. This means taking more risk with investing, not less.

## Myth 2: *Women have no aptitude for business*

From stereotypes about women's lack of aptitude with money, it's not much of a leap to stereotypes about our capabilities in business. Globally, 60 per cent of companies have no female board members, 50 per cent have no female top executives, and fewer than 5 per cent have a female CEO.[11] A government-backed report looking at why there are so few women on the boards of the top 350 companies in Britain spoke to company leaders and were given the following reasons:

All the 'good' women have already been snapped up.
My other board colleagues wouldn't want to appoint a
   woman to our board.
We have one woman already on the board, so we are
   done – it is someone else's turn.
Most women don't want the hassle or pressure of
   sitting on a board.[12]

One boss said that women would probably struggle with the 'extremely complex issues'; another said women wouldn't 'fit comfortably into the board environment'. If these were the remarks made openly to researchers, think of the misogyny behind closed doors. Sexist remarks don't just ricochet off women's backs, to be absorbed by the ether.

They are unconsciously internalized. They affect women for longer than the moment it takes to make a disparaging remark.

Sometimes, women are complicit in downplaying their competence. With the growth in entrepreneurialism among women, terms such as #girlboss, #mumpreneur and #bossbabe (which has been used 13 million times on Instagram) have emerged, which, rather than elevating or empowering women, emphasize their traditional roles of femininity ('girls'), as mothers and as objects of attraction ('babes'). Have you ever heard a man describe himself as a boyboss or a dadpreneur? Men get to drop their domestic roles by being called simply 'boss' or 'entrepreneur'. An advert on the London Underground featuring a woman with the words 'You do the girl boss thing, we do the SEO thing' was banned after the Advertising Standards Authority upheld complaints that it was patronizing to women to refer to them as 'girls'. The agency also said the term 'SEO thing' (which refers to internet search engine optimization) used in this context implied that women were not skilled at technology.

This stereotype that women lack aptitude for business is out of step with reality. It's not what the data shows. There's a strong business case for having more women in leadership roles; it's not solely a matter of social justice.

Companies with more women in senior management are more creative; they experience a phenomenon dubbed 'innovation intensity' and come up with more innovations that can be patented.[13] More women in leadership roles leads to higher corporate profits. A research report entitled 'Is Gender Diversity Profitable?' looked at almost 22,000 businesses across ninety-one countries and came back with a solid 'yes'.[14] Management consultants McKinsey & Company also delved into the issue by examining 1,000 companies from twelve nations and found that mixed-gender management correlated with higher-than-average profits.[15] Other data shows that companies with above-average numbers of women running them have fewer scandals, such as bribery, corruption and battles with shareholders.[16] Interestingly, the ninety-one-country study noted that having a woman as CEO did not, in itself, lead to greater profitability. The positive impact came from having more women in the so-called C-suite, which is the handful of top jobs, such as chief financial officer, chief operations officer, chief information officer, chief marketing officer, and so forth.

This touches on the question of whether a woman is really heard, however senior she is, if she is the only representative of her gender at a high level. Research suggests that three is the magic number; when there are three or more women in a room, a tipping point is reached where their opinions become influential.[17]

It also raises a point about the value of rectifying the pay gap. It costs money to equalize pay when gender or racial discrepancies are found, but if those staff become satisfied rather than left disgruntled, and they become more committed to long-term careers at the company, these costs can be paid back when the company performs better and becomes more profitable.

The attractions of businesses with diverse leadership are so compelling that there are now professional investors who specialize in buying shares in them. These investors argue that if companies are more effective, more innovative and generally perform better when women get to have a say in how they are run, then, logically, the 30 per cent of companies around the world that don't have a single woman running them are more likely to underperform.

One of the UK's biggest asset managers, Legal & General Investment Management, set up a fund (a basket of shares in companies) called the L&G Future World Gender in Leadership UK Index Fund ('Girl Fund', for short).[18] It ranks big UK companies on their representation of women at different levels and invests more money into the most gender equal. This strategy is intended to encourage companies to do better on diversity issues, as the ones that take diversity seriously receive more investment. Investors, too, should make more money from shares in companies with gender-diverse management.

People with savings in a pension or an ISA can invest in this fund; it accepts investors putting in as little as £30 a month. Of course, everyone should seek professional advice before they invest their money, and a fund such as this won't be suitable for everyone. But for people who appreciate the benefits of gender diversity, supporting initiatives such as these could be a practical way of encouraging more diversity in business.

## Myth 3: Women do not make good entrepreneurs

This stereotype that women aren't good with money is the reason why less than 1 per cent of investment goes to female-run start-ups, according to a government report.

'There is an underlying attitude among some men, whether family members, potential funders, possible mentors or business partners, that women do not really belong in the entrepreneurial world,' reads the Alison Rose Review of

Female Entrepreneurship.[19] The report was commissioned by the government to tackle the 'shocking' fact that only one in five small businesses in the UK is run by a woman. It concluded that the lack of female entrepreneurs is hindering the economy.

Ironically, there's evidence that venture capital investors perceive female entrepreneurs and their businesses as a riskier proposition and instead opt for the 'safer' choice of investing their money with men.[20] Male investors simply prefer backing male-run companies, concluded researchers at the California Institute of Technology (Caltech).[21] In a study of 18,000 businesses, they found that male-led companies attracted more interest from investors and were more likely to be invited to meetings and referred on to other investors.

Again, this raises the chicken-and-egg issue: there aren't enough women in the upper echelons of industry to channel money into female-led start-ups, and because there isn't money going into female-led start-ups, there is a smaller pipeline of women rising up in industry. The Caltech researchers wanted to see if perhaps the kind of businesses that women found deter male investors, but when they analysed 'gender neutral' businesses which didn't have a clear masculine or feminine focus, men still preferred to invest with male-run companies.

When women enter the dragon's den to pitch to investors, they are often assessed to a different standard. The Rose Review found that investors are far more likely to want to see confidence in women business leaders than in men.[22] Meanwhile, over 60 per cent of the questions that male entrepreneurs are asked by investors are about the potential for their business – what their plans are and what they can do. By contrast, over 60 per cent of the questions posed to female entrepreneurs are about mitigating risk – so the focus is more on averting disaster than the potential for the woman's business.

'While firms invest in men based on perceived potential, women get funding only if they can already demonstrate performance,' states the Rose Review. This is a short-sighted stance by the mostly male cohort of venture capitalist investors, as studies show that female-run companies can be as successful as male-run ones. One study of 350 start-ups found that female-run businesses generated twice as much money per dollar invested as male-run companies.

In Britain today there are 1.1 million 'missing' businesses that would be run by women, were things equal. As mentioned, entrepreneurialism is a key driver of wealth, so we cannot achieve economic equality with men unless more women are able to thrive as self-made businesspeople.

As with other aspects of inequality, there is no one quick-fix solution. Certainly there needs to be dedicated start-up and, even more importantly, follow-on capital available for female entrepreneurs. The 'chronic and unfair finance gap' faced by female entrepreneurs was highlighted in 2018, when 200 British business leaders, including Samantha Cameron, Mary Portas and Karren Brady, submitted an open letter to the government calling for action to support women-led businesses.

Often, for small businesses, the initial funding is achievable, but the money needed to take the business to scale is sorely lacking. Venture capitalists should be encouraged or incentivized to provide funds for female-run businesses. The government runs schemes which provide tax incentives to wealthy investors for putting their money into early-stage companies – the 'enterprise investment scheme' and the 'seed enterprise investment scheme' – both of which have been very popular among private investors. There could possibly be an argument for a gendered incentive scheme, given that stimulating entrepreneurialism among women would benefit the economy.

The government would also be wise to look at best practice from other countries, including the US, Canada and Australia, since the UK stands out among its peers as being a place where fewer women start up businesses. Networking is also an issue for women entrepreneurs as, since there are fewer of them, there are fewer opportunities for mingling. This stands out as an area upon which a private business could capitalize; for example, a lender could run regular meet-ups for female start-ups and also provide attractive loans to the community of female entrepreneurs.

When it comes to getting more women to work at start-up businesses or in traditionally male sectors, one solution could be for employers to use less jargon in their job adverts. Vodafone, the mobile phone network, now scans its job adverts for gender-biased language and changes words to make job descriptions more palatable to women. Jargon, abbreviations and macho language are out – for example, 'outstanding candidate', 'mission-critical', 'aggressive growth' and 'premier agency' would be changed to 'extraordinary candidate', 'critical', 'bold growth' and 'top-tier agency'. The company said that, during a trial period, rephrased job adverts helped increase the number of women recruited.

## Female visibility in finance

Women aren't given an equal platform to share their perspective on economics, business, stock markets or finance. Analysis of the experts quoted in newspaper coverage of the economy in the UK found that over 80 per cent of the people given a voice or referred to were men.[23] Fewer than one in five articles spoke to women and men equally or quoted women more than men. Consequently, the narrative around economics, tax, government spending and many other financial matters is shaped by the world views and concerns of men. They can advocate for women, but this is not the same thing as women advocating for women. When women aren't heard, their concerns are overlooked and they continue to be disadvantaged economically.

Within the media at least, this is changing. It's much less acceptable for reporters and producers to create content that features only male voices, although it does still happen. Major media organizations, including the BBC, are trying to include a diversity of voices in their journalism, while London-based newspaper the *Financial Times* has bought software that scans articles for gender balance by analysing pronouns and first names. It found that only 21 per cent of people quoted in the newspaper were women. With this software, editors will be alerted if their section does not sufficiently incorporate women's views.[24] This is a fantastic change for a publication that covers the traditionally male areas of finance, investing, business and economics, and should be standard in newsrooms around the world. But it's also an editor's job to please the audience. If readers and viewers don't take a stand and call for more gender-inclusive journalism, there will be little incentive for change.

Producers and journalists are restricted to an extent by the gender of the spokespeople available at banks, insurance agencies and accountancy practices, at fund managers and economic consultancies. Within any organization it's the company management that decide who among the staff is most suitable to be the face and voice of the company. More often than not, the spokesperson is a man. He will be given media training, be introduced to journalists and work closely with the company's press office. When journalists call, he will be the one who speaks to them. So the bias towards male voices in the media comes from the top of organizations, when (mostly male) company management look at their (mostly male) senior staff and choose a man to be spokesperson. The gender inequality that's built into organizational structures is thus reinforced when we turn on the radio or browse the news and see that it's mostly men who are portrayed as experts.

Ultimately, the lack of women's views on financial news reinforces two damaging preconceptions about women. The first is that women aren't really qualified to talk about these things. The second is that women are not impartial. The benchmark for shrewd and insightful commentary on business is the male voice. They are assumed to speak for everyone. When women enter the debate we are assumed to be giving the 'female' perspective – in other words, we're partial. Women don't speak for everyone. Legendary feminist Gloria Steinem calls this silencing of women's views the 'unseriousness of all that is female'.[25] A problem that affects men is normative; it affects everybody. Women's issues are a minority concern. To dispel the myths and reverse these preconceptions around women and finance, the balance needs to be redressed.

# 4. The Scandal of Old-Age Poverty

Women live longer than men. Throughout history, in every place with reliable records, and in every year, women have outlived men, in countries with high and low mortality from Jamaica to Scandinavia, Bangladesh to Malaysia, even in those with massive gender inequality and pay gaps. We have been doing it for centuries. Sweden has kept comprehensive public records for generations and, in 1800, the average life expectancy of a man was thirty-one years, while for a woman it was thirty-three years. And this isn't something that is unique to humans or even to grown women. Baby girls are more likely to survive to their first birthday than baby boys, and female apes outlive their male counterparts. This super-survival trait is an incredible feature of female biology, especially considering that women face the perils of childbearing.

Scientists have struggled to explain female longevity. Historically, it was believed that men died younger because they wore themselves out with manual labour, or because they went into more dangerous occupations. However, even as both sexes have taken up sedentary employment and healthcare has improved, women retain a clear advantage in longevity. It's a paradox – women experience more sickness in the course of their lives but live for longer anyway.

There may be something about male biology that limits life spans – perhaps testosterone raises the risk of heart disease or accelerates ageing. Conversely, it could be that women's higher levels of oestrogen provide some health protection for the body, particularly the heart, but no one knows for sure.

Today, women can expect to live between ten and thirteen years longer than men in parts of the former Soviet Union, including Russia and Kazakhstan, while the average difference globally is four to seven years. In Britain, life expectancy stands at 82.9 years for women and 79.2 years for men.

The fact that women live longer has been so well documented that you would think that every wealthy society would ensure that they have sufficient resources to live off through these additional years. But in nearly all developed countries, women have less money saved than men at every stage of their lives and reach old age with fewer savings to live on than men. Across Europe the pensions savings gap averages at nearly 40 per cent and is widest in Germany, at 45 per cent, while in Australia the gap widened to a shocking 70 per cent in 2018.[1] It's not inevitable; Europe's smallest gender pensions gap is in Estonia, at 5 per cent. In monetary terms, British men retire with an average £315,000 saved in their workplace pensions, while women at the same age have £157,000.[2] It's simple maths: women earn less, have more 'career breaks' (a euphemism that highlights the lack of regard given to time spent raising children), so we save less, and more of us end up in old-age poverty.

There are two sources of income for older people who can't work – individual savings and state support. The figures above refer to the amount of money people have saved as individuals; when men have 40 per cent more to live off in old age, it's essentially a doubling of the pay gap that women have experienced throughout their lives.

Those loud and insistent men who argue that the salary gap doesn't matter or doesn't exist should speak to their mothers and grandmothers about what it's like to live off a pension half the size of a man's for many years longer. Of the people living alone after the age of sixty-five in the UK, around 70 per cent are women: they're widowed, divorced or single and many of them barely scrape by. The data shows a similar trend across Europe, with women facing a 'significant risk' of old-age poverty, according to the European Institute for Gender Equality.[3] Even if women start retirement with their husband or partner by their side, the odds are they won't be able to rely on them for the rest of their lives. The brutal truth is that men tend to die first, divorce is a leading cause of female poverty, and that widows and ex-wives are often left with next-to-nothing to live on. When we talk about old-age poverty, we're really talking about women.

All societies would benefit from ensuring women have higher incomes in retirement. Women who can stand on their own two feet financially will be less reliant on state support and more able to participate in their community. Their health will be better. The so-called 'silver pound' is a vital part of the global economy and it's an important factor in fostering the success and well-being of younger generations.

The scale of female impoverishment in later life is a reflection of structural disregard for women's financial welfare. Retirement savings schemes were designed by men, for men: historically, the concept of retirement didn't apply to women, who never stopped working in the home.

Employers began offering staff pension schemes to help them save in the decades following the Second World War, but they were not obliged to do so and nor did they have to offer them to both male and female staff. The marriage bar was a huge impediment to retirement saving for women, as some occupational pension schemes let men save from the age of twenty-one but wouldn't allow women to do so until they were older and considered too old to marry, usually between the ages of twenty-five and forty. This meant that working women missed out on years of pension contributions. Often if a woman had been saving into a workplace pension she was obliged to give it up for a 'marriage gratuity' – a lump sum paid when she married and left the company. This meant her pension savings were likely to be spent on the day-to-day needs of the family. Other pension schemes didn't allow women to save into them at all, on the basis that they didn't want the hassle of returning a woman's savings when she did eventually marry. When women did save into workplace pensions, often the rules had them saving a smaller percentage of their salary than men did, since men were considered providers. Although the lucky few had a husband with an occupational pension that would support the family while he was alive, wives could not expect to inherit it when he died.

Today, there are decades of documentation that show how the pension system has failed women and how it remains biased in men's favour. Consider this anecdote: the Treasury spends more than £53 billion every year on tax relief to incentivize people to save, but over 70 per cent of this sum goes to men.[4] It happens for two reasons: men have more money to save in the first place, so they put away 69 per cent of the money that goes into pensions each year. On top of that, more men are higher earners so they receive a higher amount of tax relief. These two factors combined mean that men receive £37.6 billion from the taxpayer each year to help them save for retirement. In comparison, women save a mere 31 per cent of the cash that goes into pensions and get 29 per cent of the tax relief. Meanwhile, millions of women don't earn enough to save anything for retirement, never mind rinse the tax system for all they can.

In 2012, the UK government launched the biggest overhaul of pensions policy in decades – but completely ignored the effect its policies would have on low-earning women. New rules made it mandatory for all private employers to give workers a pension, through a scheme called 'auto-enrolment'. This policy increased costs for employers but was a massive, much-needed change to address the fact that millions of people (both male and female) are not saving enough for old age. Yet 2.7 million women, around a third of workers, were excluded from this seismic transfer of money from employers to workers' savings accounts. Why? Because their salaries weren't high enough.

The rules state that a person must be aged over twenty-two and under the state pension age and earn at least £10,000 per annum from a single employer to be eligible for auto-enrolment. Policymakers seemed to forget that 59 per cent of women are in low-skilled (and therefore low-paid) jobs and many of them don't earn above the £10,000 threshold. Male employment in low-skilled work is at much lower levels, at 37 per cent.

Another chunk of the female workforce has been excluded from auto-enrolment because they earn more than £10,000, but from several employers. Policymakers just didn't think about the women who have to fit several jobs around child-care. And so the Conservative government's landmark policy for staving off future poverty excludes a third of working women. In contrast, only 16 per cent of men earn too little to be included in the scheme.

Flip this on its head. Can you imagine addressing a problem that affects both genders, but coming up with a solution that benefits 84 per cent of women while ignoring a third of men? Think about the design flaw here – would a policy that was to the detriment of 2.7 million men get off the drawing board? There are several ways of fixing auto-enrolment, which are discussed in more detail in the notes to this chapter.[5]

The other side of the pensions problem is the amount of support from the state that women are entitled to in old age. The British government followed Germany's lead to introduce the first state pensions in 1908, after several investigations had found that those most in need were older women. A person builds up entitlement to receive an income from the state in old age (the state pension) by paying National Insurance contributions, which is a percentage of their income deducted by HM Revenue and Customs.

Sounds fair, but the criteria attached to eligibility have mostly been achievable by one part of the population – men. In the UK, people can only receive the full state pension if they have worked and paid National Insurance for thirty-five years. If they have worked for between ten and thirty-five years, they will receive a smaller amount to live off. In 2006, just 13 per cent of women qualified for the basic state pension, compared to 92 per cent of men.

It's the same old story: many women have spent time out of paid employment to care for their families – they are working and contributing to society for long periods, but in their home and not for an employer. With no money coming in, they don't pay tax or National Insurance, so they don't notch up the qualifying years for a state pension and, when they come to old age, most haven't met the criteria to receive it. And because they didn't have an income, or much of an income, for a lot of their adult lives, they haven't been able to save into private pensions either. Remember that women were doing what was expected of them by devoting themselves to family responsibilities. Many of them had no choice – they couldn't afford to pay for childcare, and there has always been insufficient government-funded help for sick or disabled relations.

Even women who are well versed in personal finance will find pensions legislation so complex that it's easy to fall foul of the rules. For example, women who take time off to care for children will lose their National Insurance contributions unless they apply for child benefit – even if they know they are not eligible for it. It works like this: people who care for a child under the age of twelve and are not in paid work can receive National Insurance credits that count towards the thirty-five years of contributions each person needs to get the full state pension. To receive those credits, they need to apply for child benefit. However, in a confusing twist, people who are not eligible for child benefit because their partner earns too much still need to apply for it, get rejected, and then they will collect the credits. People lose entitlement to the full amount of child benefit if their partner earns £50,000 to £60,000 a year, and once their earnings are above £60,000 the family cannot receive any child benefit. The tax authorities know who is working, how much they are earning and which families are eligible for which benefits. Making people jump through hoops like this is pointless – surely the government's systems could be set up to make this easier for families.

Meanwhile, the state pension has long been set at a rate that leaves people under the poverty line. Although the system has been tweaked in recent years and is supposed to give women a better deal, under the 'new' state pension, only 500,000 pensioners receive the full amount of £168.60 a week (£8,767.20 a year) – an income that is so low it must be supplemented with financial support from elsewhere, such as private savings or a partner. Yet in 2013–14, only 37 per cent of women were paying into personal pensions, compared with 63 per cent of men. These are women who will have to depend on men or family, or face living in poverty.

Here is an example to illustrate exactly how little some women are receiving. A sixty-nine-year-old woman wrote to a national newspaper column wondering why she was receiving £80 a week as a state pension. She also had a work pension which paid £30 a month.[6] Surely there had been some mistake – aside from ten years spent raising her children, she had been employed throughout her working life and had expected to be receiving much more as her state pension. The newspaper's pensions expert explained that she was receiving the correct amount from the state: she was one of 4.4 million married women who had joined a scheme that was popular in the seventies, where wives paid a reduced rate of National Insurance contributions (NICs) on their earnings and in return would receive a smaller pension when they retired. The scheme was informally called the 'married woman's stamp' and people opted into it as they would have more money in their take-home pay each month, plus it seemed obvious that wives could rely on their husbands financially. However, many women didn't know they'd agreed to it: their employers automatically put them onto the scheme. This was at a time when many workplace pensions still banned female staff from joining, so awareness of retirement savings among women was low. Many of this generation have reached retirement age and received a nasty shock when they see just how little state pension they are entitled to. Today, there are 200 women still on this scheme, which closed to new participants in 1977.

National Insurance is a contributory system – an individual can only be eligible for payouts when they're deemed to have paid sufficient amounts into the scheme. From a gender perspective, contributory systems are deeply unfair because they recognize the contribution made to society and the economy by some of the workers – the ones who can prioritize paid work outside the home. Other kinds of state support are paid on a redistributive basis – the money is raised by taxation and given to those that need it irrespective of what they have paid into the system.

A common misconception about the state pension is that National Insurance contributions deducted from your salary go into a savings pot with your name on it. Actually, the money received by current pensioners is paid for out of working people's taxes, so Britain's ageing population (with proportionally more older people to younger workers) is a problem because the system only works if there are far more younger people than older ones. A better system – which works fairly for women and men – would invest working people's contributions so that they increase in value and the money can be used to fund state pension entitlement. The Women's Budget Group is campaigning for the introduction of a tax-funded Citizens Pension, which every senior citizen would receive irrespective of contributions. It would provide an income that people could feasibly live off. This would be a form of state redistribution that is gender-inclusive, respecting mothers, fathers and carers who have prioritized others at their own expense, and giving senior citizens a level of dignity and independence that every human deserves.

Looking at retirement poverty reveals two important truths: that the impact of economic inequality can be felt decades later, and that what seem like small details in government policy can have a devastating effect on women's lives.

Here's another example. Pension credit is a government top-up to the poorest pensioners in Britain, more than 1 million of whom are women compared to 600,000 men. The annual increase to pension credit payments in 2018 was 2.3 per cent, while the state pension, which is mostly received by men, went up by a more generous 3 per cent. It's a small difference but not inconsequential, and one that reflects the relative importance of older men versus older women.

Over the past decade the government has reduced its spending on pension credits, and every 1 per cent fall in these payments between 2007 and 2013 caused an increase in deaths among old people in England.[7] Since the majority of those aged over eighty-five are women and the bulk of the elderly poor are women, these 'budget savings' the government is making are actually causing women to die. Death rates for older females in this period rose by 6 per cent.

## WASPI *women and widows*

Retirement saving is the most arcane of industries; the complex rules are frequently tweaked and the baffling jargon leaves pension savers floundering but keeps financial advisers in employment. Terms such as 'uncrystallized funds pension lump sum', 'money purchase annual allowance' and 'trivial commutation' are part of the vernacular. No wonder that the most common word women use when they contact a pensions adviser is 'sorry': 'Sorry for bothering you'; 'Sorry, I don't understand'; 'Sorry, I should know more'. Perhaps more than in any other area of social policy, in pensions, people are reliant on authority – whether it's the government, their employer or an independent financial adviser – to help them make sense of the murky legislation.

This is why the Conservative government's decision to fast-track changes to women's pensions was especially cruel. The government raised the age at which women can receive the state pension to sixty-six, up from sixty previously, to equalize it with men. Historically, men became eligible for retirement later than women. It didn't do enough to inform the women who would be affected, and suddenly 3.8 million women born in the 1950s approached the age of sixty and discovered they have to wait up to six more years to retire.

The result has been 'poverty, homelessness and financial hardships among women', according to the United Nations.[8] These 3.8 million women have lost up to £50,000 each, money they are entitled to receive following decades of contributions to the system. Many have been forced to keep working despite being in ill health. Some are suicidal. Despite campaigning from a group called Women Against State Pension Inequality (WASPI), the government has refused to provide any help to these women.

What's more, news coverage of the saga has elicited unsympathetic responses from the general public, with sentiments running along the lines of 'Stupid women should have known about their pensions, it's their fault.'

Should these women have known better? Put yourself in

their shoes. Place this all in the context of how society has infantilized women of this generation. If you were born in 1950, you would have been forty years old before you started paying income tax on your salary (your husband would have paid taxes for the household). You would have been aged thirty before you could take out a loan without a male guarantor. Unsurprisingly, fifties women were not sufficiently well versed in finance that they were aware of these changes to pensions legislation. Women of this generation were raised to be married, to be reliant on men financially. No one told them to make contingency plans.

Widows have also been targeted by government cuts. Until 2017, people who had a child and experienced the loss of their husband, wife or civil partner would receive a lump sum of £2,000 to help with funeral costs and loss of earnings following the bereavement. They would also receive financial support of up to £113.70 a week for up to twenty years. This system recognized the increased risk of poverty for lone parents, especially women, who are more likely to be widowed than men, partly because they live longer and tend to marry men who are older than them.[9] Women also take a far bigger hit financially when they are widowed, since men tend to be the higher earners and more women work part-time.

Since the payments were partly based on the deceased's National Insurance contributions, the bereaved parent was getting back some of what their partner had put into the system. Payments would stop when the widowed parent started cohabiting or remarried.

This system was decimated by government cutbacks in 2017. Since then, a parent who has lost their spouse receives a lump sum of £3,500 (£2,000 for people without children), plus £350 a month for eighteen months (£100 a month for people without kids).

The slashing of financial support for bereaved parents from up to twenty years to eighteen months was exactly the kind of policy move that leaves women poorer than men. It was another demonstration of the disregard that the male-majority leaders of this country have for women.

The retirement poverty discussed in this book is entirely avoidable. Governments could find the money to support women in their old age if they wanted to, although the political will to do this is very much absent.

Meanwhile, many employers have switched to offering staff less secure pension plans, arguing that traditional 'defined benefit' schemes are unjustifiably expensive for the business. Defined benefit pensions are the most secure kind of savings scheme for workers, as employees receive a lump sum when they retire plus a set amount of money each year until they die. In other words, the 'benefit' they will receive throughout retirement is defined at the outset. The amount each person receives will be a proportion of their salary relative to the number of years spent in the job and it will usually be increased with inflation.

Younger workers, especially those in the private sector, have 'defined contribution' pensions, which means that the only certainty is how much money is being saved in (or contributed to) the account. The savings are invested but it's impossible to predict how successful the investments will be or how much you will ultimately have on the day you retire. These are two big risks.

Employers have gradually shut down defined benefit pension schemes and nearly all in the private sector are closed to new savers. But Britain's 350 largest companies spent fourteen times more on dividend payouts to shareholders than on their pensions. So maybe it's not a matter of affordability, but of priorities. And, of course, because women live for longer, it's retired female staff who are supported for more years from a company's defined benefit pension. But women generally aren't the ones in charge of big business or making the decisions about what kind of pensions employees get.

These are trends that we can and should be railing against. But campaigners have been hindered because the retirement savings system is labyrinthine in its complexity, steeped in jargon, and misinformation is widespread. Many people don't support pro-pension campaigns, even if what's at stake is their own financial future, simply because they don't fully understand what's happening.

A cynic would say this is intentional. When the powerful (governments and employers) put in place complex practices that the less powerful (employees) don't understand, the power structure is maintained. Oppression can be as subtle as allowing confusion to cloud the air. It can also be as brazen as swindling nearly 4 million women and ignoring their calls for help.

The government ought to produce an annual report on the gender pensions gap, which would bring the issue onto the same stage as the gender pay gap. But without compensating people when they drop out of paid work to perform *socially necessary unpaid* work, female economic inequality will never be addressed.

If the government were to continue paying into some of

these carers' pensions while they do full-time caring, how much difference would it make?

The Social Market Foundation, a think tank, says that women on maternity leave perform labour worth £762.75 each week, and if they were to receive a 3 per cent contribution into their pension they would save £1,189.89 a year for retirement.[10] The Pensions Policy Institute has calculated that such a scheme could close the gender pensions gap by 28 per cent and would cost the government between £1.2 billion and £1.6 billion annually, which is 4 per cent of the cost of pension tax relief.[11]

While we wait and hope for government solutions, it's vital that women get to grips with the basics of retirement savings. Below I'll explain the key points that everyone should understand.

## Pensions explained

Being retired is like having a lifetime of Saturdays stretching out before you. Having enough money saved to no longer have to work is the most incredible freedom.

Life is a constant battle between satisfying today's demands and the needs of the future. Most women don't save enough money for retirement for one of two reasons: 1) They have a comfortable income and could afford to pay more into a pension, but retirement planning isn't on their radar; or 2) The immediate needs of their household mean saving for old age is unrealistic.

The key point about retirement savings is that having something waiting for you in a pension account is better than nothing. Every penny put into a pension is a gift to your future self.

*I know the word 'pensions', obviously,*
*but am not clear on how they work.*

Pensions are savings accounts, but they have some special features, including a ban on withdrawing retirement savings until a specified age set by the government, currently fifty-five in the UK. (In this section I'm referring to defined contribution pensions, as these are the most common schemes today. Defined benefit schemes, mentioned above, have their own rules.)

You can open a pension account through your workplace or by yourself. Employers put a percentage of each staff member's salary into their pension. Many companies will increase the amount they contribute for staff who increase their own contributions. Log on to your workplace pension account and raise your monthly contribution to the level at which you get the biggest employer contribution.

The money in your pension is invested by your pension provider so that it rises in value. Typically it will be spread across global stock markets, loans to foreign governments (called bonds) and maybe areas such as infrastructure projects, gold or property. People who want to choose their own pension investments can do so, either by contacting their workplace pension provider or by opening up a 'self-invested personal pension' (SIPP) with a provider such as AJ Bell, Aviva or Scottish Widows and then paying money in regularly. Both the Money Advice Service and Citizens Advice have some good resources on explaining how to choose a pension provider.[12]

## What is tax relief?

This is a government incentive to encourage people to save for retirement. When you save into a pension some of the money that you would have paid in tax on your salary goes into your pension. The 'tax relief' is linked to each person's income tax rate. Basic rate taxpayers receive 20 per cent tax relief; higher rate taxpayers receive 40 per cent tax relief; additional rate taxpayers get 45 per cent tax relief.

Higher earners should know that the maximum amount you can pay into a pension in a single year in order to still get tax relief is either 100 per cent of your salary or £40,000. Anyone is welcome to put more money into their pension (for example, if you receive an inheritance) but it won't get the tax benefits.

Tax relief can be a difficult concept to understand, so know this: wealthy people and their financial advisers make sure they put as much money as possible into their pensions so they receive the full tax perks. We all should aim to do this.

Because people have been 'relieved' of having to pay tax while they are saving for a pension, when you withdraw your pension you will pay income tax on the money. Most people are allowed a tax-free lump sum the first time they dip into their pensions.

## What about lower earners?

Women with no earnings or an income of less than £3,600 a year can still pay up to £2,880 into a personal pension scheme (one you open independently of any employer) and the government's tax relief will top up the amount in the account to £3,600 a year.

It would really help women if the system was changed to make it easier for working people to save for their partner's retirement. Perhaps workers should be able to designate a portion of their pension that they save into each month for their partner. Or, it could be made simple for staff to open a separate pension in the name of their partner through their employer's scheme. The employer would not pay into the second pension of course, but the employee could stipulate that X per cent of their salary goes into their own pension and another X per cent goes into their partner's. The earning spouse would not be able to view the account, see the balance, withdraw money or choose the investments – only the non-working partner could.

## How much should I be saving?

Experts have come up with a few guides to how much people should be saving, although the figures are often criticized for being unattainably high. For example:

1. One rule says that you need to have saved the equivalent of your annual salary in a pension by the age of thirty. It should be three times your salary by forty, six times by fifty, eight times by sixty and ten times your annual salary by age sixty-seven. For example, someone earning £30,000 would aim to have £300,000. Remember: with any pension savings target, not all of those figures will be money you have personally put aside. Employer contributions and the effect of investment growth should help you reach any target.

2. Put aside 12.5 per cent to 15 per cent of your monthly salary. This would be around £312.50 a month for someone earning £30,000 a year, including employer contribution. Look up the paperwork for your workplace pension or log

in to the online service to see how much you're saving each month. Bump it up if you can. If £312.50 was invested for forty years and had 4 per cent investment growth annually, it would reach the target of £300,000.

3. A savings method for people worried that they haven't saved enough is to take your age, divide it in half and put this percentage of your salary into a pension. Someone aged fifty, for example, would put 25 per cent of their income away. Of course, whatever age you are this method means siphoning off a good chunk of salary each month – but it's an excellent idea for those who are able to do so and want to ramp up their saving.

There is no fixed number that a person can have saved which ensures they won't have to worry about money ever again. People's outgoings tend to be much lower in their sixties and seventies, as by this age mortgages are paid off (ideally) so there is no monthly housing cost, they don't have to pay for much petrol or train fares for commuting, children have flown the nest and most seventy-somethings aren't saving up for a wedding, a baby or a new car. Retired people typically have between 40 per cent and 70 per cent of their former income, so someone who earned £50,000 a year might aim to have an income of £20,000 annually (40 per cent of their previous income).

That said, an individual's lifestyle and interests also dictate how much money they will need. Some people will relish spending more time with their grandchildren and learning Italian. Other people expect to spend most of their days drinking Chablis on the Côte d'Azur.

If you're serious about retirement planning, look at your life expectancy and the age at which you envision yourself retiring. This will depend on your career; if you're a police officer or firefighter you might be expected to stop working at an earlier age than someone who works in marketing or as a legal secretary. Do you have three children, and do you want to keep working until you have supported the youngest one through university? Are you planning on selling your home in fifteen years and moving to Malaga, where the cost of living is lower?

### *I have several pensions from different jobs, what shall I do?*

Around £400 million in pension savings has been 'lost' or forgotten about by people who moved jobs and years later can't remember whether they had a pension, which provider it was with, or how they can get at it. The average person has eleven jobs in their lifetime, so if you're one of the people with missing savings, you're not alone. The government has a Pensions Tracing Service which helps people do just that. It's free to use. See gov.uk/find-pension-contact-details for more information.

Should you consolidate all these different pensions into one? It depends. The drawback of having several retirement savings accounts is that each one is paying annual fees for the money to be invested. This adds up significantly over the decades that you have a pension and it can be more economical to transfer separate accounts into one, so there is a single batch of investment fees being paid from your savings. You might not want to consolidate them if the money in each pension account is being invested in different ways, you understand why and want to keep it like that.

Deciding whether to consolidate them should become

much easier in future, as the government is working on a website that everyone will be able to log in to, like online banking, in order to see the various pension pots they have all in one place. It's called the Pensions Dashboard – so look out for it when it arrives.

## *What do I actually do with my pension savings?*

I mentioned earlier that the first chance most people have to dip into their savings is after their fifty-fifth birthday. Some people use a chunk of pension savings to pay off their mortgage, buy an investment property, do home improvements, etc. You pay tax on money withdrawn from a pension and it also might affect how much you can continue saving. So anyone thinking of doing this needs to contact a financial adviser who will crunch the numbers to see how much you could withdraw while keeping enough for your later life and how much tax you will pay.

When you come to retire, there are a couple of options for the amount of money you have saved. The most popular course of action is to make the most of the rule that allows retirees to take a lump sum out of their savings tax-free and to use this little windfall to have some fun or to pay off their mortgage. (You'll obviously need to check the specific rules at the time you retire to see how much you're allowed.)

Then you can either:

1. Leave the rest of the money invested. Each year, you decide on an amount to withdraw to live on. In pension jargon this is called 'drawdown' because you are regularly 'drawing' on your savings. Caveat: this is a risky thing to do.

Because the money's still invested the amount could fall, leaving you with a smaller retirement fund. The investments could also rise, so you make more money over the years that you aren't working. Doing it this way also means your heirs can inherit the money after your passing.

2. After taking your tax-free chunk, give some, or all, of your pension savings to an insurance company in exchange for an 'annuity'. An annuity is an agreement for the insurer to pay you out a set amount of money for life. The amount you'll get depends on how much you have to 'buy' this annuity alongside the insurer's calculations about how long you'll live. Actuaries will look at your age, health, marital status, location and other personal details to predict your lifespan – if you retire at seventy and are likely to live until 100, the insurer will be paying out to you annually for a lot longer than someone who has smoked all their life or survived two bouts of cancer. The less healthy person might be offered more money each year, based on the assumption that they will have a shorter lifespan.

The benefit of doing this is that you will know what your income will be every day until you die. The downside is that you've given away all (or most) of your savings to an insurer and you may spend the rest of your days wondering if you could have made more of your money doing something else, say, through buying an investment property, having a financial adviser invest it, etc.

3. The amount of money retirees get from annuities is also dependent on how investment markets are doing. The insurer that takes your pension fund will invest it with the aim of making more money than they are paying out to you, which is where their profits come from. If investment markets are doing badly then people retiring are offered a worse deal.

Whatever you choose to do at retirement, it's vital that you make the money last as long as you do. The government needs to introduce more sophisticated budgeting tools, which could be made available through organizations such as the Money Advice Service or Citizens Advice. Retirement saving is a gendered issue, right from the moment women start working and paying into their pensions through to the day they spend the last penny in their pension pot.

# 5. Malestream Economics

Feminism has always been about economics, but economics hasn't generally been about women.

It's an industry dominated by men; in the UK only 15 per cent of academic economists are women, in the US the figure is 13 per cent,[1] and it falls to 12 per cent of professors at Europe's top twenty economics schools.[2] This is in sharp contrast with other social and natural sciences, as well as professions where women have tipped the gender balance towards equality. In the UK women make up 44 per cent of accountants (63 per cent in the US) and 48 per cent of GPs (37 per cent in the US).[3]

The most celebrated economists are virtually all men – is that because women don't have good ideas? Or because their contributions are undervalued? In her book *The Great Economists*, Oxford University professor Linda Yueh discusses twelve of the most influential economists and how their ideas can help us today. There is only one woman among them, Joan Robinson. Yueh attributes this to the 'chronic dearth of women' in the profession.[4]

The highest honour in economics, the Nobel Prize, has been awarded to two women out of its eighty-four winners: Elinor Ostrom in 2009, alongside Oliver Williamson for his separate work, and Esther Duflo in 2019 for work with her partner Abhijit Banerjee and colleague Michael Kremer. No woman has won outright.

Like other exceptional women, Ostrom swam against the tide as a budding academic in 1960s America. It was an era when 'there was no encouragement to think about anything other than teaching in high school or being pregnant and barefoot in the kitchen', she once said in an interview.[5]

To the students of economics at university level, women are a rarity in the syllabus and an endangered species among academic staff. The number of female academics falls at increasing levels of seniority, so when students are taught by women they tend to be in lower status roles: the research assistants overseeing tutorials rather than the professors sharing the ideas from their own books. With women in the minority on degree courses, students of economics go to seminars where they discuss mostly male ideas with a group of mostly male peers.

The numbers of women working towards undergraduate degrees in economics has been falling, and they now make up just 28 per cent of economics students in Britain.[6] Higher proportions of women graduate with degrees in maths, engineering, science, technology and business, so it's nothing to do with intrinsic aptitude. When women and girls don't consider pursuing economics, they may be unwittingly closing the door to some of the highest-paying careers; salaries of economics graduates, both male and female, are the second-highest after medicine.[7]

It's an open secret that economics can be a hostile industry for women, from the job-searching forums for graduates right up to the circles that Nobel Prize winners move in. One research paper examined the words that students and early career economists used when discussing men and women on a popular online forum, Economics Job Market

Rumors (EJMR).[8] Women were frequently described in sexual terms with comments related to their appearance or personality, while remarks about men focused on their academic credentials.

Not all men are antagonistic towards women; nor are all male economists or students. But men who remain silent in the presence of misogyny (whether online or in real life) are colluding in a culture that diminishes women. Men are in the best position to change this.

Economics is similar to politics in the sense that it involves a lot of impassioned debate. Competing theories of economics are like religions; students and academics hold to their beliefs as if they were the word of God. When economics is discussed the mood is rarely jocular; these are serious issues. After becoming the second woman (and youngest person) to accept the Nobel Prize in Economic Sciences, Duflo described the industry's 'aggressive' style of debating alongside its 'macho' and 'sexist' culture, all of which she believes has deterred women, leaving a 'disastrously low' number of female economists.[9] She says the mindset in economics is one of 'survival of the fittest'. If women don't reach the top, it's because they got eaten lower down in the food chain – and that's just how it is.

The French-American economist added: 'It is not intentionally sexist, but it's become sexist, because the broader social environment is such that women are trained to be polite, and not to interrupt, and to let people finish their sentences ... There is a thin line between engaging and aggressive, and it is often crossed. In an environment [like economics] where it's fair game to interrupt people and not let them finish their thought, it's more conducive to men. And also women just honestly don't like it.'[10]

## *Who economists* are *matters*

Women are under-represented in many industries and over-represented in others. But exactly who economists *are* matters because they have a huge influence on government and society. Around the world, 'chief economist' is a highly respected senior role in governments, central banks, and all kinds of private and public sector organizations. Teams of economists give their spin on current events and make predictions that guide decision-making in every area of modern life, from healthcare to education, air pollution to the location of a new airport.

Having solely male input into policymaking is like only testing medicines and protective equipment on male bodies. At best, policymakers fail to see how their ideas affect half of the population; at worst, the male bias puts women at risk of harm. One survey of male economists in the US found they were more likely to perceive dangers in government intervention than female economists, tended to think that mandatory minimum wages cause unemployment, and were less concerned about environmental protection than their female peers.[11]

In contrast, surveys of female economists in the US and across Europe found that they showed stronger support for more equal distribution of income and progressive taxation, tended to disagree that strengthening workers' rights causes poor economic growth, and had less faith in leaving problems to be solved by market forces.[12] The female economists surveyed were also more likely to agree with the statement that employers should have to provide healthcare for full-time employees, a perspective that was possibly influenced by women's more hands-on involvement with caring for sick family and friends.

One particularly revealing finding was that female economists in both Europe and America often disagreed with the statement that both genders have equal opportunities. They leaned towards thinking that men had more opportunity in higher education and at work, and much more strongly believed that men were favoured in academia.

Male economists disagreed. They were more likely to believe that opportunities are equal and that the wage gap is explained by job choices or differences in education and skills between the sexes. Perhaps the reason gender inequality hasn't been eradicated is because the people who make social policy don't even notice the problem. Getting more women into economics should mean that a broader range of solutions is laid on the table, and, more importantly, the scope of what constitutes a social problem could be broadened.[13] Since women are less likely than their male peers to believe that inequality is inevitable, economists could begin to ask different questions altogether.

The economics profession has been going through an existential crisis, one which could mean 'the rebirth of economics', the Bank of England's chief economist Andy Haldane has suggested.[14]

For the past twenty years, mainstream economic thought has struggled to explain or provide solutions for serious problems including extreme wealth inequality, the disappearance of inflation, the impact of record-low interest rates and how societies predicated on endless growth can be sustained as climate change accelerates.

Economists' inability to find a clear path around these obstacles has called into question the credibility of mainstream economic thought. This is a discipline badly in need of new ideas, and the time is ripe for women to help reshape the future of economics.

## *The malestream*

Mainstream economics has been dubbed 'the malestream' by some academics, who argue that the very foundations of the subject are inappropriately masculine. From biased, male-centric beginnings, it's not surprising to critics that economics is struggling to provide solutions to real-world problems.

The basis for modern economic thinking was laid out by Adam Smith, a Scottish professor whose views on the best way for societies to flourish were considered revolutionary when they were published in 1759 and 1776. Smith's grounding principle was that every individual's actions are motivated by self-interest, at all times and in every situation. Over the following century male intellectuals used Smith's assumptions to develop a persona called 'Economic Man' or *homo economicus*, a calculating individual who is motivated by financial gain and never swayed by the herd when making decisions.

Despite heavy criticism and the development of behavioural economic theories, which have a more nuanced understanding of human motivations, *homo economicus* remains the basis for many economic models used today. In her book *Who Cooked Adam Smith's Dinner?*,[15] economist Katrine Marçal points out that Smith lived with his mother for most of his life, a woman who tended to the home and made sure her son's dinner was on the table every evening. She did this out of love, freeing up time for Smith to work on his economic theories which, ironically, assumed everyone was entirely self-interested and took no account of the people who did things for no compensation. People like his mother.

Smith was also a staunch believer in removing regulations and taxes from buying and selling, which came to be called the 'free' market.

The thinking behind free markets is kind of paradoxical: Smith argued that by allowing every man to follow his own self-interest unimpeded, the market would self-correct into one that was efficient and socially useful. So if everyone could do as they pleased, a market economy that would benefit everyone would emerge.

In the eighteenth century intellectuals were fascinated by the emergence of physics and astronomy. Both disciplines used mathematics to explain the physical world and people believed that God's designs were revealed through scientists' measurements and calculations.

Mathematics was incorporated into economics, which gave it a scientific legitimacy and was useful insofar as maths can be used to make predictions and lay out information visually. But to do these calculations economists had to make some assumptions, namely that each of us is an Economic Man. And so our complex social world of individuals with their own histories, identities and motivations became reduced to a population of Economic Mans with just one simple desire – self-interest – and a single approach to decision-making – rational and calculated.

Economic Man is an unflattering caricature of masculinity. But over the centuries this approach has become an ideal of how men (and women) should behave. Human values and motivations that are left out of economic equations include

love, consideration, generosity, altruism, the joy of cooperation and community – all traits that are considered feminine.
By excluding these motivations from the economic frame-
work, they are devalued, even though they keep society
functioning. The parent who minds the baby while the
breadwinner goes out to work plays a part in the economic
fortunes of their family, their community and their country.
The same goes for the person who puts dinner on the table
when their children return from school, who drives their
spouse to the station so they get to work on time – these
gestures are economic activity, irrespective of whether
they're paid for or not.

They say that if you look at the world through rose-tinted
glasses, all the red flags will look like flags. And so, with
economists having a powerful role in institutional decision-
making, there's a risk that every social problem is framed as
something that can be fixed with a mathematical tweak.
Make hospitals a place to raise income and boost international trade, cut costs in care homes, encourage business
investment in education (it will increase gross domestic
product, or GDP), keep the pound strong . . . and so on.

Even among economists there is unease at how abstract and
removed from everyday concerns the discipline has become.
Duflo has criticized economists' obsession with GDP and
income as a 'distorting lens'.[16]

GDP, the figures that calculate the size and growth of
the economy, has become so embedded as a proxy for
national well-being that we fear recessions (periods of falling GDP) and live in hope of economic recoveries (when
GDP is rising). Boosting GDP has become the guiding
light of social policy: it's a tool to compare the relative success
of countries over time, and political decisions in all areas of

public life are often made with a view to making the economy bigger.

What's included in GDP formulas varies over time and between countries. The formulas are frequently tweaked by governments and statisticians, sometimes in ways that are more credible than others, and often in a bid to make a nation look as though it's doing better, economically speaking, than its rivals.

In 2014 Nigeria announced it had overtaken South Africa by becoming the largest economy in the continent. On the ground, nothing had happened, but Nigerian economists had decided to change the formula for the country's GDP by including things that were previously disregarded, such as the value of downloaded music and the burgeoning 'Nollywood' film industry.

On a different day in 2014, the UK economy grew by more than £5 billion overnight. For 67 million Britons, nothing had changed. What had happened was that economists had begun to include sex work in their GDP calculations. Despite the fact that brothels are illegal and the Crown Prosecution Service describes this profession as a form of sexual exploitation, a bit of financial wizardry gave sex work an economic legitimacy and it boosted the nation's economy by 5 per cent.

Extensive gaps in the data on sex work meant that statisticians had to make some assumptions: that, in the UK, there are 60,879 sex workers nationwide, each with roughly twenty-five clients a week and charging an average rate of £67.16.[17] The calculations also factored in figures from the Netherlands suggesting that sex workers spend £107 a year on clothes and 42 pence for each condom.[18] Clearly, this is a very crude approximation of a complex market that takes in both five-star hotels and dark streets in Holbeck, Leeds (where a legal prostitution zone has been created), involves men, women and minors, and varying levels of consent, abuse and addiction.

Debate over the inclusion of sex work in GDP figures highlighted one of its shortcomings: it takes no account of the nation's well-being. For example, if a hundred people fall ill with salmonella and go to hospital, the work and resources that go into making them better are counted as economic activity and this benefits the economy. But no one would argue that it would be good if more people became ill. Given that higher GDP is 'good' and lower GDP is 'bad', a bigger trade in sex would flatter GDP figures – although this is in opposition to current law, and will be at the expense of those who may suffer from all the related activity. (I'm not taking a stand on the morality of sex work; that's a subject for a different book. But we know it involves a mostly female workforce and that the industry is often bound up with human trafficking and organized crime.)

At the same time, GDP doesn't count work that people do for free. It only counts goods and services that are bought and sold, which includes workers providing labour in return for a salary. The unpaid work of childminding, cleaning, cooking and caring for disabled, sick or elderly relatives, which is mostly carried out by women, is not recognized. The average British woman provides 1,352 hours of unpaid work a year, but this labour, and that of millions of other women, is systematically ignored by official figures.

This is where female values have been cut out of the picture. Labours of love are simply not included when economists calculate the metrics of success by which we judge our society. It's perverse: when a hundred people spend time cooking for their families and taking care of others, this labour has a positive effect on society but, since it is uncompensated, it is deemed economically worthless. So a structure like GDP undermines the value of the caring work that is mostly carried out by women, but at the same time values an illicit form of mostly female work (sex work).

Historically, economists refused to quantify the value of work done at home by saying it would be too difficult to measure. In the past few decades, feminist economists have come up with various models to calculate women's work, such as time-use surveys where people report what they were doing each hour and statisticians estimate how much it would cost to pay someone else to do the same tasks. These kinds of models are used by official bodies including the Organisation for Economic Co-operation and Development (OECD), and Britain's Office for National Statistics has calculated that women would be paid £269 a week on average if they were compensated for household chores.[19]

There are other glaring inconsistencies in how statisticians value and measure traditionally 'male' work and 'female' work. Government spending on roads and ports is classed as infrastructure investment and recognized as vital to improving economic activity – it employs a mostly male workforce and makes it easier for goods and people to get around. But government spending on childcare is not – even though nationwide provision of childcare would be valuable to the economy: it would employ large numbers of people (likely women) and give parents more free time to participate in other parts of the economy. In the US, senator Elizabeth Warren has been calling for childcare to be classified as an infrastructure investment,[20] and studies show how the lack of affordable childcare can hold back economic growth in developed nations.[21] Maternal employment in Britain is particularly low compared to other developed economies – there is a huge gap in the numbers of women who could be contributing economically if only they could be mothers and wage earners at the same time. If Britain had the same generous provision of childcare that more gender-equal Scandinavian nations have, an estimated 1.4 million women would be working. That's 1.4 million women who would be able to catch up with men economically and build a financial future for themselves.[22]

Childcare is an essential public service just like transport and healthcare – both of which are state-subsidized because of the economic benefits of having a population who can easily go to work and earn. Childcare is an invisible force for good in the economy. Without it, the strain on household finances limits consumption, fewer adults are economically productive, as they're staying at home rather than participating in the labour force, and those adults pay less in taxes. The cost of childcare can be a deterrent to having children.[23]

Economic inequality lies at the heart of the social and political struggles that are going on around the world. Excellent resources for further reading on this include *Who Cooked Adam Smith's Dinner?* by Katrine Marçal, discussed above, *GDP: A Brief But Affectionate History* by Diane Coyle and *Economyths: 11 Ways Economics Gets It Wrong* by David Orrell. The gendered side of this inequality needs to move to the core of any discussion about how we face these challenges. There's growing recognition that the assumptions underlying mainstream economics are overly simplistic, rigid, and failing to capture the humanity within men, women and the economy.

# 6. When Governments Ignore Gender

All over Britain, women like myself are living with a rare genetic condition that slowly limits our ability to stand and walk. It's called lipoedema and it causes fat cells to fill up with a long-chain gel called glycosaminoglycan (GAG) which clogs up the lymphatics (the body's detox system), creating painful swelling and bruising. Because the fat cells don't contain fat, they're impossible to burn off through diet or exercise. Instead this diseased tissue proliferates in the legs and arms before spreading all over the body like a cancer.

Lipoedema only affects women, and while very little research has been done, scientists do know that it's linked to female hormones, as the condition usually appears at puberty and worsens with pregnancy, menopause and use of the contraceptive pill. It's a lifelong, progressive condition that will have me confined to a wheelchair before I'm forty-five unless I have surgery. (I'm lucky; there are women in their twenties with lipoedema who are already unable to walk.) But the NHS refuses to fund the surgery, its rationale being that treatment involves removing fat cells through a form of liposuction, which is classed as a cosmetic procedure, something the NHS does not cover. And yet it spends up to £88 million on Viagra in one year.[1]

Ironically, lipoedema sufferers can't just walk into any cosmetic surgery clinic and book some £5,000 liposuction on credit. There are four specialist surgeons in Britain who can treat the condition and private fees are at least £50,000 per patient. And so it's routine for women with lipoedema to raid their pensions or take out massive loans to pay for treatment, compromising their financial security. As sufferers become immobile some have lost their jobs, are forced into early retirement or reluctantly give up their careers as teachers and nurses because they can no longer stand. Because lipoedema looks like obesity, women with the condition can experience stigma and discrimination – turn to Chapter 13 to read how women perceived as obese receive lower pay.

This is a clear case of institutional gender discrimination. If lipoedema affected men, it's impossible to believe that the NHS would leave young, able-bodied men in agonizing pain, facing the choice between selling their homes or life in a wheelchair. Britain is missing a trick economically as, firstly, Germany has become the world centre of excellence for lipoedema treatment and women fly from all over the world to be seen by one of the country's many specialists. Secondly, it is estimated that for every £1 spent on public health, the median return to the economy is £14, as a population in better health is more able to participate in the economy.[2] I've started a campaign to get lipoedema treatment available on the NHS for all women – see gofundme.com/annabellelondon for more information.

NHS England's spending decisions are made by the chairs of Clinical Commissioning Groups, 85 per cent of whom are male. As mentioned above, men with erectile dysfunction in the UK have been able to receive Viagra and a generic equivalent free on the NHS – and doctors wrote nearly 3 million prescriptions for it in 2016. In comparison, the Healthy Start scheme, which gives low-income families vouchers to spend on milk, fruit and vegetables, cost the taxpayer £60 million in 2016 – £28 million less than the amount spent helping men to get erections.

It's true that Viagra is helpful to both people in a couple and not just the man. But if the NHS budgets are so tight that women are being disabled through lack of treatment, then maybe people should be buying their own Viagra from the chemist at £20 a packet.

The evidence of systemic sexism within the NHS is damning. The 2020 Baroness Cumberlege review revealed how this issue has caused women to lose their jobs, homes, partners and financial stability over the past forty years.[3] The report heard from 700 people, mostly women, who suffered after being prescribed one of three controversial treatments: anti-epilepsy drug sodium valproate, hormonal pregnancy tests such as Primodos, and pelvic mesh implants to treat incontinence and prolapse. Their problems were 'dismissed, overlooked and ignored' over years and even decades in some cases, as despite countless reports of terrible side effects, doctors failed to take women's pain seriously. These women identified by the researchers represent a much wider issue – on an institutional scale, sexism in government policy is one huge reason why women are poorer than men.

## The austerity effect

The financial prospects for millions of women in Britain have been profoundly impacted by the government's decade-long mission to reshape the welfare state. Research carried out by the House of Commons library found that, since 2010, 86 per cent of the cuts to tax and benefits were borne by women.[4] In total women have lost £79 billion, compared to £13 billion for men, which is partly due to reductions in child tax credit and child benefit, both of which are overwhelmingly claimed by mothers.[5] The Equality and Human Rights Commission (EHRC) found there had been a particularly strong adverse effect on lone parents, of which nine out of ten are women, and their children,[6] and figures from the Women's Budget Group suggest that single mothers lost 15.6 per cent of their income.[7]

There are umpteen policies which can be highlighted for their disproportionately negative effects on women. Between 2011 and 2013, there was a salary freeze for public sector workers: 75 per cent of this workforce is female, so it was mostly women who were left worse off.[8] Pay rises in the public sector were capped at 1 per cent between 2013 and 2017,[9] below the rate of inflation, so in real terms these workers experienced a 1.7 per cent drop in pay.[10] Meanwhile, researchers have highlighted how budget cuts among district nursing services have created an 'unsustainable' burden on this mostly female workforce.[11] Close to half of health visitors, who are professionals that attend to new parents and check babies' development, have caseloads of 400 – well above the 250 per visitor recommended to ensure the well-being of parent and child.[12] As with other areas of social policy, the attitude seems to be 'just cut the funding because women will carry on doing the work anyway'.

Female poverty in the UK came under the spotlight when the United Nations sent Philip Alston, its Special Rapporteur on extreme poverty and human rights, on a fact-finding mission. Alston compiled an excoriating report describing how deep cuts to public services have disproportionately affected women and children. His conclusion was: 'If you got a group of misogynists in a room and said how can we make this system work for men and not for women, they would not have come up with too many ideas that are not already in place.' Alston believes that the Conservative government has inflicted 'severe hardship' with its 'punitive, mean-spirited and often callous approach' to welfare. The report said what many were thinking when it remarked that for the fifth-largest economy in the world to have so many people living in poverty was 'patently unjust', and 'not just a disgrace, but a social calamity and an economic disaster'.[13]

Some commentators have argued that women bear the brunt of budget cuts because governments don't look at the data that shows the gendered impact of their decisions. However, there's evidence that the government does understand the impact of its policies on women – it just doesn't care. The attitude to female poverty was summed up in a report by the Department of Health on working hours for medical staff, which stated: 'any indirect adverse effect on women is a proportionate means of achieving a legitimate aim'.[14] Separately, Jo Swinson, former leader of the Liberal Democrats, said: 'There's a kind of basic truth' that when you're cutting public spending, women will be disproportionately harmed but the reforms will have been positive.[15] By comparison, the United Nations report concluded that following the welfare reforms in Britain 'men fare better than women, in every ethnic group and across every point in the income distribution'.[16]

Let's examine how women have fared with the government's flagship welfare policy.

# Universal Credit

A new welfare payment for people who are either on low incomes or unemployed was introduced in 2013 in order to consolidate six different state benefits – child tax credit, housing benefit, income support, income-based jobseeker's allowance, income-related employment and support allowance, and working tax credits – into one monthly payment, known as Universal Credit. This was intended to be simpler for people to understand and to save the government money, as many households would receive less financial support than previously. Lone parents who care for a disabled child have been among the worst affected, losing almost £3 out of every £10 they received under the old system, equivalent to an average of £10,000 per year.[17] Overall poverty among lone parents is forecast to rise to 62 per cent as a result of the austerity reforms, up from 37 per cent.[18] Eligibility for the Healthy Start food vouchers has also shrunk since Universal Credit was introduced; the number of beneficiaries has fallen by over 30 per cent, from 727,309 people in 2013 to fewer than 500,000 in 2018.[19]

Among the flaws of Universal Credit is a delay of at least five weeks between someone making a claim and receiving any money; claimants often wait up to twelve weeks. Some can receive a repayable advance to tide them over until their first Universal Credit payment arrives, but in reality people with no income or savings have found themselves being evicted by landlords who are unwilling to wait for their rent.

Philip Alston reported finding significant numbers of people (overwhelmingly women but including some men) who had been forced into 'survival sex' as a direct result of

Universal Credit.[20] Survival sex means exchanging sex for the meeting of basic needs such as food or a place to sleep, and it's likely that women are under-represented in home-lessness statistics because of this (see Chapter 9 for more on this). Survival sex has become so widespread that the parliamentary Work and Pensions Committee conducted an inquiry into the matter. Laura Seebohm, executive director at Changing Lives, a charity for women in the north of England, explains that: 'Those on Universal Credit can get a payment to keep them going but they have no idea how long that is supposed to keep them going for. One woman received £250 and she didn't know if it was for two weeks or six. In the end it was for six weeks and that didn't even cover her rent. She became homeless and had to sell sex. When people are asked to pay back their Universal Credit advance payments, it is often completely unfeasible for them to do so. That leaves them with not enough to live on at the most basic level, especially for women with children.'[21]

Another regressive aspect of Universal Credit is the requirement that couples with a child or children who are claiming the benefit appoint a 'lead carer'. It's a concept that runs contrary to other social policy attempts to equalize the roles of men and women in the home, such as introducing shared parental leave. In addition to this, Universal Credit is paid in a monthly lump sum to the highest earner in the household: the man, in four-fifths of couples.[22] This assumes that income is shared fairly between partners, but as discussed in Chapter 1, there's ample evidence that this doesn't happen.[23] Previously benefits were paid to the person who claimed them, which gave women some control over household finances.

A report from MPs on the Work and Pensions Select

Committee found that allowing one partner to receive all the money intended for the family creates a 'serious risk of increasing the power of abusers'. The committee heard evidence from one woman who said her partner 'would wake up one morning with £1,500 in his account and p*** off with it, leaving us with nothing for weeks'. Frank Field MP, chair of the committee, concluded that: 'Universal Credit turns back the clock on decades of hard-won equality for women. This is not the 1950s. Men and women work independently, pay taxes as individuals, and should each have an independent income.'[24] Benefits payments should be split between both adults in a household, something that the Scottish government is aiming to introduce but Whitehall has resisted.[25]

The Department for Work and Pensions, which is in charge of state benefits, assessed Universal Credit and found that as a policy it is 'gender neutral'. This verdict was based on the absurd assumption that if men and women were in the same circumstances, Universal Credit would treat both genders the same. But they are rarely in the same situation – to repeat, 90 per cent of lone parents are women.

This gender discrimination is in violation of the country's human rights obligations. The UK has ratified the International Covenant on Economic, Social and Cultural Rights, a human rights treaty ensuring the equal right of men and women to social security as well as 'adequate food, clothing and housing'.[26] Social security should be 'adequate in amount and duration' and reductions should be 'temporary, necessary and proportionate' according to the EHRC. The government continually fails to abide by its own legislation and we must hold it accountable. For example, it introduced the 'public sector equality duty' in 2011, which 'requires equality considerations to be reflected into the design of policies and the delivery of services'.[27] The EHRC has called on the government to urgently ensure that welfare payments provide claimants with an adequate standard of living and that its policies are fully compliant with the law.[28]

## Gender budgeting

Governments lay out their plans and priorities for taxation and spending in a budget statement once or twice a year. Gender-responsive budgeting is when a government or organization considers the effect that financial decisions will have on each gender and tries to take their needs into account.[29] This doesn't mean that the same amount of money should be raised from men and women or even that funds should be spent equally. For example, when Mexico City authorities realized that women were experiencing groping and verbal abuse on crowded public trains and buses, they invested in female-only transport. That's extra spending on women, but improved safety on public transport provides an incentive for women to travel for work, earning money to provide for their families and to spend in the community.

Gender budgeting was pioneered in Australia in the 1980s and three countries have included a commitment to this in their constitutions[30] – Bolivia, Rwanda and Austria, the latter of which allocated funds towards combating domestic violence, which has helped to reduce medical costs for the country and in the long run should mean fewer sick days and companies losing out on a day's labour.[31] Canada, France and Japan publish a gender budget statement[32] while Belgium and Spain have made strides in this area too.[33] We are doing the reverse in Britain.

The situation is similar in the US. Gender analysis of state and federal budgets is not routine and in each of its budgets the Trump administration carried out deep and savage cuts to eight of the twelve safety-net programmes that are mostly used by women trying to afford the basics – housing themselves and their children if they have them, eating and keeping warm.[34] These included the scrapping of the Low Income Home Energy Assistance programme, which helps keep the homes of the poorest warm. Sixty-three per cent of recipients are women.[35] The budget was also slashed for a scheme called Temporary Assistance for Needy Families, which supports those who are pregnant or responsible for a child and unemployed or on a low income. Eighty-five per cent of recipients are women.

Funding for food stamps was cut by a third. The Supplemental Nutrition Assistance Program (SNAP) helps people living at or below the poverty line purchase basic foods and gives an average $1.40 per person per meal.[36] Around 26 million recipients are women,[37] some of whom have resorted to illegally exchanging their food stamps to buy tampons, pads and soap, which aren't on the permitted list of products for purchase.[38] Stores that do this often charge a mark-up to make it worth their while, which further penalizes women.[39]

A further nine programmes that directly address women's needs – from domestic violence to childcare and sexual health – had their funding reduced by 18 per cent.[40] This included the decimation of the Women's Bureau, a ninety-one-year-old department that supports working women, which had 76 per cent of its funding removed.[41]

As the budget for these programmes was slashed, President Trump introduced a swathe of tax cuts for the wealthiest, which he planned to extend beyond 2025.[42] Given that men own 70 per cent of the private wealth in the world, and in a list of the world's wealthiest people the first woman doesn't appear until fifteenth place,[43] you can draw your own conclusions about which gender benefited most from these tax cuts.

US policymakers' ignorance of gender equality issues in budgeting is part of a broader, dismissive attitude towards women's needs. The US stands alongside Sudan and Somalia as one of the few countries that hasn't ratified the United Nations' Convention on the Elimination of All Forms of Discrimination Against Women. Known as CEDAW, this treaty has been ratified by 189 countries, including Afghanistan, Iraq and North Korea,[44] and has been used to protect women from discrimination, violence and poverty.[45]

Yet the US has been resistant to human rights treaties in general, viewing them somehow as a threat to national sovereignty, and CEDAW was no exception. President Bill Clinton's administration put together a list specifying the reservations the government had about the treaty, two of which are about female economic equality. Firstly, the US was reluctant to enact legislation to ensure equal pay for equal work, arguing that it already had laws in this area; and secondly, it said it did not accept CEDAW's obligation to 'introduce maternity leave with pay or with comparable social benefits without loss of former employment, seniority or social allowances'.[46] Today, the US is the only country other than Papua New Guinea that doesn't guarantee paid maternity leave.[47]

Amnesty International has been calling on the US to

ratify CEDAW to improve gender equality. One point it makes is that claims about sex discrimination in the workplace are not subject to the same strict level of scrutiny that claims over race discrimination receive.[48] Ratifying CEDAW would put this right over time and provide greater protection for female employees.

# 7. Everyday Costs . . . That Little Bit More

Pink it, shrink it and raise the price. This has been the tactic of marketing teams who have spent decades launching 'female' versions of 'male' products. These pointlessly gendered products often include designs that reinforce gender stereotypes and portray female traits as problematic. Stationery manufacturer Bic produced slimmer ballpoint pens for women who can't pick up standard man-size pens; pink Dulcolax laxatives 'for women' are 'comfort coated'; ear plugs for women are pink so we can 'sleep pretty' while men wear their blue 'extreme protection hearos' version.

Or, in the case of Doritos crisps, there were suggestions that a 'Lady Doritos' version would not be so loud to crunch. 'Women don't like to crunch too loudly in public. And they don't lick their fingers generously,' said Indra Nooyi, the CEO of the Doritos parent company, PepsiCo.[1]

It is already far more expensive to live as a woman than as a man. Alongside the cost of periods, women spend more on underwear than men because we wear bras (each woman has an average of six at one time, and spends £2,700 on bras over a lifetime),[2] and tights, which are more expensive than socks (tights cost an average £3,000 over a lifetime).[3] There's the gendered expectation that we wear make-up, use more hair products and put more effort into personal care, which all costs money. While men shave their faces, women remove hair from larger areas. A lifetime of shaving is estimated to cost a woman £6,500, while regular waxing over the course of a woman's life will cost £23,000.[4]

When it comes to gender-differentiated products, what manufacturers don't say is that the woman's version often costs more. It's called the 'pink tax' when brands put personal-care products, medicines, children's clothes – virtually anything – in packaging with a girlish hue and bump up the price. One of the most comprehensive studies of the pink tax was conducted by researchers in New York City who looked at the relative cost of 800 items with clear male and female versions from ninety brands, covering the lifespan from baby goods to the needs of senior citizens.[5] Across all categories, products for women cost more, by an average of 7 per cent, although this mark-up rose to 13 per cent in the personal-care aisle. There were also examples of 'pink shrink', where women get a lower quantity of a product compared to the men's equivalent. The pink tax is even added to girls' toys, which cost more than boys' toys 55 per cent of the time – the researchers highlighted a Rascullz brand toddler helmet, which was blue with a shark on top and cost $14.99, while the pink version with a unicorn was priced at $27.99.[6] If that wasn't enough to anger all parents of daughters, girls' clothes were also pricier 26 per cent of the time.

The pink tax follows women to the grave, as 45 per cent of products designed to help senior citizens with their health (such as walking sticks, urinals, supports and compression stockings) were priced more highly for women than for men. The report also pointed to data from 1995 which states that women pay an annual 'gender tax' of $1,351 for purchasing the same services as men, a figure that has likely risen with the increased complexity of the consumer market.

Critics say that male and female versions of most products are almost the same, but manufacturers defend the practice by saying that products marketed at women are designed especially for our needs. This was the defence of shaving company Gillette, which priced its feminine-looking 'Venus' razors at 20 per cent more than their 'Fusion' razors, which were aimed at men.[7] The razors work the same, whether they are pink or blue so, once women are aware that they are being overcharged, they can opt for the 'male' version, although it's harder to dodge the pink tax when it comes to products with a fragrance. The pink tax in gender-differentiated perfumes has been blamed on 'the cost of extracting the scent from flowers',[8] so, for example, Gillette's Mach3 shaving gel with a masculine scent was priced at 20 per cent less than its Satin Care floral-fragranced equivalent.

There are some instances where price mark-ups are justifiable. Women's clothes are often made out of several pieces of material, which makes them more expensive to stitch together than men's clothes, which tend to be cut from a single fabric. However, it is often retailers that set the prices, not manufacturers. Retailers may be doing this because women tend to make 70 to 80 per cent of a household's spending decisions, including purchases for children, partners, parents and pets.

Businesses have adopted the pink tax with gusto. It is more expensive to dry-clean a blouse than a man's shirt.[9] At the hairdresser's, short-haired women complain they are charged more than men with similar-length hair. The BBC reported the story of an Oxford University academic whose hair salon regularly charged her £37 for a quick trim of her closely cropped hair, done by a female stylist. The day she visited the salon and a male stylist was on duty, he gave her the same trim and charged £15, which is what he would charge a man with the same hairdo.[10]

The Equalities Act says that service providers should not discriminate against customers on the basis of their gender, but the onus is on the individual to fight retailers and businesses that do this.

A bill was brought before parliament in 2019 proposing to amend consumer protection law to prohibit differential pricing based on gender.[11] This would have been a nail in the coffin for the pink premium, as items that are 'substantially similar' would have to be priced the same. Unfortunately, the bill didn't pass, but there's definitely scope for feminist action against the pink tax, either targeted at retailers or through reviving similar legislation in parliament.

Redesigning products for women would be more welcome if they were things women actually needed, such as protective gear to wear in their jobs in healthcare, the police, firefighting and other occupations. Women are routinely given one-size-fits-all gloves, gowns, masks and overalls which have been designed for the standard human – a man – whose hands are bigger, face is wider, legs are longer and torso shaped differently. The problem has been simmering for years, even in the NHS where 77 per cent of staff are female, but it came to the fore during the Covid-19 pandemic. If masks and gloves don't fit, they won't protect, and an already stressful situation of dealing with a deadly virus was made worse by vital equipment that had to be duct-taped down, breasts squashed, small hands swamped in giant gloves. In 2016 a trade union report found that nearly 60 per cent of women said that their protective equipment hampered their work. This is another example of institutional sexism; management need to allocate the funds to ensure their female staff have the equipment to do their jobs as effectively as male colleagues.

## Sexist assumptions

Female motorists pay the price for the stereotype that they are clueless about cars. Research has found that women are quoted hundreds of pounds more for car repairs, with the average quote for a clutch replacement coming in at £793, while men were charged around £673 for the same job – a difference of £120. Only 6 per cent of garages in the study gave men and women the same quote.[12]

Researchers have found that women were given higher quotes on price when they indicated they were poorly informed about market prices, so start the discussion by saying you have received several quotes already. Also, stating a figure that you are willing to pay can move the conversation away from any gender bias and anchor negotiations in price. The research showed that when women and men stated what they expected to pay upfront the gender bias disappeared and both were given the same quotes.[13]

The pink premium has also been found in studies of car purchases. One study looked at 145,000 car purchases in China and found that, after controlling for a range of variables, women pay more than men for cars.[14] It also found that men who lived locally to their dealer or were born in the area tended to be offered additional discounts, but this rarely applied to women. Other research suggests subtle discrimination in negotiations results in new-car dealerships quoting a similarly significantly lower price to white males than to Black or female test buyers. While it's possible that non-economic discrimination, where the car dealer holds animosity or big-otry towards a social group, could play a part, what is happening is more likely a form of economic discrimination. Put simply, women and ethnic minorities are perceived as less informed, more gullible and thus willing to pay more.[15]

## Period products

Every girl should be given a menstrual cup on her eleventh birthday. It could save her thousands of pounds over her life-time and would normalize a product that's better for the environment than tampons or pads. It would also help prevent the most degrading aspect of female economic inequality: the persistence of period poverty, where women and girls can't afford sanitary products.

In the UK, one in seven women has resorted to putting makeshift pads in their underwear or suffering through cramps without painkillers.[16] Efforts to hide the discomfort of periods without the proper products heighten women's self-consciousness and create shame around female bodies. For the one in five American girls who has stayed home from school or left early because they lacked pads or tampons,[17] menstruation becomes one of the subtle ways they learn that girls are 'less' than boys.

Refugees and homeless women are particularly vulnerable to period poverty; in Britain, asylum seekers receive a pittance of £37.75 per week to live off, and homeless charities report that underwear is one of the most-requested items among women.

As I write, governments have committed to providing free sanitary products in schools in Scotland, Wales, England

and the Australian state of Victoria.[18] These are fantastic initiatives, but they only go some way to addressing the inequality – financial and otherwise – that women experience because they bleed and men do not. The term used to describe this is 'menstrual equity' and it was coined by campaigner Jennifer Weiss-Wolf.[19] It's worth noting here that not only women menstruate. Trans, gender queer and non-binary people also do. Menstrual equality encompasses justice for them, too. Ultimately, a society in which people who menstruate are financially equal with cis men would offer period products at not-for-profit prices or, ideally, for free.

Thankfully, most women will never experience period poverty, but having periods is an expense that does add up. Bloody Good Period, a charity fighting period poverty, calculates that the typical woman in Britain spends £11 a month on her period with costs including painkillers, heat pads, and the cleaning or replacement of stained sheets and underwear. The average female has 450 periods over a lifetime, making a total spend of £4,800.[20] On a global scale, the purchase of tampons and pads represents a vast transfer of money from the female purse to male-dominated corporations. There were 1.9 billion women of menstrual age in 2017, and over a lifetime each Western woman will use 11,000 tampons.[21]

The first patent for a menstrual cup was granted in 1867, around twenty years before pads became commercially available.[22] In the late 1930s, there were several menstrual cup brands on the market, jostling with tampons and pads for customers. All three options faced barriers to adoption; while pads were thick, uncomfortable, slipped out of place and were expensive, the safety of tampons was questioned and many women weren't comfortable with the insertion of cups or tampons. Pads and tampons have become far more popular as they have been the focus of marketing efforts by companies with a vested interest in habituating women to using throwaway products each month. Some feminists also argue that there was more emphasis on disposable products because of male disgust towards periods. The first menstrual cup company closed in 1963, having never made a profit, partly because satisfied customers made only one purchase.[23]

Today, there are a dozen menstrual cup brands on the market and they cost between £10 and £20. Each woman needs only one, regardless of her flow, and they last for up to a decade. They are sometimes perceived as being messy or tricky but a scientific review of forty-three studies into menstrual cups found they are less leaky, better for the vagina's friendly bacteria and generally more effective than tampons.[24] The one caveat is that women need access to sinks and running water for handwashing after using cups. Period pants are another promising innovation: knickers with a thick layer in the crotch that absorbs menstrual blood without the need for a sanitary pad. They are washed and dried after use like regular underwear and last for two years; there are several brands available in the US and UK, at a cost of between £20 and £30 a pair.

The notion that tampons and pads are not medically necessary is so deeply ingrained in the cultural psyche that until 2019, not a single hospital trust in Britain's state-funded National Health Service routinely provided sanitary products for women and girls. Every health trust had long-standing policies for the provision of razors and shaving foam for inpatients – so men were able to shave in hospital, but women couldn't easily access sanitary protection.[25]

The British Medical Association lobbied for change after finding that 40 per cent of hospitals said they didn't provide period products or would do so only in an emergency, and would expect patients to source their own supplies as soon as possible.[26] Despite this, there was no shop or vending machine where you could buy them at 14 per cent of hospital trusts and health boards. Often sanitary pads were available only to women on maternity and gynaecology wards, with no provision for women on other wards and those who didn't have relatives to provide them. The NHS committed to supplying period products only in the summer of 2019.

And it's not just hospitals that ought to be routinely providing women with the period products they need. Universal healthcare coverage has been accepted in most European countries for the past sixty years. Among the generous allowances that state-funded healthcare in Europe has included are: tummy tucks for 8,000 Britons at a cost of £50 million,[27] visits to health spas, Viagra, acupuncture, help with housework after a difficult childbirth, pelvic-floor-strengthening sessions, breast implants for cosmetic reasons and the removal of cosmetic breast implants that have gone wrong.[28] I find it impossible to understand how these are justifiable as medical needs but sanitary products for women are not.

When governments, employers or supermarket chains purchase items in bulk they benefit from significant discounts from suppliers. The UK government put out a tender for a company to provide sanitary products in English schools at a cost of £20 million in its first year, or £11 per pupil.[29] The cost per person could be reduced further if the provision of sanitary products was extended to other groups, or even to all women.

## Period taxes

When prominent suffragist Alice Stone-Blackwell wrote a list of reasons in 1896 why women should be able to vote, one of them was that 'laws unjust to women would be amended more quickly'. How wrong she was. Nearly 125 years later, the world's richest countries have classed sanitary products as luxuries and add tax to their purchase price, with surcharges ranging from 25 per cent in Denmark, Norway and Sweden to 27 per cent in Hungary. At the time of writing, in the US, period necessities were being taxed in thirty-five states.[30] Each of these states has a list of products that are deemed necessary and are therefore sold without sales tax. These include gun club membership in Wisconsin, private jet parts in Colorado, cowboy boots in Texas, chainsaws in Idaho, and, my favourite of all necessities: entry fees for rodeo participants in South Dakota.[31]

Taxation of products that only women need is financial exploitation. To underscore how products for men have been routinely exempted from sales tax, Connecticut and North Dakota don't tax pads used for incontinence (which men might need), but do tax pads for periods.[32]

As with the cost of buying sanitary products, there's an argument to say that the tampon tax isn't much of a burden on most women. Someone living in New York state would pay $800 (£599) in taxes on period products over their life-time, but since this is spread over thirty-plus years it wouldn't feel too burdensome.[33] But since women are economically disadvantaged relative to men in everything from retirement savings to annual earnings, that $800 is not to be dismissed. In mid-April 2015, a single share in Amazon was worth $375 (£280). A woman who took $800 and purchased two Amazon shares would find that each was worth $1,760 (£1,317) in December 2019, or $3,520 (£2,634) for both. This is a striking example of the power of money when it's put to good use. Whatever the true figures, the amount a woman has to spend on sanitary products is a poor use of her money.

Tampon taxes are regressive; they are blanket charges on all women and menstruators, irrespective of their means to pay. Campaigners have been fighting them for at least thirty years, but male ignorance of the injustice persists. Barack Obama repeatedly stated that society could benefit from having more women in power,[34] but even he admitted in 2016 that he wasn't aware at the time that period products were taxed as luxuries across America and had 'no idea' why they would be.[35]

The previous year, as its economy was sliding into a black hole, Greece increased the sales tax on tampons from 13 per cent to 23 per cent.[36] The tax was raised on other items, too, but at a time when the country's economic crisis was so bad that some women had been forced to sell sex for the price of a sandwich, tampons should have been exempt from this increase.[37]

Some thirty-two states in the US have introduced bills to tackle the tampon tax since 2016 that have later been dropped, in some cases more than once.[38] Governments defend taxation of menstrual products because they say they need the revenue. But there are countless examples of products that they are happy to sell without sales tax. It's a matter of perspective. Raise revenue elsewhere – it's unjust to tax women for their biology.

Following decades of campaigning and little change, women have had to get creative. A journalist at the *Financial*

*Times* has called on sanitary brands Always, Tampax and Bodyform to put messages on their packaging encouraging women to invest once a month.[39] It's a clever way of turning a negative (the unavoidable cost of sanitary products) into a positive (a better financial future). In another interesting innovation, a German start-up called The Female Company got around the 19 per cent surcharge on each pack of sanitary pads and tampons by selling a book with fifteen organic cotton tampons tucked inside its cover for €3.11 (£2.78/$3.46). Why? Because in Germany, VAT on books is only 7 per cent. Campaigns against this everyday economic exploitation are beginning to work. In November 2019, Germany dropped the tampon tax to 7 per cent after a landmark vote.[40] In Britain, decades of campaigning bore fruit when the government cut the tax rate on period essentials from 20 per cent to 5 per cent in 2015. The tampon tax was finally abolished on 1 January 2021. In the years preceding this, the government announced it would channel revenue raised through the tax towards charities that support women.

A noble intention. But problems have arisen with how those charities are chosen. An open letter signed by 100 academics and senior figures from the women's charity sector said that in the two years the scheme had been running, only three specialist female organizations had received funding out of the dozen that were awarded grants. The critics said that large and generic charities were receiving the cash rather than grassroots female-focused groups. This was due to the selection criteria, as charities must apply for grants of at least £1 million but the sum cannot be more than 50 per cent of their annual income.[41] These requirements rule out many women's charities and mean there are a very small number in a position to apply for funding.

Women's charities say demand for their services has increased during the past decade following austerity-driven cuts to social services. Channelling revenue raised from taxing women to women's charities was a poor sticking plaster until the tax was eventually abolished, even if grassroots organizations had been able to access the funds.

Menstrual equity is about challenging discriminatory laws that frame women's needs as invalid, and removing opportunities for governments and companies to financially exploit women and girls.

Developing nations have acted more quickly. India, Malaysia and South Africa have dropped the tampon tax, while Kenya became the first country to provide free sanitary pads in schools, in 2010, after abolishing the tampon tax in 2004.[42] Kenya went one step further by removing import taxes on sanitary products in 2011, which cut the average price of most brands by 50 per cent.[43] These changes put richer nations to shame. Female parliamentarians spoke of the disgust they were met with when trying to raise the issue at government level. Kenya is a poorer country, but it has prioritized female economic empowerment. Why have developed nations lagged behind? The answer may be that, in these countries, people tend to believe the battle for gender equality is over. It's not. Disproportionate economic outlay by women on services and products as diverse as car insurance and tampons is just another instance of this.

# 8. 'Women's Problems'

Tampon taxes and period poverty have hit the headlines, but women are still being penalized for menstruating at work.

One study found that women who 'accidentally' reminded colleagues that they menstruate by dropping a tampon out of their bag, rather than a pen, say, were perceived as less likeable and less competent and that there was a tendency for people to avoid sitting close to them.[1] In lawsuits in the US women have claimed unfair dismissal due to their employer's prejudice against menstruation.[2] But in America, menstrual symptoms unrelated to pregnancy or childbirth are not protected by anti-discrimination law under Title VII of the Civil Rights Act.

New technologies are facilitating anti-period discrimination against women. One Norwegian company made female employees wear red bracelets during their time of the month to justify their more frequent trips to the toilet. Another firm made staff sign in and out of the toilets. Insurer DNB, also in Norway, limited call centre staff's toilet trips to eight minutes per day and set off an alarm at managers' desks if a worker took two seconds longer.[3] In Spain, women working in a fruit-packing factory in the heat of Murcia, in the south of the country, were made to wear a red sign round their necks when they wanted to use the toilet, allegedly in a bid to humiliate them into not going. The company, El Ciruelo, docked thirty minutes off their wages for every toilet trip lasting more than five minutes and many workers stopped drinking water during their twelve-hour shifts to avoid the fine. The two women who made the story public were sacked.[4]

Such rules are enforced with electronic key cards or wristbands that allow employers to monitor a worker's whereabouts or sensors under desks that track when employees are sitting at the desk. In each case, the employer came under fire from local authorities, as time limits for using the toilet are discriminatory against women, who sometimes take longer. If this kind of technology becomes widespread, it represents a serious threat both to women's bodily privacy and their position in the workplace. What will it mean if employers are able to work out when a woman has her period? Will bosses favour employees with shorter, more manageable periods who spend less time in the lavatories? What if employers can spot when a woman hasn't had her period for some time? Could they pre-empt pregnancies and find a reason to dismiss women before they ask for maternity leave?

This may seem like the stuff of dystopian novels but, given what we have learned about the power and reach of modern technology in recent years, none of these scenarios is outside the realm of possibility. Shoshana Zuboff, an academic, coined the term 'surveillance capitalism' in 2014 to describe how businesses feel an economic imperative to collect data from more areas of human life with a view to increasing profits.[5] Collecting data on staff periods with a view to monitoring productivity may be the logical next step for businesses already poring over reams of employee data.

As campaigners for alleviating period poverty and the tampon tax slowly achieve their aims, the spotlight should move on to other forms of menstruation discrimination. The use of monitoring technology at work could emerge as an area that feminists have to watch closely.

## Menstrual policies

Women's bodies are not an inconvenience and showing signs of menstruation is not showing weakness. Only in a world where being male is the benchmark for normal would deviation from this (by having periods) be perceived as a defect.

Wrangling over entitlement to maternity leave continues in the West, and designated leave policies for periods and menopause aren't recognized concepts in Europe and the US. But paid menstrual leave has existed in Asian and African countries for decades, including Japan (since 1947; it's called *seirikyuuka*, meaning 'physiological leave'), Taiwan, Indonesia, South Korea and Zambia.[6]

Policies vary, but the basic point is that women can take time off work for cramps and other symptoms without dipping into their holiday days or taking sick days, which often require doctor's notes. Entitlement varies between offering women with period pains paid leave on the first and second day of menstruation in Indonesia, a day's leave per month in Zambia,[7] paid leave or payment in lieu of days not taken in South Korea, and one day a month at half-salary in Taiwan.[8] Female factory workers in Vietnam are entitled to rest an extra thirty minutes a day on the first three days of menstruation. The law in these countries has recognized the value of paid work to women, their families and the economy, and that women shouldn't have to risk their jobs or miss days of earnings because they menstruate.

What's feasible financially for employers is culturally constructed. In Indonesia, staff are allowed two days' paid leave when their son is circumcised. The country has 192 million people of working age, albeit not all of them in the formal economy, where employers have policies on leave. Theoretically, if everyone took the circumcision leave they are entitled to, that's a lot of days' paid leave.

Japan's menstrual leave was introduced after the Second World War as greater numbers of women entered the workforce. Back then, periods could be messier (they didn't have slim pads or mooncups) and pain management would have been tougher. Elsewhere, period leave was introduced based on the idea that women who work while they are on their period will have trouble conceiving – so it wasn't so much about concern for women's comfort as about the need to keep birthrates up.

Fast-forward to today, and a handful of private companies and not-for-profit organizations have introduced period leave in India and Australia in recent years. In 2017, Italian policy-makers considered introducing a new law that would have made Italy the first Western country with period leave. Yet its parliament dropped the plans over fears that, in a country where little over 60 per cent of women work (one of the lowest rates in Europe), where employers favour men, and a quarter of women have been illegally fired during or after pregnancy, the policy would further disincentivize employers from hiring women.[9] Local media reports that women are often asked by their employers to sign a resignation document in advance, so that if they become pregnant the date can be noted and their resignation will take effect from that date. If gender discrimination at work is so endemic in Italy, this country should not be used as a yardstick for how viable menstrual leave could be in other countries.

The issue with menstrual leave is that not all women need it – most don't. Critics of period leave say it's incomparable to paid leave while pregnant, because all women are diminished in their ability to work (to some degree) while heavily pregnant, but not all women are impeded at work by periods. My take on it is that if paid work was done only by women, then period leave would be a universally accepted concept. The resistance to such policies comes from comparing women to men and the fear that women will then come off unfavourably. The debate also ignores people who menstruate but don't present as female – the trans and non-binary people who also suffer with cramps. As for the potential for increasing discrimination against women, there will always be managers who frown on any kind of sick leave, while there will be others who recognize that it's part of being human. Employers who take a dim view of sick leave (or of staff who don't endlessly check their emails while on holiday) will also be the most critical of period leave. That doesn't mean menstrual leave shouldn't exist for those who need it, as periods can be a significant impediment to some women. The fairest solution seems to be extending the trend for 'duvet days', a small leave entitlement without the need to provide a sick note, which would apply to all staff, irrespective of gender. This would give menstruating people leeway while also accepting that men can also suffer with conditions which mean they need to step away from work.

In a similar vein, the issue of menopause and how it can affect women's earning capacity was brought to the fore in 2019 as Britain's Labour Party election manifesto included the promise of menopause-friendly policies. The party was also pushing for longer maternity leave. Yet these policies were derided in the press, including by Camilla Long, a columnist on *The Sunday Times* who wrote that women would be perceived as 'pathetic, hopeless, unsupported little messes who constantly need helping'. She writes that these suggestions 'infantilize women and turn them into financial burdens or victims'.[10] There's a double standard here – I don't think anyone would agree that supporting women with pregnancy-related complications or on maternity leave infantilizes women or makes them victims. There's a global trend towards better and longer maternity leave: Canada expanded its parental leave in 2018 and so did certain Scandinavian countries. If Western culture is becoming more supportive of women who have babies, why can't it be equally supportive of women who don't have babies and never have a break from monthly periods?

The question of menopause leave is where ageism and sexism at work intersect. Symptoms of menopause can be physical and psychological, including hot flushes, problems sleeping, palpitations, headaches, stiffness, irritability, mood changes and stress from dealing with all of these.[11] A woman in her twenties experiencing these symptoms during pregnancy would receive sympathy and support, but fast-forward thirty years and she's hiding them for fear of redundancy.

The average age of starting the menopause, when periods begin to peter out before stopping, is fifty-one, and there are 3.5 million women over the age of fifty employed in Britain. The change typically lasts for four or five years, although 10 per cent of women have symptoms that persist for up to twelve years.[12]

Not all women experience period cramps, not all will have children, but everyone who menstruates will go through the menopause. Yet most of the discussion about accommodating women's needs at work is in relation to childcare responsibilities, with pregnancy and maternity leave a particular focus of equality law and HR policies. Little attention has been paid to the multi-year transition that every woman goes through which entails symptoms that can have a significant impact on daily life.

Few studies have examined how the menopause affects women's economic participation, that is, their ability to work, the level of their wages and their productivity in the job. This omission highlights the lack of consideration that's been given to women's needs and means there is very little formal support for the half of the workforce who go through this.

Limited data from around the world suggests that some women reduce their hours or leave employment earlier than they would have because of menopausal symptoms, some lose their jobs, and the vast majority don't disclose the issue to managers in case there are negative repercussions.

Women over fifty are a demographic that has already had their earnings crimped throughout their careers; by the age of sixty, women typically have four times less saved for retirement than men. They desperately need to boost their income and save, and they ought to have help in tackling anything that affects their earning ability.[13]

There are racial considerations, too. A UK government report into menopause transition and work noted that African-American women are most likely to experience hot flushes, followed by Hispanic women, then Caucasians.[14] Both African Americans and Hispanic women face a wider wage gap than white women and, if their economic participation is more badly affected by the transition through menopause, they will need more support.

Aspects of the workplace can make symptoms worse, particularly hot or poorly ventilated rooms, no time for water breaks, nowhere to rest, crowded workrooms, restrictive uniforms and formal meetings. The emotional labour of hiding sweat patches and hot flushes, cramps, being in a state of preparedness for heavy periods and sleepless nights takes its toll. 'The evidence also paints a consistent picture of women in transition feeling those around them at work are unsympathetic or treat them badly, because of gendered ageism,' states the same report.[15] 'Evidence exists of women being ridiculed, harassed and criticized by colleagues and managers as a result of their menopausal symptoms or just because they are over forty and therefore stereotyped as "hysterical", "histrionic", or "menopausal-ish".'[16]

Women don't speak openly about the menopause at work for fear that it might make them seem weaker or less capable than men. That in itself is internalized misogyny, as the transition is totally normal and is not an illness. We need to move on from looking at menopause as an individual problem. Like pregnancy, it is something that affects the many, not the few.

A number of British companies don't perceive menopause-friendly accommodations as too much hassle and have introduced their own policies. These include retailer Marks & Spencer (which has a majority-female workforce), which allows managers to make reasonable adjustments for staff and has a mini-website publicizing the initiative among employees. Bosses at North Lincolnshire County Council also feel the effort is worth it and encourage management to be flexible with dress codes, where people sit in the office, and the provision of USB fans.[17]

Aside from the economic arguments, there's an ethical argument, too. It's contrary to the Equality Act 2010 to discriminate against employees suffering menopause symptoms. BT, the British telecoms company, lost in a 2012 employment tribunal against a woman who was unfairly dismissed while struggling with the menopause. She had provided her male manager with a letter from her doctor, but the manager had based his understanding of the condition on his wife's experience rather than trying to understand his employee's. The tribunal ruled that he had failed to deal with the problem in the same way he would for someone suffering a different condition.[18]

The point is that some women – not all – do struggle at times with things to do specifically with women's health, especially with conditions such as endometriosis or polycystic ovary syndrome (PCOS). In most countries there's no specific policy for dealing with this at work, and there should be. HR policies should be updated to take the realities of human bodies into account – including people who menstruate – and all managers should be informed during their induction or training.

Menopause in the workplace will become a more important issue in the future as more women work into their sixties; currently, nearly 70 per cent of women in the UK between the ages of fifty-five and fifty-nine are in employment, but thirty years ago the figure was less than 50 per cent. And there's a similar trend elsewhere in Europe and Australia.[19]

Female participation in the workforce will only increase as we live for longer, and as governments encourage women to stay in work to boost the economy. Companies, too, will want to get the best out of their talented staff and, with women outperforming men educationally, increasingly those better-educated higher earners will be women. The last stage of gender inequality at work to be tackled is the unfairness and stigma around periods and menopause. They've been ignored because these issues are tied up with misogyny and ageism, but it's in the interest of every woman to help stamp out subtle discrimination – and that includes with periods.

# 9. The Gendered Housing Crisis

Housing is a feminist issue, although it's rarely framed that way. We've come a long way since the days when women couldn't own property because they *were* property. Yet gender inequality remains in housing and property ownership, hidden in plain sight rather than enshrined in law.

On a range of measures women have a harder time securing an affordable, safe or comfortable place to call home. The pay gap, for example, means the typical woman needs twelve times her annual salary to be able to buy a home in England, while men need just over eight times.[1] There is no region in England where renting the average home is affordable (costing less than a third of income) for a woman on median earnings. By contrast, men on the median wage find the average home is affordable to rent in every region except London and the south-east of England.[2]

While the majority of Britain's estimated 5,000 rough sleepers are men, women are the majority of the 'statutory' or legally homeless. These are the women of no fixed abode, the temporarily housed, a nomadic tribe of mums and their children who move from women's refuges, to council-funded bed-and-breakfast hotels, to hostels with four people to a bedroom. Others crash on a friend's sofa, exchange sex for a place to sleep or stay with an abuser because there's nowhere else to go. It's hidden homelessness. Around 67 per cent of the statutory homeless are women and two-thirds of them are single mothers with dependent children.[3] Why isn't everyone talking about this?

Meanwhile, incidents of abuse against women in their homes have reached epidemic levels. More than 4,000 arrests were made for domestic abuse in London alone during the first six weeks of the Covid-19 lockdown – equivalent to 100 offences a day.[4] This was 9 per cent higher than the same period the previous year. 'Domestic' violence is a housing problem: fear of homelessness is one of the main reasons why women don't leave an abuser. Sadly that is an entirely rational fear given the situation with women's refuges (more on this below). Women are also the majority of those reliant on social housing and housing benefit, which is a government payment to help people who can't afford rent.

Despite all of this, gender is rarely discussed in relation to housing. Over the past twenty years Britain has nursed a serious gendered housing crisis which will require dedicated and radical government action if it is to be fixed.

Property prices have risen to record highs in parts of the country amid a shortage of around 1.2 million homes across the UK. Yet the number of homes being built in recent years has fallen to the lowest level since the 1920s. Many of these homes are too expensive for people on average salaries to rent or buy. Eight in ten working parents with children who rent privately could not afford to buy a new-build property in their area, according to Shelter, the housing charity.[5]

Government ministers have pushed housing policy to the bottom of the priority list for years. Their indifference is summed up by this fact: there have been nineteen housing ministers since 1997. Nineteen. Each of them began their role with a new strategy, a fresh focus, or a bonfire of their predecessor's ideas. Many of them lasted less than a year in the job, few stayed long enough to see new policies through, and only four of them were women.[6] The housing brief appears to be a job that politicians take in the hope of moving on and up to something more exciting. Substantive reform to housing policy has been promised but never delivered. In early 2017 the nation was in hot anticipation of the first government 'white paper' on UK housing in two decades, which had the grandiose title 'Fixing Our Broken Housing Market'.[7] The policy document did nothing of the sort.

MPs appear disinterested in tackling the housing crisis but investing in property is a popular pastime. One in every three MPs was a landlord at the last count and the list of current and former politicians making money out of the housing crisis includes prime ministers Boris Johnson, Theresa May and David Cameron, former chancellor George Osborne and former housing minister Brandon Lewis.[8] To put this in context, two in every 100 people among the general population are landlords. There is no official list of MP landlords but politicians must declare when they own property that receives more than £10,000 a year in rent or is worth over £100,000 – so each of the names listed above and their properties fall into either of those categories.

As the housing crisis has intensified the number of landlord MPs has risen by 25 per cent. The six landlord MPs who own or part-own the most properties are all Conservative and only one is a woman. Paul Howell (Sedgefield) owns sixteen properties; Fiona Bruce (Congleton) owns ten properties; Nick Fletcher (Don Valley) owns eleven properties; Robert Goodwill (Scarborough) and Jeremy Hunt (South West Surrey) each own nine properties, while Marco Longhi (Dudley North) rents out nine houses in Walsall.

People invest in rental properties in the hope that house

prices will rise while they enjoy the high monthly rents they receive in the meantime. Therefore MPs who are also landlords have a vested interest in the housing crisis continuing for as long as possible, since the desperate shortage of homes has pushed both property prices and rents higher. MPs are meant to be the voice of their constituents and are no doubt aware that lives have been ruined by the lack of affordable homes. Is an MP's allegiance to voters sufficient to override their desire to accumulate wealth? It doesn't look like it. During Cameron's six years as prime minister, the average rent rose by more than 23 per cent.[9] So much for tackling the housing shortage.

## Mortgages

The gender pay gap of 18 per cent creates a significant barrier between women and property ownership, especially if they're single. This is because lenders decide how much to offer a person on a mortgage by deducting living costs from the individual's (or household's) income and multiplying the remainder by four and a half. So the pay gap becomes amplified when women try to get a mortgage, and the average earning on a man's mortgage application is £91,292 compared to £59,036 for a woman, according to Coreco, a mortgage broker.[10] If both of these average people applied for a mortgage and were granted loans of four and a half times their earnings, the man could borrow £145,000 more than the typical woman.

With property prices at historic highs, prospective homebuyers have to stretch their finances as far as they can to get on the housing ladder. It means that even slight discrimination in a woman's pay, commission or bonuses can make the difference between becoming a homeowner and continuing to rent. Very few women are getting on the property ladder independently. Of all the first-time buyers who bought a home in 2015–16, a tiny 8 per cent of them were women buying alone. I was staggered to discover this – that 92 per cent of first-time property purchases involve men. The figure for independent male first-time buyers was more than double the women's figure, at 18 per cent.[11]

The number of women buying a first flat or house independently has shrunk more quickly over the past decade than it has for men. In 2005 single women made up 15 per cent of first-time buyers (seven percentage points higher than in 2015–16), while the equivalent figure for men was 20 per cent in 2005 (two percentage points higher).[12] The government describes the latest figures as a 'noticeable' gender difference but shows no inclination towards improving the situation. Reflect for a moment on the boost to self-confidence, sense of agency and achievement that people get from buying a home. Double the proportion of single men who get to feel this way compared to single women.

Property is the main form of wealth for Britons and Americans, but it's not held equally by men and women. One study suggests that men accumulate 30 per cent more housing wealth than women by the time they reach retirement age.[13] Mortgage-payers build up ownership of bricks and mortar through monthly payments, gradually increasing their stake in a property asset that is expected to rise in value. When people have wealth accumulated, they can use it to obtain more assets. So the gender wealth gap is perpetuated as a greater proportion of men are able to buy property independently, channelling their salary into paying down the interest and capital on their home loan rather than helping a landlord pay their mortgage.

Women's ability to accumulate property wealth might also be hampered in another way – on average they pay 2 per cent more than their male counterparts when they buy a home, according to a study that looked at 9 million housing transactions in the US over sixteen years.[14] This pattern is repeated when women come to sell their property, as they receive an average 2 per cent less than men. Women are less likely to bargain down a home's asking price when buying, and tend to undervalue their own home when selling. As a result, the highest-priced home sales consistently occur when a man is selling to a woman; the lowest-priced ones when a woman is selling to a man. The authors are careful to note that this does not mean that women are necessarily less competent negotiators. Discrimination may play a significant role. When this is extrapolated out to the eleven homes that a typical American lives in during their lifetime, the authors reckon that women lose around $1,600 in housing wealth annually.

Meanwhile, studies in the US have found that women pay higher interest rates on mortgages.[15] Lenders perceive women to be higher risk, even though research suggests that they are more reliable mortgage-payers than men.[16] This double whammy for women of higher interest rates on their mortgage alongside paying more for their homes will have a significant effect on their overall wealth. In the near future prospective homeowners may benefit from computer-aided property valuations, which use algorithms to work out how much a home ought to sell for and make the initial offers electronically.

Before reaching the mortgage stage, prospective homeowners need a deposit, or down payment, which is typically between 10 per cent and 25 per cent of the property's sale price.

Women's lower earnings translate into smaller savings piles. Around 48 per cent of female non-homeowners have nothing saved towards a deposit compared to 35 per cent of men. And among those who have built up a home-buying fund, women have an average of £5,621 compared to the £11,660 saved by the average man.[17] This could be because average rents in England take 43 per cent of women's median earnings but only 28 per cent of men's, so the typical woman cannot afford to save as much.[18] As a result, we appear to be well aware of our limitations when it comes to home ownership and have tempered our ambitions. Only 26 per cent of women anticipate that they could buy a home on their own compared to 39 per cent of men.[19]

In the meantime, finding a mortgage that fits can be easier with the help of a broker (a specialist in home loans). They will search thousands of different mortgages to find one that is suitable, advise on the best options and help with the application. They are either paid by the applicant (around £100–£200) or by the mortgage provider – but remember that this can make their advice biased.

Women who need a higher income multiple than the usual 4.5 times earnings on a mortgage could look at specialist lenders. Smaller lenders can sometimes provide more generous mortgage loans to people in certain circumstances, including those working in professions such as teaching, medicine or law. These lenders use their knowledge of the industry to predict how an individual's income may rise over the course of the mortgage and they also like the job security that comes with these professions.

# Renting

Up until the twentieth century women around Europe were unable to legally sign a lease or sale agreement on a property, which meant they couldn't pick an apartment and agree rent with the landlord without a man intermediating.

In legal terms this had mostly changed by 1907, although Italian women had to wait until 1919. But customs didn't keep pace with the change in the law and in most European countries property issues were managed between men.[20] The English term 'head of the household' referred to the man in charge of the property and was used throughout Western Europe: 'Familienvorstand' in German, 'capofamiglia' in Italian and 'cabeza de familia' in Spanish. Tenants in France had an obligation to 'reside in housing as a good father', a term which was only removed from the law in 2014.[21]

One feature of the UK's rental market is that properties tend to be owned by private individuals acting as landlords, whereas in other countries rental properties are often owned by institutions. This leaves women vulnerable to the whims of lone individuals. Since 1988 landlords have had the power to evict tenants without giving a reason any time after their lease expires.[22] This is called a Section 21 'no fault' eviction and the government has acknowledged that it is one of the main causes of homelessness in Britain. Tenants who request maintenance to their home – because the roof is leaking, there's damp in the bedroom, a window won't close – can be punished by morally bankrupt landlords. Past attempts at banning landlords from using eviction as a method of retaliation have failed. A survey by Citizens Advice found that renters who made formal complaints had a far higher chance of being evicted within the next six months.[23]

Fergus Wilson, one of the UK's most prolific landlords who owned close to 1,000 homes at one point, said in 2018 that he would evict single women who became pregnant while renting one of his properties. In a separate incident Wilson admitted to evicting four single mothers with small babies in a single week. He justified the decision by arguing that the local council's requirement for a broken boiler in a rental home to be fixed within four days was 'too restrictive'.

Eviction on the grounds of pregnancy is illegal but, since no-fault evictions are allowed at any time after the lease is up, a landlord can easily make a pregnant woman homeless. Women who are thinking of having a baby could consider asking their landlord for a long lease. Making it clear that you are happy to stay in the home as a reliable tenant should be a positive for the landlord.

The sheer outrageousness of the no-fault eviction rule finally prompted the government into action in 2019. It has promised that landlords will have to provide a 'concrete, evidenced reason already specified in law' when telling their tenants to find a new home.[24] But as I write this, over a year has passed since this proclamation and there is no sign of change. The law needs to go further than giving landlords a list of reasons to force people to move home. Tenants should be given legal protection from retaliatory eviction for a period of time after they have made a formal complaint, regardless of its outcome.

# No DSS

Alongside no-fault evictions, another form of housing discrimination still prevalent in the UK is the use of 'No DSS' on rental listings. 'No DSS' stands for 'No Department of Social Security'[25] and it means the landlord won't accept tenants in receipt of government benefits, despite the fact that its presence on adverts for property lettings is an attempt to discriminate and is in contravention of the Equality Act. As women and disabled people are more likely to be on low incomes and to receive state support, they are overwhelmingly more affected by the use of 'No DSS'.

The housing charity Shelter has been campaigning to have landlords' use of 'No DSS' banned but the term is still widespread on adverts, and a poll of private landlords in January 2020 found that 86 per cent either thought that stating 'No DSS' was lawful or they were unsure.[26]

## Rent increases and the housing allowance

Paying rent has become a much bigger problem for women since the government slashed the Local Housing Allowance, a payment to help those on the lowest incomes afford rent and housing costs. It was previously set at a rate which covered the cost of renting the cheapest 30 per cent of homes in different areas, but the rules were changed and the allowance was frozen between 2016 and 2020. The allowance is no longer enough to cover the rent on 90 per cent of properties in England.[27] In some areas it's much worse: in Thanet, Stevenage, Ipswich, Milton Keynes and Peterborough, less than 1 per cent of private rentals are affordable on housing allowance, while in Huntingdon, Cambridgeshire, just 0.44 per cent of advertised properties would be affordable.[28] The average annual shortfall in housing benefit and actual rent varies between £300 for a single room in a shared house and £3,120 for a family home.[29] People are supposed to find the money elsewhere to top up their housing benefit and cover their rent. The reality is that women are having to choose between rent, eating and heating. They are getting into debt, living in overcrowded homes, moving their children between schools frequently and dodging homelessness.

Numerous organizations including Shelter, the Chartered Institute of Housing, and Crisis are calling on the government to restore the housing allowance to levels that would cover the lowest third of rental costs. Imagine the difference this would make to the lives of poorer women if the full weight of Fourth Wave feminism could be thrown behind this campaign in order to get the policy changed.

## Financial abuse

As towns and cities went into lockdown at the beginning of 2020, authorities around the world reported steep drops in crime ranging from burglaries and murder to drug offences. The exception was violence against women. Rates of domestic abuse soared and femicide (the gender-motivated killing of women) increased too.

Domestic abuse is often tangled up with 'financial abuse', where a victim is restricted in their access to money and how it is spent or is otherwise made financially reliant so that they cannot leave. When a perpetrator has wider control over the victim's food, clothing or transport, or prevents them from improving their financial status through work, training or education, it's known as 'economic abuse'. Around one in five adults has experienced some form of financial abuse in a relationship and it affects women from all socio-economic classes – it's not about the amount of money the family has, it's about the imbalance of power within the relationship.[30] It also transcends age – charities support significant numbers of women aged over sixty-five and up to the age of ninety.

Forms of financial abuse include the aggressor confiscating their victim's debit cards, demanding pin codes, forcing them to hand over their income and making their victim beg for money to buy essentials. Financial abuse reaches far beyond the four walls of the home to influence how the victim interacts with the world. Abusers often take out credit cards and loans in their victim's name – sometimes without their knowledge – which limits a victim's ability to rebuild their lives for years to come. Survivors remain indebted or have a bad credit rating, which can prevent them from being able to do anything which requires a decent credit score, including taking out a mobile phone contract, renting a flat, finding a job (some employers run a credit check before offering employment), getting a mortgage, hiring a car and buying anything on credit, from a washing machine to a holiday.

Banks and financial institutions often fail to understand victims' situations and in the past, clumsy mistakes by staff alongside rigid adherence to company protocols have ended up aiding abusers and leaving survivors worse off. There have been cases where survivors have had to repeatedly describe the abuse to multiple members of staff or where letters confirming the survivor's new address have been sent to their abuser at their old home, blowing their cover.

UK banks and building societies have agreed to a code of conduct for helping customers experiencing financial abuse. It should be standard that when survivors approach their bank, they only need to tell their story once. Banks are also in a good position to refer survivors on to specialist services. Whether they contact the bank by phone or in-branch, there ought to be up-to-date details of local support groups that can be contacted. Surviving Economic Abuse is the UK's dedicated charity for financial abuse, while Refuge (refuge.org.uk), Women's Aid (womensaid.org.uk), Angelou (angelou.org) and Hestia (hestia.org) offer support for people affected by domestic violence.

Domestic violence and financial abuse contribute to female economic inequality, and increasing space at refuges should be considered a key pillar of tackling the country's housing crisis. Refuges are life-saving facilities, but one in six has closed down since 2010 following cuts of £7 million to council funding for shelters.[31] Nearly 70 per cent of referrals to refuges were turned down in 2018–19 because there was no room. Some of the 12,000 women who flee an abusive partner each year find that the only place of shelter they are offered is in another part of the country and others find they are only offered room for themselves, so have to decide whether to leave their children behind.

Additional refuge space could be found quite readily through collaboration with local universities and hotels, which are frequently willing and able to offer their spare capacity – this is done in France, where victims have the opportunity to stay in a hotel room at the government's expense. It's a good short-term solution but not one that is suitable for people who need specialist help.

The housing crisis has exacerbated the shortage of follow-on accommodation for families to move into after their stay in a refuge, which is supposed to be an emergency option. Incredibly, under the current rules, those escaping domestic violence are not considered a priority for housing unless they can prove to the local authority that they are 'significantly more vulnerable than an ordinary person would be if they became homeless'.[32]

There is evidence to suggest that empowering women economically and socially has been found to reduce the likelihood of financial abuse.[33] Every facet of female financial inequality is intertwined, and tackling economic abuse goes hand in hand with addressing the housing emergency.

Britain's housing crisis is much discussed but we rarely tackle its gendered aspects. The chronic shortage of homes, unaffordable rents and high property prices are all having a bigger impact on women. This doesn't just affect day-to-day life: it limits women's potential to build wealth, save for retirement and so much more. We have to change the narrative so that housing policy is framed in terms of its impact on women, today and in the future.

# 10. Free Carers

The 'sandwich generation' is the term for the 1.3 million people with the twin responsibilities of looking after older and younger relatives, typically a parent as well as a child. The ranks of this mostly female force of free carers are swelling rapidly, as our elders are living longer and the state provides limited support.

Most of the discussion about women's unpaid labour centres on childcare and, in theory, once children become young adults, mothers should have more time to focus on their careers and on retirement saving. The reality is that most women have caring responsibilities foisted on them through-out their lives, and women who aren't parents are also relied upon to take care of others – when men typically aren't.

Let's start by looking at how parenting affects the earning prospects for women versus men.

Motherhood brings a distinct salary penalty. Women who become mothers before the age of thirty-three earn on aver-age less than childless men, men with children, childless women and women who had their babies later. The average forty-two-year-old mother in full-time work is earning 11 per cent less than women without children.[1]

Fatherhood is often followed by a pay increase. Studies on both sides of the Atlantic show that men's pay begins to rise after they have children and increases when they have more children – 22 per cent extra for those with two chil-dren, while fathers of one earned 9 per cent more. These findings came from a study of 17,000 full-time working fathers in Britain aged forty-two; after accounting for men's different occupations, location and class, fathers of two still earn more.[2]

A small amount (15 per cent) of this pay boost is attributable to longer hours, as official labour market statistics show that full-time fathers work on average half an hour longer each week than men without children. But that doesn't explain the other 85 per cent of it. Several studies have highlighted that positive discrimination seems to be at play, with fathers being looked upon favourably by employers.[3] One study found that CVs from fathers were more highly scored than identical ones from non-fathers, suggesting that employers view dads as more reliable and responsible employees.[4]

By contrast, studies suggest that there is bias against mothers, that they are perceived as less competent and less employable, and that CVs from mothers were marked down against those from women without children.[5] These perceptions appear to be widely held as the Fawcett Society found that 46 per cent of people believe that a woman becomes less committed to her job after she has a baby – while 29 per cent of people believe fathers become more focused on their jobs after fatherhood.[6] It's ironic that men are likely to be beneficiaries of positive discrimination when there is so much resistance to any suggestion that positive discrimination policies for women should be brought into the workplace.

In addition, the fatherhood bonus is bigger for men at the top of the earnings pyramid. In the US, white and Latino men who are highly educated receive the biggest bump in pay, while African-American men receive the lowest.[7] Meanwhile, women on lower incomes suffer the biggest salary penalty for becoming mothers, at 6 per cent of wages per child.[8] It might be because being from a lower socio-economic class is associated with having children at a younger age and this can impede wage progression. By contrast, more highly educated women and those from higher socio-economic demographics tend to have children later, perhaps after their career is better established. Women with more disposable income can use that money to pay for childcare and other home help, which means they have more time to give to their paid work, or they may be in industries that allow them the flexibility to work from home.[9]

The motherhood penalty also affects women trying to raise capital for new businesses. One survey found that for male entrepreneurs, the amount of money they are able to raise peaks between the ages of thirty-one and thirty-five, and remains high until their mid-forties. The amount of capital that female founders raise doesn't spike until their late thirties – perhaps evidencing the pregnancy penalty – and it peaks shortly thereafter, between the ages of forty-one and forty-five. After the age of forty-five, both men and women find it harder to raise capital, suggesting that ageism in the start-up world affects the genders more equally from then on.[10]

A woman's salary may begin to rise again once her children reach young adulthood, but the damage will have already been done in those years when she was under-earning relative to her potential. This leads to the gender pensions gap, and estimates suggest that women who take time off for children retire with £15,000 less than non-mothers.[11]

# Childcare

Provision of childcare in Britain is shambolic. Some families are paying the highest nursery fees among the OECD's thirty-seven member nations.[12] Some are even spending more on childcare than rent or mortgage payments.

The government says that it provides thirty hours a week of free childcare for children between the ages of three and four, provided parents work and meet certain conditions. However, nearly 90 per cent of nurseries and other providers say that the amount of funding they get from the government for each of those hours isn't enough to cover their costs.[13] Nurseries have closed and just over half of local areas have the capacity to support all the parents who need to take their full entitlement. Half of providers have raised fees for parents to cover the shortfall – so those 'free childcare' hours become a small subsidy instead of an actual free service. A further four in ten providers say they will have to close, which means more difficulty for parents in securing a place for their child.

The crisis in childcare is pushing women out of work, as the government's own figures show that more than half of non-working mothers have said they would be working if they could afford reliable childcare.[14] It's impossible for mothers of disabled children, nearly 90 per cent of whom say they can't work as much as they would like because there's no suitable childcare.[15] Women are the highest earners in one in three British families now – something that's changed rapidly since 1996, when it was less than one in four.[16] How many more female breadwinners would there be if childcare was provided by the state?

In Britain, maternity pay ends when a child turns nine months old and parents start going back to work, but free childcare doesn't begin until the child's second birthday. This gap is a hugely stressful time for women; many need an income, many want to go back to work, but the sums don't add up. Putting one child under the age of two into part-time childcare (twenty-five hours a week) at nursery or with a childminder costs £9,100 a year in London. Across England, Wales and Scotland the average is £6,600 a year.[17] Often, most of a mother's take-home pay will go straight to childcare, especially if she has two children, and in other cases she will be better off not working.

On top of this, the hours that childcare is typically available are incompatible with modern work. Childcare needs to be available at the hours when all parents are working – not just the office hours that some people are working. This includes early morning from 5 a.m. – there's no reason why a nursery cannot open at this time – and there needs to be nationwide provision of later childcare shifts, from 2 p.m. to 10 p.m.

As it stands, the system is so broken that it needs a complete rethink. At the very least, local authorities ought to be provided with the funding they need to provide the childcare that parents are being told they are entitled to. In Chapter 5 I explained how governments ought to view state investment in childcare the same way that it views spending on decent roads or public transport. Childcare is a form of essential infrastructure which requires expense and upkeep, but has benefits to society and the economy which outweigh the costs. The Childcare Levy Campaign is calling on the government to put in place comprehensive childcare infrastructure that would enable women to go back to work if they wanted to. Other organizations campaigning for better childcare include the Coram Family and Childcare Trust and Save the Children.

## Gender and housework

In Britain, official figures show that women do more than double the amount of unpaid childcare and housework that men do, and they do it in every age bracket, from the under-twenty-fives to those over fifty-six years old.[18] There's a gender gap in how the work is divided too. Stereotypical men's jobs are infrequent and outdoors: mowing the lawn, household repairs, taking the rubbish out or washing the car. Women's jobs tend to be indoors and frequent. There's a relentless element to 'female' jobs: plates need to be washed after every meal, children's noses and faces have to be wiped, a mopped floor is dirty hours later. There is little gratification in tasks that come undone and need repeating so soon. The average man would earn £166.63 more a week if he was paid for his unpaid work, while the average woman would earn an extra £259.63, according to the UK's government data body, the Office for National Statistics (ONS).[19]

Women also take on more of the 'worry work', the emotional labour of keeping track of everything that needs to be done in order to prevent things going wrong. This involves being the person who has to remember about parents' evening, that there's a costume to be made for a school play, that someone needs a doctor's appointment or help with homework, to respond to letters from the school, to make sure the children have their PE kit . . . This labour is literally invisible; no one else knows that a mum is thinking of ordering school lunches when she's in the shower or worrying when the next payment for ballet classes is due when she's walking to work.

Women also become chief delegator, expending more energy requesting that their spouse does their chores or reminding them of things they have promised to do. Lack of initiative in one partner is draining for the spouse who continually has to act as field marshal and prompt them into action.

'I had been conditioned my whole life to think one step ahead, to anticipate the needs of those around me and care about them deeply. Emotional labour was a skillset I had been trained in since early childhood. My husband, on the other hand, hadn't received the same education. He is a caring person, but he is not a skilled carer,' writes Gemma Hartley in her book *Fed Up: Navigating and Redefining Emotional Labour for Good*.[20] It's a valuable resource for women who are struggling with this dynamic at home.

Studies have found that partners who share housework more equally have more frequent sex.[21] Yet the gender division in housework persists in many couples – why? One theory is that the partner with greater resources (typically the man) always does less housework. This is called the 'relative resources theory', and it suggests that the greater the division in resources between a husband and wife, the less housework he will do. If this theory is right, it would mean that if more women enter higher-paying and more highly skilled jobs than their spouses, they will be doing less unpaid labour at home. The caveat is that one study found that even when the woman significantly out-earns her husband, he still does less housework.[22] The authors suggested that men felt emasculated by being the lower wage earner and didn't want to exacerbate this by taking on a 'feminine' role at home.

So far, all of this data is about mixed-sex couples. Research looking at same-sex couples consistently reveals that they divide up housework more equally. Maybe the relative resources theory is at play here: if there isn't such a great divide in earnings or occupational prestige between lesbian or gay partners, there is less incentive for the lower earner to take on all the 'extra' jobs at home.[23] Another theory suggests that same-sex couples are more relaxed about gender roles so they can pick chores that suit them.

However same-sex couples manage it, it's working. They report feeling a greater sense of fairness in the division of household jobs than heterosexual couples. Studies suggest that it's not only attributable to each partner getting to choose the tasks they want to do but that satisfaction depends on good communication about the division of housework.

## Discrimination against part-time workers

The 'part-time penalty' is a term that statisticians use to describe the fact that part-time jobs have far lower prospects for pay rises or promotions,[24] while hourly salaries for part-time work can be up to 25 per cent lower than the equivalent role done full-time. This is a feminist issue, as most of the 8 million people working part-time in Britain are women; only 27 per cent of mothers have returned to full-time work three years after their child is born, compared to 90 per cent of fathers. Among the widest part-time penalties of any sector are found in Britain's arts and culture sector, where senior women in part-time roles are paid an average of £8,000 less than senior men doing the full-time equivalent job.

Women looking for part-time work are hindered by the kinds of jobs that are available on a part-time or job-share basis. Roles tend to be lower-skilled, with higher-paid jobs typically demanding full-time hours. As a consequence, people working in part-time jobs also tend to be under-utilizing their skills. This has a profound impact on women's ability to achieve economic equality with men and to save enough over the course of their careers to sustain themselves in retirement. Cultural change is needed within the workplace so that it becomes acceptable for a wider range of jobs to be part-time – combating presenteeism at work generally should help towards this.

Discrimination against part-time roles is specifically outlawed in Denmark, so employers cannot pay someone working ten hours in a week a lower rate than they would someone else doing the same job for thirty-five hours. Similar rules are needed in the UK, perhaps forcing employers to reveal the average hourly pay of part- and full-time work, as transparency is essential to ensuring that remuneration is fair.

## Parental leave

Sweden is one country with progressive parental leave policies: it began offering men three months of leave on a use-it-or-lose-it basis, instead of giving couples an entitlement that they could choose to split. Their culture has changed since then: fathers now tend to take up their full allocation of paternity leave and, because everyone is doing it, they are not penalized in salary or career progression.

Swedes also have an additional 120 days per year of paid leave to care for sick children, which removes the dilemma that women around the world face: compromising their jobs and incomes to take up ad hoc caring for children or parents who fall ill. An additional benefit is that social scientists believe the sharing of caring responsibilities (and thus the financial burden) is contributing to lower divorce rates and the greater involvement of fathers in children's upbringing after separation.[25]

Britain could benefit from following the Swedish example. In 2015, the UK introduced shared parental leave, which gave couples the option of splitting fifty weeks of time off and thirty-seven weeks of pay. The take-up is thought to be as low as 2 per cent.[26] And there's a snowball effect: when some men don't take parental leave, other men don't want to stick out by taking leave either.

The low statutory pay that's available during parental leave is a deterrent to men taking up some of their paternity entitlement. For any couple, financial considerations play a major part in decisions about who works more hours and who spends more time caring. It makes more sense for the higher earner (usually the man) to go back to work while the lower earner receives the maternity pay. This further entrenches women's reliance on their partners, limits their ability to work and contributes to gender gaps in pay and representation.[27]

Changes in a country's parental leave policies can cause a shift in social attitudes.

Spain introduced paid parental leave for fathers in 2007,

which started with two weeks and increased to five weeks by 2018. The numbers of fathers taking time off for their new baby went from virtually zero before the policy was introduced to more than 50 per cent of men afterwards. However, economists studying the effects of the change noticed something curious: once fathers in Spain had been given paternity leave, they wanted fewer children. Couples who took up the paternity leave were 15 per cent less likely to have more children over the following six years than those who missed the eligibility cut-off. Moreover, surveys of Spanish men aged between twenty-one and forty showed they wanted fewer children in the wake of the policy's introduction. Economists suggested that spending more time with their kids may have made men more aware of the effort and costs associated with child-rearing and encouraged them to focus on 'child quality, not quantity'.[28]

Despite the benefits that could emerge from better-designed parental leave, in some countries there's hard-core resistance to change. Switzerland has been slower than other European countries to adapt to women's financial needs: until 1985, Swiss women had to get their husband's permission to work or have a bank account. Until September 2020, Swiss fathers were entitled to paternity leave of a single day, with the government arguing that two weeks' leave would cost too much at 230 million Swiss francs (£179 million). This has now been increased to ten days of leave,[29] which sounds more reasonable until you consider that, by law, Swiss men have to do three weeks' military service, plus around nineteen days of refresher training annually. Although Switzerland hasn't fought a war for 200 years, the country still voted against scrapping the training in 2013, despite criticism that it's more about male bonding than national security. So the issue isn't whether it's okay for men to take time out of work, but what's considered a good use of their time – and parenting pales into insignificance against military service.

## *Caring breaks*

The trends for rising longevity and limited taxpayer-funded care for elders mean that more women will end up having to take time out of paid work to look after their relations – unless more men begin sharing these responsibilities.

This has key implications for how well women reintegrate into the workforce. Returning from a caring break often marks the start of a period where promotions and career progression become scarce, and women often slot back into jobs that are below their previous level (this contributes to 'the Paula Principle', which will be discussed in Chapter 12).

People who have left the workforce are an untapped resource and the return of their skills and experience should be welcomed.

There's an unflattering perception that returners are out of touch or have outdated skills, but some employers are recognizing the value in returners and focusing on how they can refresh their professional skills. Special 'returnership' schemes have appeared at global IT companies Capgemini, IBM and Amazon Web Services and telecoms provider O2, offering paid internships or training programmes of three to six months which are specifically aimed at people wanting to rebuild their careers. Hopefully, these kinds of initiatives can destigmatize breaks from work. Other organizations that can help with building confidence to re-enter the workforce include the Women Returners Professional Network.

## *Divorce*

Multi-million-pound divorce settlements won by top-tier law firms frequently hit the headlines, reinforcing the widely held belief that women do well out of divorce.

When the super-rich resort to a courtroom fight to divide their assets during divorce, newspapers pore over the details, revelling in who got what: the Surrey house and Swiss chalet, nannies, school fees and six-figure sums to care for the children.

These glimpses into the private lives of the super-rich are fascinating to most of us, as we envy those who are winning at the Game of Life. Yet these reports are almost never made without sly judgement. Media columnists opine on whether the wife's demands were reasonable – as if they are in a position to know – before insinuating that her share of the couple's assets was unduly large.

The sheer number of high-net-worth divorces going through London's courts has created the popular perception that separated women shake down their husband for every penny he has. The language used to describe divorce settlements is revealing; the ex-wife is always said to have 'walked away' from the marriage with such and such, as if she was last seen heading towards the horizon and never looked back. Painting a carefree image of a twenty-first-century Thelma or Louise covers over the mundane truth: that most divorcees drive home to their children and carry on being a mum much as before, but single, maybe in a different home, and with a new ritual of anticipating the monthly bank transfer from her former life partner.

In reality, women suffer a financial penalty from getting divorced while men do well for themselves, according to studies from Britain, Canada and across Europe.[30] The typical woman experiences a 22 per cent drop in income after her marriage ends, and five years after separation her income still hasn't returned to pre-divorce levels. By contrast, a man's income rises 'immediately and continuously' by an average of 25 per cent, suggesting he is not spending as much supporting a partner and children. The poverty rate for divorced women is triple that of divorced men, at 27 per cent – so nearly a third of divorced women experience poverty.

London is known as the 'divorce capital of the world' because the world's wealthiest head to England to legally end their marriages. Unlike in other countries, couples do not need to have been married in England to file for divorce and nor do they have to be British nationals – it's enough for one spouse to be habitually resident in Britain. Those with the means to take legal action wherever they like know that England and Wales have among the most generous divorce rules for the financially weaker spouse – usually the woman – as judges start from the assumption that assets should be divided 50:50. A judge can also use their own discretion in awarding the final settlement and can decide if a prenuptial agreement is valid under English law on a case-by-case basis. And so the capital calls out to disgruntled wives around the world. Sometimes this sparks a race between warring spouses to see who can file for divorce first in which jurisdiction – with both choosing the legal system that will favour their interests.

Ironically, it's really in divorce that we can see the feminist aspect of marriage. The English system has enshrined the principle that breadwinners and homemakers make equally important contributions to a marriage, that wealth should be divided 50:50 because most men wouldn't have the time to make the money they do if they didn't have women supporting them.

Unsurprisingly, husbands try to subvert the system by saying they made a 'special contribution' to building the family's wealth. For example, a judge ruled in 2014 that billionaire hedge fund manager Sir Chris Hohn was a 'financial genius' who only had to leave his ex-wife with a third of their £1 billion fortune, rather than the half that she had sought.[31]

But even though this point has been argued many times, it has rarely succeeded and a recent case suggests the 'special contribution' line isn't going to work as frequently in future.

An already wealthy man co-founded a company prior to getting married in 2008, worked as its CEO and became hugely successful. The business was sold, some of the proceeds were invested and by the time the couple (whose identity has been protected by the courts) separated in 2015 they had assets of £530 million. During the divorce the husband argued 'it is plainly a case in which she [the wife] is not entitled to share in the value of the company at all'. He said that his wife hadn't done paid work during the marriage and so she should receive, at best, a financial settlement based on 'needs' rather than the 50 per cent she claimed.

However, what the husband didn't emphasize was that his wife hadn't worked outside the home because she had been a full-time carer for their disabled child, who had a rare, life-threatening condition, a role she continued with after the divorce. The husband described her as being 'an excellent mother who is totally devoted to the well-being of [the child]'.[32] So there was a good reason why she hadn't worked outside the home, and another good reason why he was able to work as many hours as he did – his kind wife sacrificed her own chance at making money to look after their child.

However, the court agreed that the husband had more of a claim on their wealth and awarded the ex-wife a 29 per cent share. The wife took the case to the Court of Appeal which, in 2019, overthrew the original ruling and gave the ex-wife half of the assets. The judgment stated: 'I must be particularly careful not to undervalue the domestic contribution of the homemaker to the welfare and happiness of the family as a whole. In this case, the wife's enormous contribution . . . has freed the husband to a very considerable extent to enable him to pursue the business activities which have generated the enormous wealth now available.'[33] This sets an important precedent in case law, and will make it much harder in future for one party to argue that they deserve a bigger share of the wealth on divorce.

Among the biggest misconceptions is that divorced women receive lifelong support at their husband's expense. Historically this could happen following a long marriage to a very wealthy man, but in recent years judges have increasingly been placing time limits on spousal payments.

In a landmark case in 2015, the Court of Appeal upheld a ruling that Tracey Wright, ex-wife of a millionaire racehorse surgeon, should not be supported indefinitely by her former husband. She had been receiving £75,000 annually following the divorce in 2008 as part of a package that included a mortgage-free house and stables for several horses.

Her ex-husband applied to the family courts in 2014 arguing that the payment ought to be reduced, as he was approaching retirement and she had made no effort to find work. The judge found in Mr Wright's favour and told Ms Wright in no uncertain terms to 'get a job'. The payments from Mr Wright were to be gradually reduced over five years before stopping entirely, a judgment reaffirmed by the Court of Appeal when Ms Wright tried to have the decision over-turned. This case is going to have significant implications for spousal support payments in future, and it suggests that judges won't entertain the idea of a woman living off her ex-husband's income for life or even until the children reach adulthood. Women in this situation should expect their ex to be able to put a stop to maintenance payments once they reach retirement or perhaps when the youngest child turns seven.[34]

Unfortunately, when it comes to divorce too many women are disadvantaged by limited access to legal support, often in comparison to their higher-earning ex who can afford to pay lawyers. Ex-wives often end up with fewer financial assets than they are entitled to. For example, since 2000 it has been possible for divorcing couples in the UK to share pension savings, usually with the lower-earning spouse receiving a portion of the other's pension. These rules were put in place to protect women – it's an acknowledgement that retirement savings are a valuable asset built up during the marriage, usually the biggest asset after the family home, and that both parties need the means to support themselves in old age.

So the spirit of the law is in the right place. But in 2012 the government massively reduced public funding for free legal advice and representation, called legal aid. Help has been abolished for many of the issues that go through family courts, including divorce, child contact, welfare benefits and employ-ment and housing law, except in very limited circumstances.

Since then, those involved in a legal dispute have to either pay a solicitor or barrister, or represent themselves in court.

This has resulted in a huge drop in the number of women fighting for their fair share of their ex-partners' pensions. In 2019 only 13 per cent of divorces included some kind of pension settlement, which goes some way to explaining why the average divorced woman reaches retirement with less than a third (£26,100) of the pension savings accrued by the average divorced man (£103,500).[35]

The government's failure to ring-fence access to legal aid during divorce means that the vast majority of women can't benefit from rules designed to protect them. If a person can't exercise their rights, those rights effectively don't exist. This is a huge issue because, as we know, one in three marriages ends in divorce in Britain. Globally divorce rates have risen 260 per cent since 1960, so ensuring women get a fair deal in divorce is essential in every country.

Divorce is a massive financial shock. It radically changes what a woman's retirement will look like and she will have to get her financial plans back on track. Unfortunately, doing this in one's fifties or sixties makes it very hard to accumulate enough money to provide a basic standard of living in later life.

A society where justice is only accessible by a privileged few isn't a just society at all. But this is the situation in Britain today. Since the Conservatives introduced the 2012 Legal Aid, Sentencing and Punishment of Offenders Act (known as LASPO), funding for legal assistance has been reduced by more than £600 million a year. Public access to justice and a fair trial has never been so restricted in this country, according to the Law Society, the organization which represents solicitors.[36]

Legal aid is available in some circumstances but the rules are complex. The big impediment is the means-test, where the maximum income level is set so low that everyone except a tiny minority is considered able to fund their own legal team. Having a mortgage, for example, can make someone ineligible for legal help even if they have little income.

The government's own guideline figures for legal professional charges state that in London a trainee solicitor can cost up to £138 an hour, while a solicitor with more than eight years' experience can charge £408 per hour.[37]

Wealth has become a prerequisite to justice and there is ample evidence that women find these fees harder to pay. An industry of specialist finance providers has emerged in Britain and America, offering litigation loans mainly to women who cannot otherwise fund the legal costs of divorce. Demand for these loans has ballooned since legal aid was slashed even though they come with shocking interest rates of up to 16–18 per cent.

Those who can't pay solicitors often represent themselves. Only 20 per cent of cases dealt with by the family court in 2017 had legal representatives for both parties, and in a further 35 per cent of cases neither party had a solicitor or barrister.[38] Delays, confusion, overrunning and extra costs have become the order of the day for the courts as bewildered litigants-in-person try to do the jobs of barristers and solicitors. Imagine how daunting it would be to represent yourself in court against your ex-spouse and their barrister, and how galling it would feel if the case did not go your way.

Women who find themselves facing divorce or in need of legal support should first look for free advice via a voluntary agency such as Advice Now or Citizens Advice, which also has information on mediation services. This is where an independent person helps two opposing sides to work through their dispute, and it is often cheaper than seeking the help of a solicitor. It is always better to come to a resolution outside of court, and some family court matters require people to have attended a mediation session first.

The Money Advice Service is another good resource with a large section of articles on all aspects of divorce. Support Through Court is a charity that helps people who are facing a court battle without representation. While it doesn't provide legal advice, it can help at most stages of a legal dispute, including filling in forms, deciding what to say in the courtroom and even accompanying people to court.

Paying for a session or two with a solicitor can be useful, if you can afford it. There are many online legal advice services where the contact is over the phone or through emails, which will cost less than face-to-face meetings with an established firm. If you could put a set amount towards legal fees, explain this to the solicitor, who may be willing to work with you on a fixed-fee basis or could advise you on how much help they could give for your budget. Establish upfront how much you will be charged, and bear in mind that you could save a good deal of money by filling out necessary forms yourself, as solicitors will charge for their time in doing this. In any meeting with a solicitor, ask specifically whether you should stop the case or if it's worth continuing. If you are told your case is weak, drop the matter and move on. If you do have a case, ask for an outline. You don't have to enlist a solicitor from the start to finish of a case but you can return for help if you need it, for example when the case reaches a later stage. Before any meeting or phone call about the legal situation, do your homework and make a list of points that you want to raise. This will help you get the most out of the time.

If you end up representing yourself in court, the Bar Council has a guide which explains how the legal process works, how to prepare a case and what to expect when going into court. There is a link to the document in the notes to this chapter.[39]

## *Rights for girlfriends*

Divorce law places gender equality at the core of rules about the division of financial assets. But when it comes to rights and protections for girlfriends and cohabiting partners, there's a gaping black hole.

Only people who are married or in a civil partnership are covered by laws about couples dividing shared assets when they divorce or separate. Cohabiting couples have no legal obligation to support one another financially, so if one of them ends the relationship they could leave the other in the lurch. This has affected thousands of people who have lived with their partners, shared everything and perhaps given up their livelihood to raise children, but then realize when the relationship breaks down that they aren't entitled to anything that isn't in their name or owned jointly.

Unfortunately, the law in England is drastically out of sync with modern life, as the number of cohabiting couples more than doubled from 1.5 million in 1996 to 3.3 million in 2017, but they have not been granted similar protections to married couples. Scotland made legal changes in 2006 to allow cohabiting partners to apply to the courts for financial provision if they have been left with nothing. These are protections that women badly need for all the reasons outlined in this book. In the meantime, unmarried but cohabiting partners should be aware of the following points:

1. If your name isn't on the title deeds of the house you've been living in and paying the mortgage on, you have no claim to it. The same goes for a car that's owned by one person but used by both.

2. The unmarried partner of a tenant cannot stay in the property if they are asked to leave. However, both people in a marriage have a right to remain in their matrimonial home after the relationship breaks down.

3. Unmarried mothers who prioritized their family and homemaking over work are not entitled to maintenance support payments or their partner's pension, both things which married couples can claim.

It is also vital to get a will if you are in a cohabiting couple. The unexpected death of one partner leaves their other half in a pickle; the surviving partner cannot legally access their bank account. If they were married the widow would be allowed to withdraw reasonable amounts from the account.

If one half of an unmarried couple dies without leaving a will, their assets don't automatically pass to their partner. Any assets will go to the next of kin under inheritance law.

## Prenuptial agreements

Prenups date back to the ancient Egyptians, who had some surprisingly feminist attitudes towards financial rights. Prior to marriage a bride could make her husband sign eight-foot-long contracts ensuring that, if the union failed, she got back the property and wealth she had brought to the marriage, plus alimony. One of these nearly 2,500-year-old contracts guarantees a wife 1.2 pieces of silver plus thirty-six bags of grain every year for the rest of her life. These legally binding documents were arranged between the couple in the presence of several witnesses and a scribe. If either party wanted to break the contract they would have to appear in court, and most importantly, women could file for divorce.

Thousands of years later, pre-marriage contracts remain controversial. They are especially useful for: people who own a business and don't want to risk it being sold or split after divorce; those who have children from a previous relationship and want to ring-fence assets for their future; people who have substantial wealth of their own going into the marriage; people expecting a significant inheritance in future; or, when marrying someone from abroad, you may want to protect your assets from financial orders outside of the UK. The aim is to create a contract strong enough to withstand legal challenges, should the marriage end and you need the contract to do what it promised. Courts are more likely to respect a prenuptial agreement if it has been made with the full and frank disclosure of assets by both parties. Both partners need to have had independent legal advice. It's also a good idea to include a provision that allows the contract to be revised at a later stage.

Prenuptials and postnuptial agreements (made after marriage) are not legally binding in the UK but judges can use their discretion to decide whether a prenup holds on a case-by-case basis. Over the past few years the stipulations of pre-and postnups have been taken into account more often by courts in England and Wales – which means there's a good chance that they will be more respected in future.

## *Child maintenance*

Child support payments from former partners can be a vital part of the household budget for women. When couples separate they can come to a private agreement about payments to (usually) the mother, but if the pair can't settle on an arrangement they can go to the Child Maintenance Service (CMS) which can calculate how much should be paid and collect the money.

There is a one-off application fee of £20 followed by a fee every time money is passed from one parent to the other; currently 20 per cent from the paying parent and 4 per cent from the receiving parent. Over a quarter of receiving parents have said that the fees are difficult to afford.[40] But given the ubiquity of electronic money transfers and how cheaply these automated transfers can be made – often for less than 3 per cent of the sum being sent – it's not clear why the charges are as high as 24 per cent. The CMS needs reform, including the removal of the £20 application fee. It may sound like a small amount but since this fee was introduced the number of applications to the CMS has fallen substantially, which suggests that the poorest cannot spare the money to make an application.

In the case of many life events, from parenthood to divorce, the financial cost of being a carer needs to be borne more equally. There is no reason why women should be 'better' at looking after children and relatives – but whoever the job falls to, we must ensure that 'breaks' from paid work don't leave carers financially damaged for life.

# 11. Reproductive Rights

When the contraceptive pill became available in the sixties, women were set on the path to gaining economic power. In the decades since, women have overtaken men educationally, moved into paid employment in droves and risen through the ranks to some of the highest-status and best-paid jobs. After centuries of female economic inequality, gaining the ability to control decisions about having children changed everything.

The Pill delays the age of first motherhood, which in turn means more women can obtain university degrees, go out to work and earn higher wages.[1] Yet too often discussions about being pro-life or pro-choice are not based in women's economic reality. When women have more control over their bodies, they have more opportunities in employment. Forcing women to give birth to babies they will struggle to look after is a direct cause of female impoverishment. And yet, the systematic erosion of the most fundamental of human rights – to choose when, how and with whom we have a baby – is under attack in the US. By extension, women's financial rights and economic freedoms are also in jeopardy.

In a nation where private health insurance is critical and where most people have it arranged through their workplace, it is legal for some employers to ban the insurer from providing free contraception.[2] If a boss's religious or moral opinions dictate that it's wrong for female staff to take birth control pills or have a coil fitted, those women will have to pay for them out of their own pocket in addition to their insurance costs.

This measure was introduced with the 2014 'Hobby Lobby' ruling, and the Trump administration wanted to take it further: it pushed for legislation that would allow more employers to take contraception cover out of health insurance. One of the virtues of hormonal contraceptives is that women get to control how and when they use them. This policy would have allowed powerful men to get a say in whether many women could access birth control.

At the time of writing, the so-called Birth Control Coverage changes have been blocked by a federal court, which ruled that they would affect 70,500 women. But the fact that this legislation was even on the table illustrates the way in which women's financial freedom is bound up with our reproductive freedoms – and how easily both can be taken away.

Although the restrictions on contraception are being framed as a moral issue, policymakers have chosen to sanction women seeking birth control through their finances. Women are already restricted by economic factors – the pay gap, limited parental leave, costly childcare – and now those who want to manage the costs of parenting by spacing out their pregnancies or preventing them will face extra costs.

Even with their health insurance, many women in the US had to pay towards the cost of the Pill prior to 2010, when female contraception was classed as a medical need for the first time under President Obama's Affordable Care Act. Despite this, one Republican commentator argued in the *Wall Street Journal* that contraception is an unnecessary expense for the American taxpayer: 'In a spending crisis with trillions in debt and many in need, in a nation in existential doubt as to its standing and purpose, in a time when parents struggle to buy the good sneakers for the kids so they're not embarrassed at school . . . that in *that* nation the great issue of the day, and the appropriate focus of our concern, is making other people pay for . . . birth-control pills.'[3] This is a very different perspective from more than two dozen countries, rich and poor, which don't see the provision of free or subsidized contraceptive pills as an undue burden on the taxpayer, including Algeria, Angola, Argentina, Bolivia, China, India, Iran, Kyrgyzstan, the Philippines and the UK.[4] Countries where the Pill isn't subsidized, or only partially, include Brazil, Ireland, Japan, Norway and Spain.

In the US, the cost of contraception adds up substantially over a lifetime. Birth control pills can cost up to $50 per month and are typically between $240 and $600 a year, plus the cost of an initial consultation with a doctor and regular check-ups at $35 to $250 a time.[5] If a woman takes the Pill for ten years and has two annual check-ups, that could cost up to $11,000, and many women use female contraception for up to thirty years.

America is the only developed country where employers are not obliged to provide paid maternity leave.[6] So employers could bar female staff from receiving free birth control pills and expect them to self-finance time off work when the baby is due. Yet women's income is vital to the survival of their families; in the US, 55 per cent of working women bring home at least half of the family income.

Since January 2011, over 400 separate restrictions on access to abortion have been introduced across America.[7] These include mandatory waiting times of up to three days between the termination counselling session and the procedure, and allowing medical professionals to withhold information about the pregnancy to deter a woman from seeking a termination. Some states used the Covid-19 pandemic as an excuse to further restrict access to abortions. Although abortions are a time-sensitive, necessary procedure, the Texas attorney general declared them non-essential and banned doctors from providing them during the crisis. Similar moves were made in Alabama, Iowa, Ohio and Oklahoma. The increasing number of restrictions imposed in recent years has put pressure on the network of independent clinics which provide most pregnancy terminations in America. But there are fears that shutting down clinics during the pandemic will have a lasting effect on their ability to survive financially – permanently removing the option of abortion.

Studies have shown that the number one reason for seeking a termination is that a baby would cause financial instability and interfere with work, education and caring responsibilities.[8] Research suggests that having a termination can help women follow through on work and educational aspirations.[9] Women living in states that have abortion restrictions experience more 'job lock', where they struggle to move between employers and into higher-paying roles.[10] Virginia tried to pass a law forcing women to undergo a transvaginal ultrasound prior to an abortion, hoping they would think again after seeing the foetus inside them. There is no medical reason for a woman to view a vaginal ultrasound, and mandating this is forcible penetration, which in any other situation would be called rape.[11]

This attack on women's reproductive rights gained intensity in 2019, with eight states passing laws that effectively ban abortion after the earliest stages of pregnancy, often before a woman knows she is with child.[12] They are Arkansas,

Georgia, Kentucky, Louisiana, Mississippi, Missouri, Ohio and Utah.[13] A ninth state, Alabama, has taken the most extreme approach and has banned abortion in virtually every circumstance, including rape and incest. Doctors who perform the procedure face up to ninety-nine years in prison. Restrictions on abortions will deepen the divide between wealthy and poor women, as only those who can afford it will be able to travel to other states to have the procedure. The late Ruth Bader Ginsburg, an associate justice of the US Supreme Court, had called for more social action on the issue. 'The truth is that with all these restrictive laws, the only people who are being restricted are poor women. They normally can't pay a plane fare or the bus fare, they can't afford to take days off of work to go.'[14]

Meanwhile, the Trump administration placed new restrictions on a scheme that funds birth control and reproductive healthcare for low-income women, called Title X. Healthcare providers that participate in the programme can inform women of the full range of pregnancy-related options, including termination, but new rules state they can no longer provide referrals to abortion clinics, even on the patient's request.[15] This immediately marks out abortion as illegitimate – 'I can tell you it is an option but I can't say where.' In a country where availability and laws governing abortion differ widely from state to state, this confusing and illogical rule will hurt vulnerable women.

These are all examples of how rapidly attitudes towards women's bodily autonomy have changed in the United States over the past decade. There are now legitimate fears that the right to have an abortion, which has been in place since the Roe v. Wade court judgment in 1973, will be removed.

## Global reproductive rights

The US's anti-abortion agenda is able to reverberate around the world because of its status.

Within days of taking office in 2017, President Trump withdrew funding for global healthcare organizations that assist women in developing countries. He resurrected the so-called Mexico City Policy (also known as the Global Gag Rule), whereby the US refuses to give any foreign aid to organizations that provide abortion counselling, referrals and advocacy for abortion law reform. The rules restrict where $8.8 billion of funding can be allocated, which has had massive ramifications for healthcare organizations globally.[16]

Meanwhile, the United Nations Population Fund (UNFPA) is the world's largest provider of contraceptives, and it helps 12.5 million women in forty-six countries reduce the likelihood of unintended pregnancies and maternal mortality. It also advocates for an end to child marriage and for reproductive rights.[17] The Trump administration withdrew funding for the scheme in 2017, ostensibly because it believed UNFPA supports 'coercive abortions' in China, something which UNFPA has denied.[18]

Again, it is poor women who have suffered – women who rely on free maternity care, contraception or HIV medication. The Trump administration dismantled decades of economic progress for women all over the world by restricting their ability to control what happens to their bodies. America is driving an anti-woman agenda that limits female economic power in communities around the world.

Far from preventing abortions, the Global Gag Rule has led to a 40 per cent increase in terminations and has reduced the use of modern contraception in twenty-six African countries that depend on foreign aid.[19] These are women who simply cannot afford contraception, but neither can they afford to have more children. Given that abortions are a leading cause of maternal mortality, it's likely that the policy has led to a greater number of deaths, particularly since the abortions are more likely to be back-alley procedures.[20] Other studies have found that the policy has had a negative effect on prenatal care and increased poor child health.[21]

## Vasectomies

Women put up with injections, implants, coils, cervical caps, regular visits to the doctor and the responsibility of having to take a pill at a regular time each day, all in the name of not getting pregnant. The freedom women have to choose a birth control method is a joy, but it's also a burden: we are expected to take responsibility for contraception. Social scientists call this 'the feminization of responsibility' and it's an additional form of labour that women take on. This is reinforced by male attitudes that perceive getting the snip as going above and beyond the call of duty. One clinic in the US gives men who go through a vasectomy a certificate for 'uncommon bravery' and 'meritorious performance'.[22] A 2017 article in the *Guardian* was headlined 'Man up, guys, you're a snip away from being heroes', as if sharing the burden of contraception is an act of heroism.[23]

It's been sixty years since hormonal contraception arrived for women, but little progress has been made on creating a male equivalent. So there remain twelve kinds of female-specific contraception and only two for men – condoms and sterilization. Pharmaceutical firms seem reluctant to invest in a product that men say they wouldn't want to take if it had side effects.[24]

The humble vasectomy – a reversible, fifteen-minute procedure that's more effective than female sterilization – would seem an ideal solution for couples in long-term relationships who have had children. But vasectomies are very much out of favour: in the UK, the number of vasectomies performed fell 64 per cent between 2006 and 2016.[25] In the US, vasectomies are one of the least popular methods of birth control and fewer than 6 per cent of women rely on their partner having a vasectomy for contraception. Vasectomies are an outpatient procedure with few complications and men can return to work in a few days. They cost six times less than female sterilization (up to $1,000 in the US, depending on medical cover,[26] and around £400 in the UK)[27] so they can work out cost-effective over time. Meanwhile, female sterilization is the most popular form of birth control in the US, used by 18 per cent of women, even though it is expensive and is a more invasive procedure.[28] Talk about taking one for the team.

Medical professionals say that misconceptions abound about vasectomy: it will hurt; it will hinder an erection; it will somehow diminish manhood. This nonsense reinforces the burden on women for family planning – in time, money and emotional labour.

## Maternal mortality

The statistics for maternal mortality reveal how female economic inequality, health and race intersect. It's defined as women dying during or up to forty-two days after complications giving birth, and while people might think of this as an issue for 'poor' countries, in Britain twice as many women die from childbirth as in Sweden.[29] The figures have increased in recent years alongside infant mortality rates, which rose for the first time in a decade – a worrying development that academics believe has been caused by austerity cuts.[30]

The racial divide in maternal mortality is also shocking: in the UK, Black women are five times more likely to die during pregnancy or in the six weeks afterwards than white women.[31] Asian women have maternal mortality rates twice as high as white women in Britain. In the US, Black women die at the same rate from pregnancy complications as women in Uzbekistan, according to the World Health Organization, and there are also much higher rates among Native American women.[32] A society that valued Black and ethnic minority women's lives equally would channel more resources into ensuring they receive the care needed to combat those risks.

The Covid-19 pandemic threatened to worsen the risks facing pregnant women. They were under extra stress from the uncertainty – could they still attend routine health checks? – and when antenatal classes were called off, leaving women feeling less prepared for childbirth. There was initially very little data about how pregnant women would fare if they caught the virus or what effects it could have on the baby.

Although women make up 70 per cent of the global health force, healthcare in many nations is so stretched that there was a very real risk that funding for the reproductive and maternal care that women need would be diverted to other areas. The United Nations predicts higher rates of maternal mortality, young pregnancies and sexually transmitted diseases as access to care in these areas is restricted or downgraded in priority. The pandemic has highlighted how budgets for both pre- and postnatal maternity care need to be sufficient and ring-fenced so that continuity of care can continue during periods of high stress on local health services.

Meanwhile, the US has been dubbed the 'most dangerous place in the developed world to give birth', following an investigation by *USA Today*. Maternal mortality rates have risen rapidly, even as childbirth has become much safer around the world.[33] The number of women dying per 1,000 births in America is up from 9.8 in 2000 to 26.4 in 2015.[34] These figures do not include the women who are left with disabilities, which can limit their ability to undertake paid work after giving birth. By contrast, in Sweden, there are 4.4 maternal deaths per 100,000 births, and 7.3 in Canada.[35]

Most people think of maternal mortality as a crisis during labour or delivery, but over a third of deaths happen in the week after birth and, in the year afterwards, suicide becomes the leading case of maternal deaths.[36] Deaths after births are the result of a lack of healthcare before and after having a baby. Even for women with private health insurance, maternal health services are often not covered, which is why more than half of deliveries in the US are covered by Medicaid, the government health service. This isn't generous: it stops paying for pregnancy-related care six weeks post-partum, which some doctors say isn't long enough to identify problems.[37] Ultimately, at least 60 per cent of maternal deaths in the US are preventable.[38]

More than a third of women in the US say they have avoided seeking the medical care they needed because of the cost, which is far higher than in other developed countries.[39] Women with no prenatal care are up to four times more likely to die.[40] It's both a cause and a symptom: women die from pregnancy when they suffer higher rates of poverty, lower earnings and lack of access to good healthcare, and maternal deaths can trap families in a cycle of poverty.

Reproductive rights and adequate maternal care should be available to all women – and this shouldn't be seen solely as an issue for women: we all have a responsibility for the social well-being and health of children, mothers and those who choose not to have children.

# 12. The Pay Gap

Political interest in women and money has increased after a concerted campaign to bring the gender pay gap under scrutiny. Thanks to these efforts, since 2017 companies in the UK with more than 250 employees have had to share details of average pay for male and female staff. The results have been shocking. For example, the British arm of Condé Nast, the publisher of magazines including *Vogue*, *Vanity Fair* and *Tatler*, employs three times as many women as men and has more women working at every level of seniority. Despite this, it still managed to pay female staff less than two-thirds of their male colleagues' salaries, on average. And Condé Nast is far from alone in this.

There are also clear examples of women being paid less for doing the same jobs as men. TV presenter Louise Minchin, fifty, was sitting with her co-host, Dan Walker, forty-two, on the couch presenting the *BBC Breakfast* show when he cracked a joke referring to his presence on the television company's list of high earners. Minchin shot him a dirty look live on air – she wasn't on the list, despite working side by side with Walker and being the more experienced of the pair. Often we have no idea how much other people earn because there's little transparency over pay.

There are places in the world where women earn more than men for working in sewers, waste management, construction and water supply. Slovenian women working in these traditionally male industries earn an average of 11 per cent more than men, while Romania's construction industry has a gender pay gap of 20 per cent in favour of women. In Hungary the figure is 11.5 per cent.[1] This is one of the legacies of socialism. At a time when women in the West were at home with their washing machines, socialist regimes needed female labour to contribute towards industrialization. Women were encouraged to gain technical skills, find employment in male-dominated industries[2] and gradually new representations of women emerged, including the female tractor driver, labourer and engineer.

Training and employment weren't the only factors. Russia was ahead of Britain and America in granting women financial rights: since 1753, women had been able to earn their own money and keep it independently of their husbands. Under socialism, some regimes saw female emancipation as part of a wider plan to create more 'advanced' societies. Social policy in the Eastern Bloc included free childcare and generous maternity leave, and the Bolsheviks attempted to socialize domestic labour by investing in public laundries and canteens, removing the burden of chores from women. This isn't a paean to socialist ideology and neither is it a denial of the grotesque and inhumane government policies that were in place in this era. But there were ways in which women benefited from socialism.[3]

With the collapse of socialism, paid maternity leave and childcare disappeared, reversing some of the progress that had been made towards female economic independence. Yet even today women hold more senior management roles in Eastern Europe than in any other part of the world.[4] Around 85 per cent of companies have at least one woman in their senior leadership teams.

The gender pay gap is culturally constructed: in every

nation, it's assumptions about the value of women's labour and what we should be doing with our time that shape how much women earn relative to men. Chile is a country where traditional notions of gender roles persist; the country didn't introduce the principle of equal remuneration for men and women into law until 2009. In this context, it's not surprising that the gender pay gap is close to 50 per cent among professionals, the worst of any country in the OECD. In Chile, 79 per cent of women who have been to university have a job that is appropriately paid for the level of education they have acquired, in comparison to 91 per cent of men.[5]

I have left it until now to discuss what women are paid because female economic inequality runs much deeper than the pay gap. But with misconceptions about the pay gap rife, this chapter will deconstruct the main myths surrounding it.

## Myth 1: It's illegal to pay women less, so pay discrimination doesn't happen

Statisticians around the world consistently report finding 'unexplained' elements when analysing national gender pay gaps. The UK's Office for National Statistics (ONS) says that two-thirds of the pay gap 'cannot be explained' and only a small part (36 per cent) of the male pay premium is justifiable by the types of jobs men and women do or the characteristics of each gender in the workplace, such as average age, length of service or the size of company.[6] The pay gap remains in favour of men in all occupations; however, the ONS declined to pinpoint discrimination as the cause.

'It is possible that this plays a part,' it states. At least 25 per cent of companies in the UK pay female staff at least 20 per cent less than men.

It's the same all over the world. New Zealand's government describes 80 per cent of the country's gender pay gap as unexplained and says that discrepancies in salary are now driven by 'harder to measure factors, like conscious and unconscious bias that impacts negatively on women's recruitment and pay advancement'.[7] Switzerland's federal statistics agency says that 42 per cent of the wage gap can't be explained,[8] while the World Bank talks of a 'persistent and sizeable portion of the wage gap that cannot be explained' across the European Union.[9] In the UK, the pay gap is 9 per cent for people in full-time work, 18 per cent for all workers, and when looking at some of the most important industries, including banking, it widens to 40 per cent.

This 'unexplainable' part of the pay gap remains mostly ignored. Instead, women's lower pay is written off as the impact of maternity leave on a woman's career, or the different kinds of work women do. This misses the point: the fact that women are concentrated in lower-paying jobs and struggle to raise their income (especially after having children) is a reflection of their inequality. To suggest there's an inevitability to the pay gap, that women should earn less or fail to progress in their careers because they are mothers, or because they have taken eighteen months of maternity leave during a thirty-five-year career is ludicrous. A year or two out of work during a lifetime of labour is not that much. Men also have gaps in their careers, when they are out of work, on gardening leave, changing careers, travelling or having personal problems. When a woman goes on maternity leave she returns with a black mark on her card. Women are penalized financially for being parents in a way that men aren't.

## Myth 2: Men are better workers

In the late sixties, there was a well-known saying: 'Every employee rises to his level of incompetence.' It's called the Peter Principle and the term was coined by author Laurence Peter, who said that workers (i.e. men at the time) keep on being promoted for demonstrating competence in their jobs until they arrive at a level at which they don't show enough competence to be promoted any further. This means that workers settle into a role that's one rung above their ability, which Peter believed goes some way towards explaining the ineptitude encountered in the workplace.

Today, academic Tom Schuller uses this once-famous saying to suggest that there's a corresponding rule for women: they consistently work in jobs that are below their level of competence. He calls this the Paula Principle: 'Women's competences are not recognised and rewarded as men's are. Women's work is given less recognition at every level and women's careers have a lower and flatter trajectory.'[10]

Men's labour is perceived as more valuable. Recruitment company Hired.com says that in 60 per cent of job offers men are offered higher salaries for the same role at the same company, and that when a job is available around 40 per cent of the time only male candidates are interviewed. Rather than women choosing low-wage industries – something that pay-gap deniers chide women for – plenty of evidence shows that some occupations become lower-wage when more women work in them.[11]

Another hidden form of discrimination is in the salaries paid in jobs predominantly occupied by women versus the wages of traditionally male jobs. An Australian study found that childcare workers were being paid around half the wage of metal fitters who had the same level of qualifications.[12] The men who bash metal are valued twice as much as the women who shape children's lives.

For women to be working below their level of competence is a waste of potential for individuals, companies and the economy. It's also astounding, considering that girls have outperformed boys at every stage of school and university for the past thirty years around the world. Fewer girls drop out at each stage of academic transition, so they are more willing to be educated, and when they do participate their achievement is higher.

## *Myth 3: Education will solve the pay gap*

Studying STEM (science, technology, engineering and mathematics) subjects or working in high-earning roles can guarantee a higher salary, but not one that's equal to that of similarly qualified men. Among the twenty best-paid STEM occupations, women hold 20 per cent of jobs and earn 89 cents to every dollar a man makes.[13]

American women in architecture and chemical engineering out-earn men in the field, despite holding 8 per cent and 15 per cent of the jobs respectively. But the pay gap persists in other STEM fields, the worst being operations research, actuarial science and environmental science, where women earn 81–2 cents for every dollar a man makes.[14]

In Europe in 2010, the top 10 per cent of high-earning

women earned close to €700 per month less than the top 10 per cent of male earners, according to the International Labour Organization (ILO).[15] In its 2018–19 global wage report, the ILO highlighted the fact that in many countries women are more highly educated than men but are paid less, even when they work in the same roles.[16]

Other data shows that women are offered lower starting salaries than men straight out of university, while a report from the American Association of University Women found an unexplained 7 per cent pay gap for women just one year following graduation – even after accounting for factors including college major and occupational choice.[17] Having an elite education does not remove the pay gap; women who attended Ivy League colleges earned $85,000 a year less than their male peers by the age of thirty.[18] Other studies have found direct evidence of discrimination – for example, more jobs went to women when the applicant's sex was unknown during the hiring process.[19]

## Myth 4: Women are distracted from careers by motherhood

Motherhood is consistently given as the reason why women lag behind men at work. Sheryl Sandberg, author of *Lean In*, argued that some women begin to disengage from their careers before they have children, in some cases even before they have found a partner. Yet this perception that women do not commit as fully to their jobs is undermined by the fact that women hugely outnumber men in workplace training and adult education. Around 76 per cent of adult learners in Britain are women, and they have been the majority in adult education for the past twenty years.[20] There's a similar trend across Europe, where women keep learning as adults, showing more commitment to increasing their vocational skills throughout their careers and widening the competence gap over men.

This doesn't fit with the stereotype of 'working women who are so distracted by family duties that they can't give their all at work'.

## Myth 5: Women aren't good leaders

No conversation about the gender pay gap is complete without some discussion of the 'glass cliff', a phenomenon where women are appointed to positions of power just when the organization is on the brink of crisis or in a precarious situation.[21] They then face a hostile environment, which makes the job tougher to do. Britain got its second female prime minister, Theresa May, when the country was mired in the crisis of its exit from the European Union and the government was a shambles. An example from the corporate world is American retailer JCPenney appointing its first female CEO, Jill Soltau, after making losses and closing dozens of stores. Female CEOs are 45 per cent more likely to be sacked from their own companies – is this because they were tasked with leading a sinking ship and were blamed when it went down?[22]

The term 'glass cliff' was coined by academics at Exeter University after they examined a 2003 article in *The Times*, which suggested that FTSE 100 companies that 'decline to embrace political correctness' by having a woman on their board had a better share price performance. By contrast, those that appointed women to their boards had a worse share price performance, which meant that women in leadership roles were 'wreaking havoc on UK companies'.[23] The study investigated the context of these claims and concluded that those companies' share prices were already declining before women were appointed.

## Competency bias and the pay gap

White male candidates are judged as more competent than women or ethnic minority candidates and are given higher starting salaries, even when their CVs are identical. In one study, faculty members in the biology, chemistry and physics departments at a number of leading American universities rated the applications of students applying for a laboratory manager position. The identical résumés had been randomly assigned male or female names, yet the 'male' candidates were rated as more competent, were more likely to be hired and were also offered higher starting salaries. It was an especially interesting discovery, given that scientists have undergone rigorous training to be objective and not give in to unconscious bias. It also made no difference whether the faculty staff reviewing the application were male or female, which suggests that women have also internalized the notion that men are more competent.[24]

Beliefs about gender competency are formed before people enter the workplace. Studies of university students have found that they consider the course materials chosen by male lecturers to be superior to those chosen by female lecturers. Students perceived female academics as taking longer to give feedback, even when male and female staff take the same length of time.[25] Gender bias can be subtle and research has found that men are perceived as better workers. They are more likely to be given 'brilliant' and 'exceptional' performance ratings and rated more highly even when their qualifications and behaviour are identical to those of female colleagues.[26] Managers hold women to higher standards of competence and interpersonal warmth;[27] they discount women's skill and give them less credit for performance;[28] and assessors scrutinize women's work more heavily for errors. People rate male staff as more likeable, capable and worthy than female staff.[29]

Competency bias is important because it also explains some of the prejudices behind the pay gap: how can men and women achieve equal pay status when they both internalize sexist assumptions about ability and, by extension, whether someone 'deserves' to be paid a certain amount?

There are ways, however, of tackling this prejudice in the office. When President Obama was elected, two-thirds of his staff were male and, worried that their voices would go unheard, the women on his team adopted a tactic called 'amplification'. Every time a female employee made a good suggestion, all the other women reiterated it and gave credit to its author.[30] This was a way of combating something which many women have experienced at work: being interrupted, ignored or instantly contradicted.

Negotiation is also something that often comes up in reference to the pay gap. It's an excellent life skill that can be used in any number of personal and professional contexts. But attributing the pay gap to the power of male bargaining is a form of essentialism – it's saying that there is something intrinsically better about men that means they warrant higher pay.

Where are men supposed to have learned these superior negotiation skills? Did all the women miss class on the days negotiating was taught? The idea that all men have skilfully negotiated their salaries throughout their careers, using guile and diplomacy to achieve higher pay without compromising their reputation in the workplace, is absurd. Many companies do not have the funds available to award pay rises whenever a woman asks. Surely there are times when both women and men can be knocked back for business reasons.

To every person who maintains that women just need to be better negotiators to achieve financial equality, I would say: stop making women jump through hoops. Men don't have to. They just get paid more. Stop telling women to be more like men. Being male isn't the only 'right' way to be in the workplace.

The belief that women can rectify any inequality in their salary by having the nous to ask for a raise ignores the power imbalances within political and social structures, discrimination and the historical basis for economic inequality. When a woman finds out she is being paid unfairly, this is not an aberration, a blip in an otherwise perfectly functioning job market. It's part of a wider social phenomenon where women work below their level of competence and are underrewarded for their labour. This cannot be fixed solely through individual action, however canny a person may be in demanding higher pay.

## Confidence

Western culture is obsessed with female self-doubt. Confidence, or the lack of it, is frequently cited as the reason why more women aren't in high-flying jobs. Public declarations of self-abasement have become almost a rite of passage for exceptional women. Nobel laureate and civil rights activist Maya Angelou nodded to her imposter syndrome (where a person feels inadequate, believes they do not belong in their job and fears being exposed as a fraud) when she said: 'I have written eleven books, but each time I think, "Uh-oh, they're going to find me out now."' Former First Lady Michelle Obama has also spoken of feelings of imposter syndrome that 'never go away'.[31]

Psychologists Pauline Clance and Suzanne Imes coined the term imposter syndrome in 1978 and initially it was thought to affect predominantly women: 'Despite outstanding academic and professional accomplishments, women who experience the imposter phenomenon persist in believing that they are really not bright and have fooled anyone who thinks otherwise.'[32]

The idea that imposter syndrome is a peculiarly female phenomenon persists.[33] An article from *Forbes*, the business magazine, states that 'more women than ever are susceptible' to imposter syndrome.[34] 'Female teachers are plagued by imposter syndrome,' screams a headline in the *Times Educational Supplement*, a classic example of an article blaming women's self-doubt for their lack of progression.[35]

Most of the discussion about women and imposter syndrome has been in the context of female self-improvement and positive thinking. Confidence is treated like a kind of magic dust; just by sprinkling a bit on herself every day, a girl will go far. But we ought to be careful not to pathologize feelings of insecurity or inadequacy at work; it can be a natural response to pressure, scrutiny and exposure.

One study looked into whether imposter syndrome was

causing women to drop out of scientific careers. In astronomy, for example, young women comprise the majority of America's society for budding and professional members, so they are more engaged in the subject as youngsters.[36] But after studying astrophysics and astronomy, women go on to leave the discipline in higher numbers at every stage of academic transition, and at university level, female astrophysicists make up only 19 per cent of university faculty members.[37] Researchers found that while feeling like an imposter did make women think about leaving their field, there were bigger issues at play to do with the nature of academia that contributed to the attrition rate.[38] Women were more likely to have moved region because of their spouse and report problems with the so-called 'two-body problem', where the need to move frequently between regions and countries (which is part and parcel of a successful academic research career) makes it difficult for a couple to find suitable jobs at the same university or within reasonable commuting distance of each other.

An often-quoted statistic that is supposed to illustrate how women are hamstrung by a lack of self-belief is: 'Men apply for jobs when they have 60 per cent of the qualifications, while women only apply for jobs when they meet 100 per cent of the requirements.' This came from an internal study done by Hewlett-Packard, the computer company, and it was widely shared, including in Sandberg's book *Lean In*. It's something of a zombie statistic – Hewlett-Packard has not published the study. Can we really accept that women don't apply for roles when they fulfil 90 per cent of the criteria?

Nevertheless, it is worth investigating whether women do hold themselves back at application stage, contributing to a pay gap when it comes to more senior roles. Tara Sophia Mohr, writing for the *Harvard Business Review*, conducted a survey where she asked a thousand men and women why, if they didn't meet all the requirements for a job, did they not apply for it anyway? The results were interesting: most of the respondents said they didn't think they would get the job because they didn't meet the requirements so wouldn't waste their time applying. This was irrespective of gender. The least common reason was lack of confidence or whether they thought they couldn't do the job.[39] Recruiters ought to provide more clarity about roles advertised – if there's a list of desirable qualities in a candidate, are they must-haves or will they be willing to consider people who match some of the criteria, or people from different backgrounds altogether? It's also possible that if men have seen their male peers jump up a few rungs into roles they don't seem qualified for, then that emboldens them to apply for jobs on a speculative basis. Men are often promoted on their potential, while women are promoted based on what they have already achieved.

## Fixing the pay gap

Having to talk about the gender pay gap (again) is disheartening. It's the problem that won't go away. But I believe it's the easiest aspect of female economic inequality to fix, if only employers and policymakers have the will to do so. Historically, the impetus has been very much lacking. The concept of equal pay for equal work was first mooted in the 1830s in Britain, but it wasn't taken up by any political party until the 1960s. Unions had been championing workers' rights for decades but were often reluctant to support women in their pursuit of equal wages for fear that this might negatively affect men's pay. The Equal Pay Act became law in 1970 but didn't come into effect until 1976.[40] The justification was that employers needed time to adjust, but making women wait six years longer for fairness they had spent decades fighting for was justifiable only because their needs weren't that much of a priority. In the years since, employers have consistently preferred to fight claims of unequal pay rather than admit wrongdoing.

After fifty years of equal pay legislation, what have we learned? That existing legislation isn't sufficient. That allowing employers to interpret the rules and provide no sanction for transgressions allows pay inequality to persist. That expecting each woman to end the pay gap on her own is ridiculous. So what can be done about this? None of the solutions below are difficult. We know that the current set-up of work and remuneration leaves too much space for discrimination and inequality to emerge, and a do-nothing approach from employers and the government is not an answer – unless we are all happy to wait 257 years for women to be economically equal.[41]

## Solution 1: Just pay staff fairly

Employers must accept that pay discrimination on the basis of gender can exist within any organization, take steps to identify it and immediately rectify the problem with pay increases. Remuneration committees need to be gender equal – research has shown that gender diversity on the committee can make a difference but there needs to be a critical mass of 30 per cent of women for this to happen.[42]

San Francisco-based software company Salesforce spent $3 million on rectifying its pay gap in 2015 after finding that 6 per cent of employees (mostly women, but some men, too) were on lower salaries and the only explanation was their gender. Even after doing this, new gaps emerged each year as the company expanded, and it spent another $3 million on the problem in 2017. After three years of pay audits, Salesforce has spent close to $9 million to address race, gender and ethnicity-based pay gaps. Former CEO Marc Benioff said that prior to seeing the analysis of pay at Salesforce, he had been 'utterly convinced' the business he ran was gender equal: 'I simply did not believe that pay disparities could be pervasive.'[43]

When someone finds out they have been receiving unfair pay, this isn't a financial loss that's confined to a single year; it could have been going on for years or decades. This will have affected whether that person was able to buy a home, how they were able to bring up their children, and so forth. Companies ought to rectify historical pay discrimination by raising pension contributions, which will help to mitigate the risk of old-age poverty.

## Solution 2: Non-disclosure of previous pay

Prospective employees are often asked to share their previous salary when applying for a job. This immediately provides a benchmark for employers to base their salary offer on, regardless of whether the candidate's previous pay was commensurate with their experience and contribution. This means a person who has been underpaid because of their gender, race or class risks having that discrimination carried forward into their pay at their new employer.

In the US, a number of states have banned employers from asking this question, and this should be standard in other countries, too.[44] Remuneration levels should be based on what a newly hired person will be doing and what they bring to the company, not what a former boss decided to pay them.

## Solution 3: End pay secrecy

In some US states, including California, Colorado and Washington, it is mandatory for employers to share the minimum salary or pay bracket for a role when asked.[45] Similar rules in Britain would provide some much-needed transparency in the jobs market. Currently women and men have no way of knowing if colleagues are earning more without going to an employment tribunal to clarify the facts. Men can be underpaid too, and they also lose out by not knowing how much others are being paid.

There are ripples of change in the water. A group of 100 senior women from business, law, politics and the arts is calling for a new Equal Pay Act that will give staff the right to find out from their employers what their colleagues are earning.

The only people who stand to lose from greater transparency are unscrupulous employers, and implementing this act would reverse the situation where women are stigmatized for trying to get the truth out of their employers.

## Solution 4: Sanctions for pay discrimination

There is no point in creating legislation that tells companies to check whether they are doing the right thing but not including a sanction for when they don't. Companies in Ontario, Canada, are given financial penalties for failing to comply with gender pay rules, while Swedish law requires companies to take action over discrepancies. In 2018, Iceland became the first country in the world to make employers prove that they were not paying women less than men for the same job. Companies and organizations with at least twenty-five full-time employees must obtain government certification proving that their pay policies are based on factors such as education, skills and performance, not gender. Employers who do not comply face hefty fines that roll over each day. We need sanctions and enforcement of employment law – from equal pay to discriminatory dress codes.

## Solution 5: Make HR teams more responsible

HR departments have a lot to answer for. In some companies, there's a hotchpotch of job titles and a lack of pay grades and salary bands to put a ceiling and floor on similar roles. When a role is unique within the organization, the HR team needs to assess carefully the knowledge and responsibility required, plus the value it gives to the business, before a salary is finalized. HR departments ought to monitor promotions to check for bias and ensure pay rises aren't just in line with what the company can afford but with what people in similar roles are being paid.

A female employee at the London office of bank BNP Paribas came to work one morning to find a witch's hat on her desk, which her 'visibly drunk' male colleagues had put there the night before as a 'joke'. You can laugh that off as childish behaviour, but the hostility towards her was reflected in her salary. It was later established that she had begun on a salary 25 per cent lower than that of her male equivalent and been given a bonus half the size of his, even though they received equal grades for performance. After three years at the company, she was earning 85 per cent less than this male colleague.[46]

There is no compulsion for British employers to have an annual appraisal meeting with their staff, but it should be standard practice. This gives staff a formal opportunity to discuss the specific tasks and responsibilities of their role and is an opportune time for employees to raise the question of salary, should they want to.

## Solution 6: Active inclusion of women

It is not in the interests of any employer for staff to be working below their level of competency or to feel frustrated in their efforts to progress. Initiatives to address the gender imbalance need to come from the top of each organization. However, implementing change is often the responsibility of middle management and there needs to be proper, regular supervision of team leaders to ensure they are supporting their staff.

Women in senior management may be excellent role models, but the assumption may be that they have beaten a path that other women can tread. Mentoring can benefit both mentor and mentee, giving both the chance to experience perspectives on the same career. Mentors who care about the gender pay gap are in a great position to inspire change. They have the benefit of hindsight, can be open about their salary progression and how hard or easy it's been and offer advice on getting promoted. However, mentoring has limitations. It is often an add-on activity that takes place away from day-to-day work and it's usually a relationship between two people.

Salesforce's Benioff said that one of the statistics that made him realize the company had a gender problem was learning that women made up 14 per cent of those in leadership positions. He implemented a policy where at least 30 per cent of the participants at any meeting had to be women, so they would actively be given opportunities to contribute within group settings.[47]

Having women's voices heard at work and implementing the solutions outlined above would go a long way towards closing the gender pay gap.

# 13. Beauty Standards and Social Expectations

In Argentina, girls grow up believing astrophysics is a career for women. The country has had a long tradition of gender diversity within astronomy; in 1988, 25 per cent of Argentina's professional astronomers were female. For comparison, in Japan at the time the figure for women was just 2 per cent.[1] Today, the Japanese figure is 8 per cent,[2] whereas in Argentina, it's 40 per cent, an unusually high number that contrasts with single digits or low teens in most other countries.[3]

In Iceland, a generation of girls has grown up believing that presidents and prime ministers are female. Vigdís Finnbogadóttir became the world's first democratically elected female president in 1980 and she remains the longest-standing female head of state, having been re-elected three times for a total of sixteen years in office. She was followed by Jóhanna Sigurðardóttir, prime minister between 2009 and 2013, and the world's first lesbian prime minister.

President Finnbogadóttir's election immediately led to a huge jump in the number of women in Iceland's parliament: in 1983 the number of female MPs went from fifteen to sixty. This set off a domino effect that led to Iceland becoming ranked as the most gender-progressive country in the world for eleven years running. By comparison, the UK ranked 21st in 2020 (down from 18th in 2015) and the US placed 53rd.[4]

In Iceland there's a pretty much unshakeable belief that

having women in power is good for women and families and there is research to suggest that this may be true. A study from the US found that politicians' preferences in social policy are influenced by their gender, with elected women being more involved in welfare issues, for example.[5] A separate study found that female politicians are far more active. They introduce more bills and pass more of them by working together with greater frequency than male politicians; they also work with politicians on the opposing side more often.[6] Iceland has become Niceland because its citizens understand that when legislature includes women equally, it benefits everyone.

Following the global financial crash in 2007–8 Iceland was one of the worst-affected countries, left bankrupt with debts amounting to 850 per cent of GDP. In the few short years leading up to the crash, Iceland had become an international hub for finance and banking, an astounding feat for a nation with a population the size of Newcastle. The masterminds behind it were mostly men; while women worked in Icelandic financial institutions, they were rarely in risk-taking leadership positions, as was the case in the UK and US. Investigative journalist and author Michael Lewis said of the crash: 'One of the distinctive traits about Iceland's disaster, and Wall Street's, is how little women had to do with it . . . As far as I can tell, during Iceland's boom, there was just one woman in a senior position inside an Icelandic bank. Her name is Kristin Petursdottir, and by 2005 she had risen to become deputy CEO for Kaupthing [a bank] in London.'[7]

The gender of most of the protagonists did not go unnoticed by Icelanders. There was a widespread view that the crash was due to hyper-masculine behaviour. 'It was man-made. It's always the same guys,' said Halla Tómasdót-tir, a businesswoman who described the antics of the financiers in the run-up to the crash as being akin to a 'penis competition'.

The subtext of this Icelandic perspective is that women can do finance as well as – and maybe even more sensibly than – men. During the crisis, women were appointed leaders at two of the country's failed banks and given key positions at the financial regulatory body.

Compare this attitude with other parts of the world. President Jair Bolsonaro of Brazil once publicly stated that female congresswoman and federal deputy Maria do Rosário was 'not worth raping, she is very ugly'.[8] In the US, Donald Trump won the presidential election despite being recorded boasting about sexual assault and accused of rape and sexual misconduct by more than twenty-five women.[9] During the 2016 election campaign Trump's Democratic competitor, Hillary Clinton, received four times as much negative press for alleged scandals than Trump's treatment of women did.[10]

We don't have to look abroad for examples of national leaders who publicly denigrate women for being women. In articles Britain's prime minister Boris Johnson wrote for *The Spectator* magazine during the ten years that he was its editor, he advised that the best way to respond to advice from a female colleague was to 'just pat her on the bottom and send her on her way'.[11] In a separate article he criticized the British man for 'his reluctance or inability to take control of his woman'.[12] These men were still endorsed and elected as representatives by millions of members of the general public.

Their shameless misogyny normalizes such attitudes and behaviours. One study found that white women born in areas of America with more prevalent sexist attitudes will grow up to earn less and work fewer hours than women born elsewhere.[13] The negative effect on a woman's salary continues even if she moves to a less sexist area as an adult, which suggests that the levels of sexism a woman is exposed to during childhood shape her behaviour and lifelong earnings. This stuff sticks.

A separate US study confirmed that exposure to attitudes of 'hostile sexism' encourages both men and women to accept financial inequality between the genders, to 'victim-blame' and to believe that gendered income inequality is the result of women's choices or their fault.[14] The effects were stronger on people who held conservative political views.

Research has shown that up until the age of five, girls and boys don't perceive gender as an impediment. But six-year-old girls start to develop self-limiting beliefs. They start to avoid activities that are suitable for 'really, really smart' people and begin to categorize more of their male peers as highly intelligent.[15] Some researchers believe that at this age, girls are internalizing cultural stereotypes that 'promote the idea that being intellectually gifted is a male quality'[16] and that gendered perceptions of intelligence have an immediate effect on girls' interests.

The takeaway for caregivers and educators is that girls need to be encouraged to have a 'growth mindset', which means believing that practice and effort matter more than natural ability. We can foster a growth mindset by emphasizing that the whizz-kids in maths, gymnastics, football can be overtaken if they don't put the effort in.

Maybe they're getting it from their parents. Data scientist Seth Stephens-Davidowitz crunched Google search information and found that American mothers and fathers search 'Is my son gifted?' two and a half times more than they ask the internet 'Is my daughter gifted?' Any other search term related to intelligence was more likely to be asked of sons rather than daughters.[17]

Meanwhile, parents google 'Is my daughter overweight?' some 70 per cent more often than they ask the same of their sons, and were more likely to google whether their daughters were 'ugly' or 'beautiful'. Stephens-Davidowitz pointed out that these weight concerns aren't even grounded in reality, as girls are 11 per cent more likely than boys to be in programmes for gifted children and fewer girls are overweight. In this context it's no wonder that 87 per cent of girls aged eleven to twenty-one think that the world will judge them more on their appearance than their ability.[18]

Sexism is the expression of the belief that women or men are inferior because of their sex and it can be unconscious – a person doesn't have to know they are sexist to be sexist. No doubt all of the Google-searching parents cited in the research above want their children to thrive regardless of their gender. But it does highlight that before we blame 'the culture', we need to remember that we're all participants in it. How would society differ if mothers and fathers asked Google about their daughters' aptitude and intelligence?

## Investment in beauty

Western culture provides a contradictory narrative of what it is to be a woman. Women are visible in leadership positions like never before: New Zealand's prime minister Jacinda Ardern was re-elected with a landslide victory, Germany's chancellor Angela Merkel has led the country for fifteen years, and Britain's highest-ranking police officer is Dame

Cressida Dick, while countless initiatives encourage girls to step into formerly all-male spaces, from engineering to plumbing, coding to weightlifting.

But amid these freedoms, the expectation that girls and women place their appearance front and centre has not waned. If anything, beauty pressure has intensified, thanks to the impact of social media and online porn, both of which have encouraged a culture of greater physical scrutiny. Although there's greater diversity in the fashion industry, with better representation of different ethnicities and body types, female beauty is still considered a marker of value.

The female ideal has become hyper-feminine (think of Kim Kardashian's impossible proportions) while the male ideal has become hyper-masculine. Through porn, music videos and computer games boys are increasingly exposed to a model of masculinity that emphasizes muscles, tattoos, sexual prowess and aggression. An excellent book which delves more deeply into hyper-femininity is *Cinderella Ate My Daughter* by Peggy Orenstein, in which she argues that girls are being primed from younger ages to prioritize their appearances and become consumers in pursuit of the 'right' image.[19]

While it's a normal part of adolescent development to become concerned with one's appearance, beauty culture has normalized such a high standard of gender-specific grooming for girls that increasingly their time is eaten into by what they consider to be non-negotiable beauty regimes. In the recent past hair extensions, false nails and semi-permanent eyelashes were treats to look good on nights out or holidays, but growing numbers of girls need them daily to feel they look 'normal'. A major study of more than 1,200 British girls found that half of primary school pupils aged seven to eleven wear make-up to lessons.[20] Nearly half of eleven- to sixteen-year-olds wax or shave their bikini lines, while fake tan is a must for over a third of girls. Up to half of girls wear padded bras to school and a third alter their uniform to appear sexier.

Self-consciousness means young women are devoting hours of their evenings after school maintaining the 'right' appearance. Some will grow up to become one of the 50 per cent of Britain's adult women who say they feel under pressure to look good at all times. Others will get into debt to pay for cosmetic surgery and nearly a third will spend an entire week of each year getting ready to leave the house.[21]

When they are in the classroom, self-consciousness is a barrier to participating and achievement. A large-scale review of studies covering 49,000 girls and women from five continents found that at least 20 per cent of teenage girls won't engage in classroom debate because they don't want to draw attention to their appearance.[22] Regardless of how much they weigh, girls in China, Finland and the USA who think they are overweight achieve lower grades academically. Is this because a significant minority (15 per cent) of teenage girls stay home from school on days when they feel bad about their looks?

The typical spend for high-school girls and university-aged women is around £45 a month on clothes, make-up, nails and hair – that's £540 a year – which is a considerable drain on their parents or their student loans. A solid 20 per cent say they spend more than £50 a month, while for 6 per cent of them, beautification costs over £100 monthly.

It may be unsurprising to learn that girls cost an average of £30,000 more than boys to raise from birth to the age of eighteen. The overall cost of bringing up a girl is £108,888 compared to £79,176 for a boy, with girls' clothes, toiletries and cosmetics making up a big chunk of the difference.[23]

## *Aspirations*

The ultimate outcome of beauty pressure is a narrowing of girls' aspirations and social participation. The study of 49,000 females mentioned above found that a significant minority of adult women do not turn up to work or job interviews due to body image concerns. In a separate study, two-thirds of young women said they wouldn't want to appear on TV because of the criticism they'll face about their looks.[24] This is worrying: becoming a leader or excelling in one's field means being visible.

At the other end of the spectrum, some young women increasingly aspire to careers that have arisen through the ideals presented by social media – as influencers or Instagram models, work that is based on presenting an idealized image of a woman's face, body, home, relationships and lifestyle. Researchers asked 10,000 fifteen- to nineteen-year-old girls in Britain to indicate what their ideal profession would be from a list of varied careers and many chose options that emphasized their bodies: glamour modelling was the ideal profession for 63 per cent of the girls, while a quarter cited lap dancer as their top choice.[25] This data suggests that beauty pressure is influencing women's career choices to a greater extent than you might think.

## The penalty for non-conformance

High heels, lipstick, mascara, blusher, foundation and eye shadow worn at all times and regularly applied – these are some of the discriminatory dress codes that women must abide by in twenty-first-century Britain.

These grooming requirements from British employment agency Portico were brought into the spotlight in 2016 after Nicola Thorp arrived for a nine-hour shift as a receptionist wearing flat shoes.[26] Although the role involved walking with guests to meeting rooms and back again, Thorp was told that she needed to be wearing shoes with a heel of between two and four inches, and was sent home without being paid for the day.

Thorp started an online petition demanding that the law change so that companies can no longer require women to wear high heels, which soon gained 152,000 signatures. A subsequent parliamentary inquiry found that discriminatory codes remain widespread. It received complaints from women who felt sexualized by uniform requirements; others said they were forced to wear heels while carrying heavy luggage, taking food up and down stairs or walking long distances.[27] The inquiry concluded that 'physical instability caused by wearing high heels reduces the wearer's presence and authority when communicating'. So much for power dressing.

The parliamentary report stated that the dress code Thorp had been asked to comply with broke existing law, as the 2010 Equality Act already prohibits dress codes from being more onerous for one gender than another.[28] Yet despite the overwhelming evidence that discriminatory practices are widespread, the government shied away from toughening the law and reiterated that individuals could take their employers to a tribunal if they felt they were being discriminated against. As we have seen, the government has removed legal aid for employment tribunals, which means that many women can't afford to take their employers to court. So the law isn't enforced.

## Body size and salary

Large data sets from Canada, Europe and the US show that if you were to plot women's weight against their average wages on a graph, you would see that thinner women tend to earn more. The graph would show how women's wages tend to fall steeply as their weight increases from thin to average, and then fall further as their weight moves into the overweight and obese categories.[29]

Meanwhile, women perceived as having larger bodies are less likely to be selected for an interview, their performance is rated more harshly and they are considered to have lower productivity and ambition. They are deemed less suited for challenging or customer-facing work and they are more likely to be placed in lower-paid or menial roles, to be evaluated more negatively by supervisors and colleagues and to be punished more harshly for misconduct.[30]

Research in the US has found that men display greater levels of disgust towards and dislike of obese people than women do. In contrast to women, average male wages increase with a man's weight. The exception is underweight men, who receive a wage penalty. Overweight men enjoy the highest pay premium across Europe and the US. This levels off until obesity, when men do experience a wage penalty, although some researchers have suggested that this isn't the case for obese men in the US, possibly because higher rates of obesity across the country normalize larger bodies.[31]

The US state of Michigan is one of the few places that prohibits discrimination on the basis of weight and height. There is little public appetite for this kind of legislation in Europe, yet women continue to be impeded in their working lives by scrutiny of their weight and appearance.


## Gender-neutral childhood

The concept of raising children in a 'gender-neutral' way has gained traction over the last decade. Some parents have tried to limit the impact that society's more restrictive gender norms can have on their children by carefully choosing their activities, toys, clothes and bedroom decor. The aim is for children to develop their own authentic interests and preferences without the influence of culture's ideas about what they 'should' do or like because of their gender.

Outside of the home, Icelanders have found a way to limit the effects of traditional gender norms at schools. Around 8 per cent of nursery children are enrolled in a Hjalli school, which encourages boys and girls to actively behave in ways that aren't expected of their gender.[32] Uniforms and toys are gender-exclusive and boys are encouraged to put on nail varnish, give each other hand massages and play with dolls. Girls aren't given dolls; instead they're led through activities that will help them develop confidence and a daredevil nature – running barefoot into the snow without screaming, or climbing trees.

The Hjalli school model was founded in 1989 by feminist Margrét Pála Ólafsdóttir, who argues that girls and boys have natural strengths which become exaggerated through cultural conditioning. When girls slip into the 'pink haze' their strengths tip over into weaknesses; their sensitivity and caring becomes self-pity and victimhood. Boys embroiled in the 'blue haze' find their strength and power becomes aggression, and so Hjalli schools keep boys and girls separate for most of the day.

In the UK, there are some excellent playthings available that are aimed at broadening girls' horizons. The website AMightyGirl.com has a huge selection of products that feature women in 'different' roles (not princesses and cooks), construction and science toys, and knick-knacks like the 'Women Who Dare' card game and a colouring book of famous women's artwork.

I like 'The Little Feminist' jigsaw puzzle from the brand Mudpuppy, which has the faces of nine fantastic women including aviator Amelia Earhart, astronaut Sally Ride, tennis player Billie Jean King, education campaigner Malala Yousafzai and writer Maya Angelou.

A series of children's books called *How the World Really Works* by Guy Fox is another good resource. Each explains how a different part of business and finance works: asset management, investment banking, savings, the law. They're intended for children but many adults could probably do with a refresher too. If you think your child might be interested but know she or he isn't going to read it, it's worth reading it yourself so you can talk to them about different possible careers.

Why does a gendered upbringing affect whether women are poorer than men? If girls are socialized to believe that their aptitude is related to their gender, or if their interests are shaped by ideas about what they 'should' or 'should not' pursue, then they are already on the back foot at school, in further education and in the workplace. The data's clear: girls who are bound by gender norms are more likely to limit their aspirations, to succumb to beauty pressure and, ultimately, to earn less. Let's lift up future generations of women and encourage them to achieve everything that they deserve.

# 14. Money as Self-Care

Resilience is the ability to weather anything life throws at you, and it's become one of the biggest buzzwords in wellness. It's a learned trait, one that's increasingly advocated by psychologists, who see it as essential for creating a life of contentment and success. There is also the concept of financial resilience, which is taking the steps to ensure that you will have the money to pick yourself up if you get knocked down. Building financial resilience is a kind of self-care. Putting money aside today shows that you care about your future self as much as you do about your current self. Once you've strengthened your finances to be resilient over the coming year, you can focus on future-proofing them for the next five years and into the decades ahead. The goal is to have the money to do the things you dream of and to support loved ones. One day, your seventy-five-year-old self will be grateful you were thinking of them today.

Looking after yourself financially is the best kind of self-care. Here are the basics.

## *The foundation*

Every person needs to have enough cash saved to cover between three and six months of expenditure, which includes rent or mortgage payments, essential bills, food, getting around and some reasonable leisure costs. If you work in a profession where it's easy to find a new job, savings towards the lower end of that scale will do. If you have children or moving between jobs is hard in your industry, aim for at least six months' worth of outgoings.

In practical terms, this is the cushion against potential bad times (however unlikely they may seem), including job loss, a break-up, a death in the family or serious illness. I prefer to think of it in psychological terms: as building a more solid foundation from which you can grow. Simply having savings builds confidence. Often, it's money, or the lack of it, that stands in the way of people achieving their dreams, so having some put aside allows you to dream, as well as giving you headspace from worrying.

This money should be saved in cash in an interest-paying 'easy access' account. This means you can take the money out on demand; without easy access there is a notice period where you request your money and have to wait for it. There are also 'fixed term' accounts, where you must wait until the end of a set period (from three months to five years) to take out your money. These accounts pay more interest but are no good if you need the money in a hurry. Fixed-term savings accounts are more suited to people who already have quite a bit of money saved and know they will have no need of £3,000 or £5,000, say, in the coming years.

What constitutes decent interest rates? Unfortunately, in the past decade, interest rates on bank accounts have been very low and the top-paying accounts pay interest of around 1 per cent. In Britain, there's a trend for banks to offer current accounts that pay much higher interest on balances up into the thousands. Banks typically need the account holder to pay in a certain amount of money each month (often around £1,000, the average monthly wage), and they need direct debits to be coming out of the account, too. So the catch with a high-interest current account is that you may have to use it as your main account for receiving your salary while also keeping your savings in it. People who find it impossible to save should avoid this kind of set-up; instead choose a separate savings account and transfer money into it every month.

## Zilch to 10k

The foundation fund of three to six months' expenses is meant to be kept aside for the unexpected. Saving is also about having money to enjoy life, so once you hit the target for a foundation fund, move on to a bigger goal. I call it Zilch to 10k, but you can break it down into Zilch to 1k, 2k or go higher. The next steps are how you can get there.

### Set aside time for life admin

There are 168 hours in a week. If you sleep for seven hours a night, you have 119 hours left. Subtract another 9.5 hours a day for working and commuting for five days, and you have 71.5 hours remaining. Essentials such as cooking and housework, ferrying children around, appointments and spending time with people may take up another 20 hours per week. This leaves 51.5 hours. Everyone has the same amount of time in a week: it's the one true equality in life.

Doing money stuff takes a couple of hours a month if you are really committed to it, or maybe one hour on a Sunday evening each month if you are taking it easy. You don't even have to do anything – just spending time thinking about your money can help. What did you spend this month? Did you have enough to last until payday? Is there anything you need to buy soon that you should plan for? Did you pay the water bill? Do you regret any purchases? Do you have any contracts that are due for renewal soon? This kind of thinking gets you organized and puts you in the right frame of mind.

If you have more time, sit down after work and spend thirty minutes looking at your online banking and various accounts, or look up a price comparison site to see if you could get your house insurance or broadband for less. You don't have to commit to anything.

## Work out your net worth

An enduring feature of modern life is that most people are in debt while at the same time saving. Traditional wisdom says you should always pay off debts before saving, but this kind of thinking has become skewed, partly because the cost of living is so high now that many people have a credit card or overdraft they dip into each month to manage their outgoings. On top of this, it's normal to have car loans, massive mortgages and student loans that are being paid for into our thirties.

Thinking of your net worth is a good mindset to get into. This is the sum of all your assets (what you own) minus your liabilities (debts). It gives a much fuller picture. Calculating it can make you feel richer (when you factor in the money you have stashed in a pension), but poorer, too (your savings will be diminished when you subtract any debts).

To work it out, add up the money in your savings accounts, workplace pension fund, the rough market value of your home and vehicle, plus any valuables you could sell. Then subtract any outstanding credit cards, loans, the balance on your student loan and the remainder of your mortgage. Check in yearly and see where the trend is going – is your net worth increasing, stagnant or declining?

## Divvy up your income

How much of your salary could you realistically live on? A popular way of setting a budget is called the 50/30/20 rule. Try to keep your essential living costs, including housing, bills and food, to 50 per cent of your income. Then see if you could keep non-essential spending to 20 or 30 per cent of your income. What amount you can achieve will depend on where you are in life, but either way you will then have either 30 or 20 per cent left over for financial goals. These will be savings and paying off debts, whichever you prioritize. Savings should go straight into a separate account soon after payday. Don't wait a couple of weeks to see how much you think you can save.

It's important to be realistic about these parameters because often people set a budget that's too low or put too much into their savings account and then end up using their overdraft or a credit card, which usually means paying interest charges.

## Take proper action

Once you have got into the habit of thinking about where your money goes, where you are financially and where you want to be, force yourself to take one piece of proper action this month, or next month.

Scroll through your online banking and, if there are debits and subscriptions for things you do not really want, cancel them. Pay particular attention to utility bills. If any of them seem larger than expected, go through your email or log into the account to find out when you signed up and when the deal you agreed to came to an end. Use a utility switching website to see if there is a cheaper rate – new customers tend to be offered better deals than existing customers, so there is often little reward for loyalty. Switching suppliers for electricity, gas and internet providers doesn't usually involve anything more than filling in an online form and maybe giving a meter reading. The suppliers will sort it out among themselves.

If you have credit cards, look at the interest payments you make in the average month and multiply that by twelve. That is how much you are spending on top of the debt itself. There is no reason to pay interest on a credit card, unless you have a poor credit rating. Just as the interest rates on savings accounts are very low at the moment, credit card interest rates are at record-low levels. Card companies have interest-free periods for balance transfers that can last up to two years, plus interest-free periods on purchases. Balance transfers are where the money you owe to one card company is transferred over to another for a small fee. Move your credit card balances on to an interest-free credit card so that any repayments you make go straight towards paying off the money you borrowed, rather than on interest.

## Prioritize yourself

Women always put their monetary needs at the bottom of the pile. Couples tend to pay for childcare out of the woman's salary and save for their children's future before their own – it's incredible how often people admit that they have money in a savings account in their kid's name but barely anything put away for themselves. Women often stop paying into a pension when they are on maternity leave or working part-time. It's understandable that the short-term needs of keeping the family afloat are the priority, but even the odd £20 put into a pension can add up. Whoever is the higher earner in a couple has to take more responsibility for this and help their partner with the epic task of saving for retirement.

## Know the passwords to your joint accounts

Both people in a couple must know how they could access shared savings if they need to. This is more about emergencies than splitting up, and if you need to have this conversation with your other half, frame it like this. When a loved one dies unexpectedly, it can be such a battle to get into online accounts, and this could be made much easier if couples kept each other informed about where money is held and what the account details are. Keep a document in a safe at home, on a hard drive in a secure location or in an encrypted electronic file.

## Reflect on social pressures

In 1968, *The New York Times* ran an article discussing the strange new pastime of jogging. At a time when smoking and drinking excessively were normal and only athletes went running, anyone exercising in public was treated with suspicion. One US senator was stopped by police while out running, while a magazine article about the dangers of the sport quoted a doctor who described it as 'physiologically insane'. Men tended to run at night to avoid attracting attention and, slowly, the pastime grew in popularity as people realized how good it made them feel.

It's easy to feel like a sixties jogger when it comes to money. We are confronted by conflicting forces. On one side, there's the high cost of living, which drains our income, and the pressure to 'have things' – stylish clothes for work, an attractive home – which has never really gone away. What is newer to our generation is the displays of experiences that people share on Instagram and social media – the holidays, food and days out. On the other side, there's the knowledge that we live in societies where we need to become financially secure in order to thrive and to give our loved ones opportunities. Reflect on the pressures you feel (if any) on your spending. Is all your spending for your own enjoyment and quality of life or is some of it influenced by the desire to display, to show you have done things, that you can afford things?

Anyone curious about spending less should look up the ideas shared on the thriving online communities for frugal people, who have motivations as varied as wanting to buy a first home or to feed their families for less, and include people exasperated by having mountains of stuff or by our wasteful consumption culture, and those who just want to have more money. They set no-spend challenges, work towards zero waste, try to eat like a gourmet with free or cut-price food, throw deceptively cheap parties or weddings and share tips on day-to-day money saving. Try reddit.com/r/UKPersonalFinance, moneysavingexpert.com or Money Shed.

# 15. Let's Talk about Investing

The gender investment gap is a key reason why women struggle to boost their wealth. The pay premium that a lot of men receive is multiplied when they invest their savings and make a return far and above the interest rates that can be found on cash savings accounts. Starting to invest is a big hurdle to overcome, even for women who have considerable amounts of money saved. The barriers are practical: people don't know how to physically transfer their cash savings into shares; they are emotional, as women are often frightened they will lose money; and there's a mental barrier, too, as the odd terminology, the baffling jargon, masculinity and elitism of the investment world is off-putting. Culturally, finance has become a macho sport, and it carries connotations of greed, gambling and one-upmanship. But like the weights section at the gym, there's no reason why investing should be intrinsically male.

I've spent over a decade writing about stock markets and I believe that the principles of investing are easy to understand, even though most people have had no exposure to this world.

At its simplest, investing is about spotting something that might be more valuable in future – whether it's a property, a fine wine or future trend that you could invest in by buying shares in a particular company. This could include businesses that have an innovative product (Amazon twenty-five years ago), are creating a new market (Fevertree's premium mixers for spirits) or do something fairly ordinary but do it better than competitors (Hotel Chocolat's boxes of chocolates). Investing can be exciting – the kinds of areas that are being tipped for their long-term investment potential today include driverless cars, clean energy, biotechnology and China. Investing can be socially positive – companies need investors to raise money, so directing your savings into those which create better outcomes for people and the planet is one way to put your ethics into action.

One caveat: I'm not a financial adviser and the information in this book is not financial advice. This is guidance and information about how various aspects of money work. Most people just want to be told what to do with their savings/mortgage/inheritance/debt, but the only people who are legally able to do that are called independent financial advisers, who take a proper look at your situation and help you decide the best course of action. It does cost money but a) you will get it back in the long run and b) in the old days when financial advice was free, it wasn't always objective as the adviser was being compensated by product providers.

You can make decisions about money feel a lot less stressful by learning the basics, which are simpler than you have been led to believe. And note that the companies discussed in this chapter have been chosen because they have interesting stories – I'm not saying they're a good investment!

## What is investing?

Investing is about putting your money into something that will grow in value, so you can sell it later at a higher price than you paid for it. Many people do this inadvertently when they buy a home; they have the expectation that it will appreciate in value. Often, when people talk about 'markets', 'investment markets' or the 'stock market', they are referring to the electronic world where people swap shares in companies. (There are also 'markets' in oil, gas and gold, called 'commodities', markets in loans called 'bonds' or 'bond markets' and other things that investors like to buy and sell, such as cryptocurrency.)

Shares are tiny stakes in a business; a company as large as Facebook, for example, could be offering up to 3 billion shares for investors to buy.[1] The idea is that you buy shares in companies that you believe will go up in value in the coming years. As the company's sales and profits improve, the little stakes in those companies become more valuable as more people want to buy them. The basic point of the stock market is that you buy shares when they are low and sell them when they are high to make a profit.

In Facebook's case, each share costs $267 (£200).[2] If you have £1,000 and you think that Facebook is a company that is going to become more profitable, expand and improve its business over the coming decade, you would be able to buy six of its shares and pay the small charge for every time you buy and sell shares, usually up to £10 for each purchase. For comparison, shares in the parent company of Google, called Alphabet, cost $1,823 (£1,360) each, so you would need a lot more money to think about buying shares directly in the company. There are ways around this for people with smaller amounts – skip to the part below about funds for more information.

Buying and selling stocks is known as trading, and you can do it through dedicated websites (more on this below). Every kind of industry that you can think of is represented on the stock market, from Manchester United Football Club, whose shares are listed on the New York Stock Exchange priced at $19 (£15.08) each, to Greggs the baker, famed for its cheesy bean pasties (shares cost £1,795 each on the London Stock Exchange), and YouGov, the polling company (£800 a share).

A good example of how investing in stocks can be profitable is the internet giant Amazon. Its shares started trading on the US stock market in 1997. Each share cost $18. Today, they are worth $1,901. This was a fantastic investment for the people who had the foresight to buy some of them back when Amazon was a young online retailer.

Looking at Amazon's share price today and twenty years ago does, however, mask the ups and downs in their value. In 2011, the shares fell by 26 per cent, so people who owned Amazon shares would have lost just over a quarter of their money. Over time, the shares started to rise again, until 2015, when they fell by 20 per cent. At that stage, they cost $534 each. People who bought some of the shares at that stage and kept hold of them until today would have made a considerable amount of money. That said, past good performance doesn't mean it will continue that way.

Shareholders are not only in it for the money. Owning a share in a business entitles you to vote on some of the key decisions that its management make and attend their annual general meeting. At the meeting shareholders grill the company's board of directors with questions about chief executive salaries, company performance, products and policies on everything from environmental degradation to human rights. 'Shareholder activism' is the term for when the people who own the shares reject the company's proposals. There has been growing unrest among shareholders in the past decade. For example, in 2019 the owner of well-known hotel chain Premier Inn, called Whitbread, sold its high-street coffee shops Costa Coffee to The Coca-Cola Company for £3.9 billion. Whitbread sold Costa after pressure from shareholders, who thought it should focus more on the hotel industry.

This kind of activism is driven by big shareholders, typically professional investors who have bought up a significant proportion of a company's shares with a view to changing how the business is run.

Businesses that are not on the stock markets are called private companies and you cannot buy shares in them. Once a business has grown to a certain size, the management team will consider whether to 'go public' by listing shares on the stock exchange. The process is called a 'flotation' or an IPO (an initial public offering) and by selling shares management will raise huge amounts of money which can be invested into the business and give the owners a nice payday. Snapchat, the picture-sharing app, IPO'd in 2017 and raised $3.4 billion, leaving the company's founder Evan Spiegel fabulously wealthy at the age of twenty-six.[3]

The drawback is that public companies have to release detailed information about how the business is faring so that shareholders know where they stand. Management have to put up with intense scrutiny and heavy criticism when the investors aren't happy. Many thriving businesses have kept themselves private, including Wilko, the discount retailer, and Dyson, which makes household appliances.

A quick note on jargon: Britons and Australians tend to say 'shares' and 'share prices' while Americans tend to say 'stocks'. They mean exactly the same thing. Some people make it complicated by referring to 'investing in stocks and shares'. I use 'shares' because I am British.

## What makes investing interesting?

Investing is a forward-looking activity that's about predicting the future of companies and industries while also having a good knowledge of their past in order to understand what has gone right or wrong previously.

As I write this, investors are eagerly looking at Beyond Meat, a manufacturer of plant-based burgers and sausages. The popularity of veganism and clean eating doesn't seem likely to fade away any time soon. It could be the case that those with the prescience to buy shares in Beyond Meat when it floats on the stock market are vindicated in thirty years' time, when killing animals and eating meat may be considered totally bizarre. Or it may turn out that Beyond Meat is overtaken by a better company, one that makes animal proteins in a Petri dish, for example. Either way, investing in shares can be a fun way of trying to predict the future. The bonus is that when you get it right, you make money, too.

Company shares rise and fall with news about how the business is doing. ITV, the broadcaster, found that its shares started soaring in 2011 after the success of *Downton Abbey*, an award-winning period drama. ITV was on a roll, and the popularity of another series, *I'm a Celebrity . . . Get Me Out of Here*, also boosted its share price. However, its shares tumbled when one of the presenters of *I'm a Celebrity . . .* , Ant McPartlin, was involved in a car crash and later admitted he was having problems with addiction. McPartlin was seen as a vital part of the show and investors worried that ITV would struggle for viewing figures without him.

I've discussed company share prices as they are a simple way of getting your head around stock markets. Looking at a company's share price over the last six months, three years and five years will give you a snapshot of what everyone else is thinking about its worthiness as an investment. Ask yourself whether the share price has fallen sharply, or risen consistently, and by how much. When the shares fell, was this due to something company-related or was the wider stock market having a bad patch?

But looking at a share price won't tell you the full story about whether it's a good investment. For example, the company with the highest share price in the world is called Berkshire Hathaway, a global giant based in Nebraska, USA, which has an array of underlying investments including Duracell batteries, American Express credit cards, Apple computers and The Coca-Cola Company. It was founded by Warren Buffett, a man who's frequently referred to as 'the world's most successful investor'. With that nickname, you might be tempted to buy shares in Berkshire Hathaway to get the benefit of his genius. But buying a single share in Berkshire costs $300,000. Many people would have to sell their own house and their mother's before they had enough money to buy one tiny share in this massive company.

So does that mean it's a more attractive and successful investment than Alphabet (Google) or Apple, whose share prices are a fraction of that? No, not at all.

Buffett has structured the stocks available to be bought so that it keeps the price of each one high, as he doesn't want people buying shares in his company and selling them a few months later to make a quick buck. The stock market has a bad reputation because there's a relatively small but powerful group of professional investors who spend all day playing the markets like they're in a casino – and increasingly computer algorithms are set up to do this too. There has been a backlash against this kind of behaviour from others in the industry who believe that investing in companies for years, decades or a lifetime is the best way to grow their wealth slowly.

Buffett only wants the kind of serious (and super-rich) investors who would be happy to part with $300,000 and leave it there for the long term. But, as with shares in Alphabet, people without six-figure sums can invest in the company through 'funds', discussed below.

This is another reason why you shouldn't fixate on share prices: they can be manipulated by company management, who don't like to see the brand's share price falling too low. A CEO's reputation and remuneration packages are often tied to how well the share price does, so there are technical things (such as 'share buybacks') that they can do to bump the price up.

Now we know what investing is, let's look at the most common myths that hold people back from doing it.

## Myth 1: Investing is gambling

This is a big misconception. There is a clear difference between investing and gambling, and it's this. Placing a bet tends to have a binary outcome: you win or you lose. You could put money on a horse and, when it loses, your money's gone. If it wins, you win big.

Investing doesn't tend to have binary outcomes. For example, if you buy £1,000 of shares in Amazon or the global drugs company GlaxoSmithKline, the likelihood that either of those companies goes bust in the next five years and you lose all of your money is small. It's possible, of course, but it is one outcome of many potential outcomes over the coming years; a company's shares could fall in value over the following two years then rise substantially over the next five, followed by a fall again. You could sell your shares at any point; you may make money, or you could lose some. This is very different from buying a lottery ticket, placing a bet or backing a horse in a race.

## Myth 2: You have to be wealthy to invest

This one holds most people back from making more out of their savings. In the old days, it was mostly wealthy people who had a stockbroker or investment manager who looked after a portfolio of shares for the family. The internet has changed this, and online investment managers allow people who have £50 a month to spare to begin buying shares in the world's biggest companies via their websites. Small amounts can turn into something massive. For example, £100 a month invested in the FTSE 100, a list of the UK's biggest companies, would hopefully grow by 5 per cent a year. After thirty years, you would have around £88,000, rising to £152,000 after forty years. Those are life-changing sums of money and they came from £100 a month.

## Myth 3: It's only adventurous/pompous/ greedy people that invest

A lot of people think they are just not the type to invest in the stock market. Most don't realize that if you have a workplace pension, then you already have investments. The company that keeps your retirement savings is investing them every month in a diverse portfolio of shares, bonds (loans to governments or companies) and maybe property or infrastructure projects. Your money will be invested around the world.

## Myth 4: Stock markets are always crashing and I'll lose everything

In 2020 stock markets around the world plunged when the Covid-19 pandemic brought the global economy to a standstill. The impossibility of predicting how long shops would be closed and aeroplanes grounded, and what impact the virus would have on companies' sales and profits, meant that hordes of people sold their investments and got their money back. Having cash in a bank account felt safer, even at very low interest rates, than keeping wealth tied up in shares which could fluctuate in value.

Crashes such as the Covid-19 pandemic and the previous stock market blow-up, the 2007–8 global financial crash, are rare. Trouble on the stock market begins when there's a whiff of uncertainty in the air. Ambiguity about the outlook for a company/economy/industry makes people frantically start selling their shares. Sometimes it's an exaggerated reaction to a reasonable concern, and shares drop much lower than they ought to. People sell shares immediately because they can get their money back at today's price – they worry that if they wait until later they will have to sell at a lower price.

No one talks about what usually happens immediately after stock markets tumble: they often go back up again. When share prices fall they are cheaper to buy so professionals buy more. For example, if you could buy Netflix shares at under $300 after they slumped during the Covid-19 lockdown, when the month before they were $380, why would you stop yourself? As the pandemic worsened, the uncertain outlook led many investors to sell their shares in all kinds of companies. But Netflix shares bounced back, and by the end of the year they were worth around $500 each.

History tells us that soon after crashes, the share prices of many companies rise again. Over the past thirty years the overall direction of most stock markets has been upwards. Do a Google search for 'FTSE 100 index chart thirty years' and you will be able to see how the jagged line has moved steadily up with a few big dips along the way. Anyone who invests will have to get used to logging on to their account and seeing that some of their investments are up, and some have fallen.

These episodes seem worse than they are because the mainstream media covers them extensively. It's really only in the specialist press that's read by serious investors that you will find the good news, the stories about which markets are doing well and the shares that the professionals are optimistic about. The positive side of investing is hidden from the general public as it's only people who specifically look for information on what shares to invest in that find these stories. See below for more information on where you can look for more objective coverage of investments than you will find on the front page of a newspaper.

Aside from these global crises, from time to time serious problems within a company emerge and investors sell off their shares. This can happen completely out of the blue. In 2014 Tesco's shares dropped to the lowest level for more than eleven years after the company revealed it had over-stated its profits by £250 million. Supermarkets are a cut-throat business as the Big Four (Tesco, Asda, Sains-bury's and Morrisons) control most of the food market in Britain. Forensic accountants and lawyers were brought in, there was a fraud investigation and it emerged that some of the company's head office staff had indulged in a bit of cre-ative accounting when compiling the figures to make it look as though Tesco was doing better than it was.

This kind of thing is where investing gets challenging for people who have full-time jobs and lives away from the finance industry. When something like this happens, you may have to seriously consider selling your shares. This is another benefit of 'funds' (which I have mentioned a few times), as they have a professional who buys and sells shares on your behalf. More on this below.

## *Why investing is important*

In this book, I've explained why investing is necessary for women. Some people treat it as a hobby, a nice-to-try, but in reality, making your savings grow through investment is vital for increasing your wealth. The reason for this is that keeping savings stashed in cash is a ruinous strategy for the long term. This is partly because banks are paying such low interest rates (often around 1 per cent per annum). But, more importantly, investing is important because it can combat inflation. Remember how you could buy a chocolate bar for 30 pence when you were a child and now they cost 75 pence? That's the effect of inflation, where the value of money is gradually eroded over time. So if you have £5,000 in a cash bank account earning barely any interest, in thirty years' time that sum of money will feel a lot more like £2,000. You will look back at your £5,000 savings and wonder why you ever thought that was a lot of money.

## Should I start investing?

Despite everything I've just said, there are circumstances when investing your money is not in your best interests. Ask yourself the following questions:

- Do you have an emergency fund?

If you don't have three to six months of expenditure in cash as a safety net, forget about investing. There is no point putting money into stock markets, where it will be subject to ups and downs, if you may need that money for an emergency.

- Do you have debt?

If you have debt, aside from a mortgage, there's no point in investing. This is because any money you make will be outweighed by the amount of interest you are paying on your debt. Focus on dividing your spare cash between a savings account (for your emergency fund) and making overpayments to your credit card or loan. When you have accrued an emergency fund, consider increasing the debt overpayments so you can pay it off more quickly.

- Do you need the money in the next five years?

Only invest if you don't need the money for at least five years – ideally, ten.

One of my best friends invested £5,000 of her £15,000 savings, money which was intended for a deposit on her first home. She invested in Asia and emerging markets (up-and-coming developing economies such as India and Indonesia). The markets fell and she lost £4,000. I remember her dismay when she told me over drinks one night. Her investments did later recover and she made some money on them, but the pain of losing a lot of her savings at a crucial time would have been worth avoiding.

- Do you own a property?

When you invest in the stock market you are taking some risk. If you own a home, a relatively risk-free way of using your money is to make overpayments on your mortgage. This way, you will pay for your home, an asset that could potentially rise in value, more quickly. The downside to this is that you're putting all your eggs in one basket: a property. But if you live there and want to own a home outright one day, it's sensible.

- How do I actually start investing?

This is the barrier that stops most people from investing. You know how the stock market works, you know why you should do it, but you don't know how.

The main question people always have is: 'So how do I actually start investing? Do I go to my bank?'

Let me answer that here. There are investment websites, known as 'platforms' or 'investment supermarkets', which allow people like you and me to invest their money in stock markets. In the UK, among the most popular are Hargreaves Lansdown, AJ Bell and Interactive Investor. In the US, it's Charles Schwab, Fidelity International and TD Direct.

Each platform will allow you to open an account online, although it may ask you to verify your identity by sending in paper documents. Your account will look similar to an online savings account, and you will transfer money into it from your main bank. Then you search for different investments and see their current values. It's good to play with the site for a while before you commit any money. Look up ASOS at 11 a.m. and see its share price, then log in again at 2.30 p.m. and see whether it has gone up or down. Some of these investing websites also allow you to set up a virtual portfolio, similar to fantasy football. If you have the time, it's a good way to see how you feel when the investments you have chosen rise or fall. It's human nature to be excited when you gain money and to feel terrible when you lose money.

## Girls just want to have funds

So far I have discussed company shares because these are the nuts and bolts of investing. Actually, most people don't spend their time choosing specific companies to buy and sell through their pension or ISA. There are three reasons. First, unless you're a professional investor, it's difficult to know whether a particular company is worth investing in today or whether you should wait until after its next financial results statement is released. Are the shares overvalued? Have they risen massively and are they now due to fall? Is the company's chief executive planning to retire? Is the company in a lot of debt? Is it planning to expand internationally? Was the company's last product a hit and now analysts think that success cannot be replicated with the follow-up product? These are all things that can affect a company's share price and, unless you have the time to do extensive research, you will find it difficult to have the answers to these questions. Second, the big problem with shares is that if you hear about a company doing well, it's likely that all the professionals have already bought shares in it. At that stage, you would be investing in shares that have already risen, so the potential for them to rise further would be muted.

Third, women working in senior positions at multinational companies or certain industries such as finance or media may find that their employer's policies do not allow them to invest in individual shares. This is because some positions give people specialist knowledge of company shares that gives them an unfair advantage. Women in this situation can invest through funds instead.

For all of these reasons, many people invest in funds, which are baskets of company shares compiled by a professional investor, called a 'fund manager'. (In case you were wondering, 86 per cent of fund managers in the UK are male. The percentage of women doing this prestigious job has remained unchanged for twenty years.)

The fund manager picks anywhere between thirty and 100 (sometimes more) companies that they think have the best prospects. Financial advisers and other investors see the fund advertised and if they like the look of it, they put some money into it. The fund manager amasses a large sum of money from lots of people and uses it to buy up shares in each of those companies. They usually buy more of one company's shares and fewer of another's, and their job is to sell shares when something goes wrong and buy more of the better performers.

Over time the value of all those shares should rise and when you sell those shares they will be worth more than you invested. When one company's shares fall the loss is usually offset by gains in other shares in the fund.

Market crashes reveal the value in having a professional to choose investments for you. During the good times, selecting successful companies to buy shares in can seem obvious, especially when you are looking at well-known British companies. But during a crisis a professional will not just be trying to protect the value of your investments but also use the turbulence as an opportunity to make more money.

Funds all have a particular theme: US funds invest only in US companies; Asia-Pacific funds invest solely in that area; and smaller European funds are the same. There are specialist funds investing in trends such as luxury goods, the rise of artificial intelligence or healthcare companies, and the funds that invest globally, or in a particular region such as emerging markets (otherwise known as developing economies – think Vietnam, Poland, Mexico and the United Arab Emirates).

Funds have slightly odd, long-winded names. For example, at the time of writing one of the most popular funds among UK investors was the Baillie Gifford American.[4] 'Baillie Gifford' is the name of the management company and it invests in American companies, although it's not clear from the name whether it focuses on the biggest companies, smaller ones or a mix. Other funds may specify their focus in the name. You will have to look at the fund's information page, called a 'fact sheet'. Search online for the name of a fund and the words 'fact sheet' to find more details.

Others in the top ten list include:

**Lindsell Train Global Equity:** Lindsell Train is the name of the management company, which invests in companies from around the globe. 'Equity' is another word for 'share'.

**Baillie Gifford Positive Change:** As above, Baillie Gifford is the management company and this fund's focus is on companies which make a 'positive change'. Its fact sheet says it invests in twenty-five to fifty companies from around the world which make an impact in four areas: social inclusion and education; environment and resource needs; healthcare and quality of life; and addressing the needs of the world's poorest populations. Funds are a simple solution for people who want to invest ethically, as the manager screens companies for their environmental and social impact. This is a fast-growing area as people increasingly realize the value of channelling their savings into businesses which could make the world a better place, or at least try to mitigate their footprint on earth. Names of other most popular ethical funds in the UK include the Kames Ethical fund, which focuses on UK companies; the First State Asia Focus fund, which invests throughout Asia; and the Royal London Sustainable World fund, which has a global remit.

**Polar Capital Global Technology:** Polar Capital is the management company and this fund invests in 'global technology', which the fund fact sheet says includes the likes of Microsoft, Alphabet, Alibaba (China's version of eBay) and

Tencent (a Chinese giant which owns all kinds of online ventures including a version of WhatsApp, called WeChat, and an equivalent of Netflix). Technology funds have been hugely popular over the past decade owing to the growing power of the tech giants.

All of these funds, and others, can be found by searching an investment supermarket such as Hargreaves Lansdown or AJ Bell. The big drawback of investing through funds is the costs. Fund managers need to get paid and a percentage of the money each person invests will be sliced off as fees – which really does add up to a significant amount over years of investing. These fees are in addition to the ones charged by the investing supermarket/platform for using their services.

## Investing globally

I've been using examples of companies from around the world because some of the most innovative and promising businesses are found on the other side of the globe. Typically, people have more investments in their own countries – something called 'home bias' – which leaves Britons with mostly UK-based investments, Americans with a majority of their shares in US-based companies and so forth. This can be quite limiting. Investing globally is vital in today's world.

However, it's a little harder to buy shares in companies listed on foreign stock exchanges. The simplest way to buy international shares is through a fund and it manages any tax implications associated with foreign companies.

It's harder to buy shares directly in international companies. Not all investing platforms offer non-UK shares, partly because it means dealing with foreign currencies and sometimes because there is paperwork to fill in. The two most popular investing websites in Britain for international shares are Interactive Investor and Saxo Capital Markets. Also bear in mind that British people who want to own shares in US companies need to complete a form called W-8BEN, which American tax authorities use to make sure people aren't hiding wealth abroad.

## *Doing your research*

If you want to choose specific company shares to invest in, it's good to get a feel for what professional investors are choosing and the prospects for different industries in the current climate. The websites listed below have plenty of articles on how to get started with stock markets, and they also have good information on being savvy with money in other areas – cheaper broadband, travel deals, asking for a pay rise and so forth.

Fool.co.uk – The Motley Fool is a fab resource for both beginners and more experienced investors. Its simple, no-fuss approach means that articles go straight to the point of what readers want to know. As I write this, headlines on the site include: 'These are the best two stocks in the UK' and 'Should I buy oil shares like BP now?'

Citywire.co.uk – Its Funds Insider section has articles on what the experts think about popular stocks and there are forums where you can post questions. Citywire's other sections are good for more knowledgeable investors who want to know what the professionals are doing.

Telegraph.co.uk/money – The money section of *The*

*Telegraph* newspaper is another good source when it comes to finding out how to invest and what to invest in.

In addition, investment banks and other finance companies make regular predictions about the prospects for specific companies, rating shares as 'buy' or 'sell', giving them a 'target price' which they think the share price will reach, and generally sharing their views on what they consider to be the best investments. They are called 'analysts' notes' or 'broker forecasts'. As I write this, Goldman Sachs, the investment bank, has announced that it thinks shares in a company called Peloton Interactive should rise to $84 from $66 currently. Peloton sells stationary bikes and online workout programmes for exercising at home.

These predictions are often reported in the press and investing platforms keep records of them for their users to look at. The names of companies which make these predictions include JP Morgan, Credit Suisse, Jefferies Group LLC and RBC Capital Markets. Shares Magazine (sharesmagazine.co.uk/broker-views) has a subscriber service where you can see these and the website's editors also tell you how well analysts have done with previous predictions, too.

## How do I choose investments?

Investing websites such as Fidelity and Hargreaves Lansdown have sample portfolios for newbie investors.

A 'portfolio' is a collection of investments – if your neighbour owns and rents out eight houses, she is a 'portfolio landlord'. The list of investments in your pension is a 'pension portfolio'. Investing websites put together portfolios of funds chosen by experts, and all you do is transfer your money into one. A portfolio of funds might have five to ten different funds that the expert in charge thinks will:

a) be sensible investments
b) include a range of investments that complement one another
c) be an easy option for people who don't want to trawl the internet researching different funds and deciding which ones go well together.

Portfolios and funds each have a risk rating. There's no reward without risk, but higher risk means a great chance of losing. Cash is considered 'risk-free' but remember, there's risk in doing nothing, because leaving your money in cash for decades means inflation will erode its value.

They can be 'cautious', which are the lowest risk and are expected to make only modest returns of perhaps 2–3 per cent of the amount you have invested; 'balanced' or 'medium risk', which are intended to take more risk and could potentially make more money, perhaps 3–6 per cent a year; or 'adventurous' or 'high risk', which are going to be invested in the most ambitious way. The potential here for making money is highest (perhaps 6–10 per cent a year), but the amount by which your portfolio could fall in value is also much larger. Think back to the example I gave of my friend investing her house deposit in a high-risk portfolio – she lost a chunk of the money for a period of time.

Here I'm talking about the risk of losing some money, which is a possibility with any investment. But in monetary terms there are other kinds of risk too: 'shortfall risk' is the possibility that you won't meet your savings goals to achieve the things you want or need, such as a deposit for a home for yourself or your children, travelling to a place you've always wanted to see, or having enough money saved for a comfortable retirement. There's also 'longevity risk', the possibility that you live for longer than your pension savings last.

There are people who wouldn't go near stock markets and put all their money into property in the belief that it's safer. But what happens when they need the money soon? Say you lose your job and urgently need to get hold of some cash to pay your children's school fees. You don't want to pull them out of school but don't know when you will find another job. You put your investment property on the market, but what if it doesn't attract any buyers for a year? When someone has stored their wealth in an asset like property but they cannot get at the money it's called 'liquidity risk'. This is why it can be sensible to spread your money around investments with different liquidity levels. Montenegro may be the next best place to buy a holiday home, but think about doing that with money you can afford to live without – if you want to sell the property, it's probably not going to happen in a month.

And finally, the next steps would be to read about the following: 'passive' investing; different kinds of investments such as commercial property, commodities and bonds; how company shares are valued by analysts as either 'cheap' or 'expensive'; and the different ways to make money from investing, such as 'income investing' where you focus on companies that pay the highest dividends.

# Afterword

In the summer of 2020 a statue of Mary Wollstonecraft, Britain's 'mother of feminism', was unveiled in the leafy London suburb where she lived, worked and founded a girls' boarding school at the age of twenty-five. Wollstonecraft published one of the earliest works of feminist literature, *A Vindication of the Rights of Woman* (1792), but died aged just thirty-eight shortly after bearing her second child, Mary Shelley, who became the author of *Frankenstein*.

Feminist campaigners felt that Wollstonecraft was not as celebrated as other influential women of her era. Keen to elevate Wollstonecraft to the status she deserves, they fought a ten-year-long battle to raise the £147,000 needed for a commemorative statue in a city where 90 per cent of statues are of men.

But the sculpture caused immediate outcry. The ensuing furore became a microcosm of contemporary debate about female success and status. It depicts a tiny, naked figure, her physique as honed as a twenty-first-century supermodel's body. The silver figurine stands atop a giant tree-trunk shaped plinth, a woman dwarfed by the enormity of the support underneath her. Campaigners clothed the statue in a T-shirt.

Did its nudity diminish Wollstonecraft's achievements or did its unashamed nakedness and bold stance reflect her spirit of defiance? Why was the figurine so small – successful women couldn't take up too much space back then, and perhaps they still can't now? If Wollstonecraft's likeness had been sculpted into a towering figure, would it have been considered masculine? Or ugly? Perhaps female artists always attract more criticism for their works than male artists, and this was what was happening to the creator of this monument, Maggi Hambling. Defending herself, Hambling said the statue was not *of* Wollstonecraft but *for* Wollstonecraft, with the figure symbolic of 'everywoman' – which again was a confusing idea. All these questions highlight the difficulties faced when deciding how best to elevate and celebrate women.

It has been nearly 230 years since *A Vindication* was published and the world is dramatically different for women. But some things remain the same. Women are poorer than men. We own less of the wealth and assets in both rich and poor societies all over the world; we are not equally represented in the jobs where the most money is made, or in the industries where public funds are spent and private wealth is invested. Most troubling is that we are still debating how we should elevate women.

This book has exposed some of the myriad reasons why equality in money and wealth continues to elude us. Female economic inequality is like a bowl of spaghetti: dozens of strands entangled, and it's hard to see where each begins and ends. But pull on a single strand and others begin to unravel.

Parts of this book made for uncomfortable reading, but it is not a misery memoir. This discussion marks the beginning of the next phase of gender equality, in which women earn, save, start businesses, invest and become wealthy at the same rates that men do.

This ideal is within our reach. Landmark legal changes that support women financially have been made around the world, providing a model for other nations to follow.

Scotland became the first country in the world to make sanitary pads and tampons available free of charge for anyone who needs them, and in a way that ensures recipients have 'reasonable dignity'. Period products are likely to be distributed in the same way that free condoms have been for years.

In New Zealand, prime minister Jacinda Ardern has implemented a policy of 'pay equity', where salaries must be determined by the skills involved in the role regardless of which gender predominates in the job. A government-led review concluded that the majority-female workforce of social workers has comparable skills to majority-male police detectives, air traffic controllers and engineers for Auckland City Council, and therefore should be remunerated accordingly. Similarities include the high sensory demands for focus and alertness, managing stress levels, and calculating potential risks of harm. No two roles were identical: for example, interpersonal skills were less necessary for air traffic controllers.

Ardern's policy was the kind that every society needs if it's going to tackle gender equality – we don't need hollow gestures but legal and practical changes that demand a fundamental, objective rethink of old perceptions.

Elsewhere, a growing list of state and local authorities have been implementing the one remedy that could have the most profound effect on women's finances.

Universal basic income allows every person to receive a set amount of money from the state regardless of their earnings, assets, life situation or behaviour. Crucially, the amount is enough for each person to have the dignity of a basic standing of living, with a little left over which could be used to improve their own or someone else's prospects. No one would be financially sanctioned for failing to meet terms or conditions.

It's a centuries-old concept that has garnered greater support in recent years for its potential to address the seemingly intractable problems of vast wealth inequality, generational poverty and, importantly, women being poorer than men. Benefits for women are manifold: mothers in receipt of basic income might worry less about maternity pay, while families with two parents in receipt of basic income might opt for the father to be a stay-at-home dad. Perhaps gender will become less of a barrier to entrepreneurship if a woman opts to use her basic income to get a business off the ground.

Advocates include Mark Zuckerberg, the billionaire founder of Facebook, and influential economist Milton Friedman. The concept picked up more support during the Covid-19 pandemic, which opened our eyes to the social and economic benefits of universal basic income. Places that have dabbled in basic income policies include Finland, Germany, Iran, Kenya, and the US states Alaska and North Carolina.

For Britons, universal basic income couldn't be more different to the welfare system that's currently in place, particularly when it comes to the government's Universal Credit policy. It cannot be said enough: it's mostly women who suffer from the design of state benefits, with the tight conditionality, the harsh sanctions and the below-subsistence level payments. Universal basic income is badly needed for a more equal Britain.

There has never been a better time to be a woman; among our generation are some of the freest, best-educated and highest-paid women to have walked the earth. The speed of these changes have been exceptional. From achieving universal suffrage across the Western world, to overtaking men educationally on every continent and right up to PhD level, to reaching a point where nearly a third of the top 10 per cent of earners are women, we should never stop reminding ourselves what an incredible century it has been for women. Here's to the next phase of the battle for gender equality – to societies where women aren't poorer than men.

# Notes

*Introduction: Finance Is a Feminist Issue*

1  'Gender Diversity is an Imperative for the Financial Services Industry', Mercer website, www.mercer.com/our-thinking/gender-diversity-financial-services-industry-report.html (accessed 10 February 2020).

2  World Economic Forum, 'The Global Gender Gap Report 2018', available at www3.weforum.org/docs/WEF_GGGR_2018.pdf (accessed 10 February 2020).

3  According to Senator Elizabeth Warren: Elizabeth Warren, 'Valuing the Work of Women of Color', *Medium*, 5 July 2019, https://medium.com/@teamwarren/valuing-the-work-of-women-of-color-c652bf6ccc9a.

4  Anthony Breach and Yaojun Li, 'Gender Pay Gap by Ethnicity in Britain Report, March 2017', Fawcett Society website, www.fawcettsociety.org.uk/Handlers/Download.ashx?IDMF=f31d6adc-9e0e-4bfe-a3df-3e85605ee4a9 (accessed 10 February 2020).

5  MP Sarah Champion quoted in Heather Stewart, 'Women bearing 86% of austerity burden, Commons figures reveal', *The Guardian*, 9 March 2017, www.theguardian.com/world/2017/mar/09/women-bearing-86-of-austerity-burden-labour-research-reveals. Fullfact is a fact-checking charity and this analysis explains the methodology behind the statistic that 86

per cent of the reduction in government spending has been in spending on women.

6  'New study suggests women do ask for pay rises but don't get them', Warwick University website, https://warwick. ac.uk/fac/soc/economics/news/2016/9/new_study_suggests_ women_do_ask_for_pay_rises_but_dont_get_them (accessed 10 February 2020).

7  Janine Brodie, 'Reforming Social Justice in Neoliberal Times', *Studies in Social Justice* 1:2, 2007, available at http://citeseerx.ist. psu.edu/viewdoc/download?doi=10.1.1.916.2411&rep=rep1& type=pdf (accessed 10 February 2020).

8  'Health at a Glance: Europe 2018', OECD and European Union report, available at https://ec.europa.eu/health/sites/ health/files/state/docs/2018_healthatglance_rep_en.pdf (accessed 10 February 2020).

9  'Gender at Work: Emerging Messages', World Bank Group report, available at www.worldbank.org/content/dam/World-bank/document/Gender/Gender%20at%20Work,%20Emerg ing%20Messages,%20Official.pdf (accessed 10 February 2020).

10 According to the government-commissioned independent report 'Race in the Workplace', the McGregor-Smith Review, 2017, available at https://assets.publishing.service.gov.uk/gov ernment/uploads/system/uploads/attachment_data/file/594 336/race-in-workplace-mcgregor-smith-review.pdf (accessed 28 November 2020).

11 Alex Christen, 'How Does Gender Pay Gap Reporting Affect Transgender Employees?', Personnel Today website, 13 July 2018, www.personneltoday.com/hr/how-does-gender-pay-gap-reporting-affect-transgender-or-non-binary-employees and 'Does Gender Pay Gap Take Transgender and Non-Binary Employees into Account?', Lawson-West Solicitors website, 17 September 2018, www.lawson-west.co.uk/for-

people/services/other-employment-matters/articles/gender-pay-gap-reporting-issues.

12 Michael Savage, 'Half of frontline care workers paid less than living wage', *The Observer*, 19 April 2020, www.theguardian.com/society/2020/apr/19/half-of-frontline-care-workers-paid-less-than-living-wage.

13 'Coronavirus: Public spending on crisis soars to £190bn', *BBC News*, 9 July 2020, www.bbc.co.uk/news/business-53342271.

14 According to the International Monetary Fund, 20 May 2020. See here: https://blogs.imf.org/2020/05/20/tracking-the-9-trillion-global-fiscal-support-to-fight-covid-19.


*Chapter 1: Where We Are Today*

1 HM Revenue and Customs, 'Identified Personal Wealth: Assets by Age and Gender', National Statistics report, 2016, available at www.gov.uk/government/statistics/table-132-identified-personal-wealth-assets-by-age-and-gender (accessed 10 February 2020).

2 Figures from 2007: Mariko Lin Chang, 'Women and Wealth in the United States', Sociologists for Women in Society website, available at https://socwomen.org/wp-content/uploads/2018/03/fact_2-2010-wealth.pdf (accessed 10 February 2020).

3 Ministry of Justice, 'Statistics on Women and the Criminal Justice System 2017', National Statistics report, 2017, available at https://assets.publishing.service.gov.uk/government/uploads/system/uploads/attachment_data/file/759770/women-criminal-justice-system-2017.pdf (accessed 10 February 2020).

4 'Gender Disparity Report: TV Licensing', TV Licensing and BBC report, December 2017, available at www.tvlicensing.co.uk/about/gender-disparity-AB23 (accessed 10 February 2020).

5  Office of the High Commissioner for Human Rights, 'Report on Austerity Measures and Economic and Social Rights', United Nations High Commissioner for Human Rights report, 2013, available at www.ohchr.org/Documents/Issues/Development/RightsCrisis/E-2013-82_en.pdf (accessed 10 February 2020).

6  International Institute for Labour Studies, 'World of Work Report 2012: Better Jobs for a Better Economy', International Labour Organization report, 2012, available at www.ilo.org/global/research/global-reports/world-of-work/WCMS_179453/lang--en/index.htm (accessed 10 February 2020).

7  'Gender at Work: Emerging Messages', World Bank Group report, available at www.worldbank.org/content/dam/Worldbank/document/Gender/Gender%20at%20Work,%20 Emerging%20Messages,%20Official.pdf (accessed 10 February 2020).

8  Mizuho Aoki, 'Poverty a Growing Problem for Women', *Japan Times*, 19 April 2012, www.japantimes.co.jp/news/2012/04/19/national/poverty-a-growing-problem-for-women.

9  Kayla Fontenot, Jessica Semega and Melissa Kollar, 'Income and Poverty in the United States: 2017', United States Census Bureau report, 12 September 2018, www.census.gov/library/publications/2018/demo/p60-263.html.

10  Social Metrics Commission, Measuring Poverty 2019 report, July 2019, https://socialmetricscommission.org.uk/wp-content/uploads/2019/07/SMC_measuring-poverty-201908_full-report.pdf (accessed 28 November 2020).

11  Gertrude Schafner Goldberg, *Poor Women in Rich Countries: The Feminization of Poverty over the Life Course* (Oxford: Oxford University Press, 2009), p. 3.

12  Around 23 per cent of single men are in poverty, down from 26 per cent in 2016/17: 'DWP Data Reveals Women and

Children Continue to be Worst Affected by Poverty', Women's Budget Group website blog, 29 March 2019, https://wbg.org.uk/blog/dwp-data-reveals-women-continue-to-be-worst-affected-by-poverty (accessed 10 February 2020).

13 According to the Women's Equality Party: www.womens equality.org.uk/equal_health (accessed 1 October 2020).

14 Mary Daly and Catherine Rake, *Gender and the Welfare State* (Cambridge: Polity Press, 2004), p. 122.

15 A. B. Atkinson, 'Basic income: ethics, statistics and economics', unpublished paper from Nuffield College, University of Oxford, 2011, available at www.nuff.ox.ac.uk/users/atkin son/Basic_Income%20Luxembourg%20April%202011.pdf (accessed 1 October 2020).

16 Alyssa Schneebaum and M. V. Lee Badgett, 'Poverty in US Lesbian and Gay Couple Households', *Feminist Economics* 25:1, 2019, pp. 1–30.

17 M. V. Lee Badgett et al., 'New Patterns of Poverty in the Lesbian, Gay, and Bisexual Community', The Williams Institute website, June 2013, https://williamsinstitute.law.ucla.edu/research/census-lgbt-demographics-studies/lgbt-poverty-update-june-2013 (accessed 10 February 2020).

18 Alyssa Schneebaum and M. V. Lee Badgett, 'Poverty in US Lesbian and Gay Couple Households', pp. 1–30.

19 Data from the Government Equalities Office, 'Ethnic Minority Women's Poverty and Economic Well-Being', September 2010, available at https://assets.publishing.service.gov.uk/government/uploads/system/uploads/attachment_data/file/85528/ethnic-minority-women_s-poverty.pdf (accessed 2 November 2020).

20 Jane Millar, 'Gender, Poverty and Social Exclusion', *Social Policy and Society*, 2:3, 2003, pp. 181–8.

21 World Economic Forum, 'Global Gender Gap Report 2020', p. 11, available at www3.weforum.org/docs/WEF_GGGR_2020.pdf (accessed 1 October 2020).

22 'More Steves than women are FTSE 100 CEOs', ICAEW website, https://economia.icaew.com/news/august-2019/more-steves-than-women-are-ftse-100-ceos (accessed 10 February 2020).

23 Laurence Mishel and Jessica Schieder, 'CEO pay remains high relative to the pay of typical workers and high-wage earners', Economic Policy Institute report, available at www.epi.org/files/pdf/130354.pdf (accessed 10 February 2020).

24 Ibid.

25 Julia Kollewe, 'GSK's Emma Walmsley becomes highest-paid female FTSE 100 chief', *The Guardian*, 12 March 2019, www.theguardian.com/business/2019/mar/12/glaxosmithkline-gsk-emma-walmsley-highest-paid-female-ftse-100-chief-executive; 'Former Persimmon boss was paid £85m in two years', *Financial Times*, 18 March 2019, www.ft.com/content/4c23d282-498e-11e9-8b7f-d49067e0f50d.

26 Cahal Milmo, 'Britain's 600 aristocratic families have doubled their wealth in the last decade and are as "wealthy as at the height of Empire"', *iNews*, 19 July 2019, https://inews.co.uk/news/long-reads/aristocrat-uk-britain-families-double-wealth-empire-exclusive-study-498179; Rupert Neate, 'Richest 1% own half the world's wealth, study finds', *The Guardian*, 14 November 2017, www.theguardian.com/inequality/2017/nov/14/worlds-richest-wealth-credit-suisse; Larry Elliott, 'World's 26 richest people own as much as the poorest 50%, says Oxfam', *The Guardian*, 21 January 2019, www.theguardian.com/business/2019/jan/21/world-26-richest-people-own-as-much-as-poorest-50-per-cent-oxfam-report.

27 'The Distributional Effects of Asset Purchases', Bank of England website, 12 July 2012, www.bankofengland.co.uk/-/media/boe/files/news/2012/july/the-distributional-effects-of-asset-purchases-paper.

28 'The World Ultra Wealth Report 2017', Wealth-X report, available at www.wealthx.com/report/exclusive-uhnwi-analysis-world-ultra-wealth-report-2017 (accessed 10 February 2020).

29 It is generally understood that there have been four waves of feminist activity in the UK and US. Individual countries have their own number of waves; however, the term 'Fourth Wave' has come to refer to the phase of global feminism since 2012.

30 Nadia Khomami, '#MeToo: how a hashtag became a rallying cry against sexual harassment', *The Guardian*, 20 October 2017, www.theguardian.com/world/2017/oct/20/women-worldwide-use-hashtag-metoo-against-sexual-harassment.

31 See their website at: www.feminismforthe99.org.

32 World Economic Forum, 'Global Gender Gap Report 2020', p. 8.

33 Jane Merriman, 'After gender bias, women face gender fatigue', *Reuters*, 2 November 2009, www.reuters.com/article/us-gender-fatigue/after-gender-bias-women-face-genderfatigue-IDUSTRE5A13HE20091102.

34 Helen Russell, *The Year of Living Danishly* (London: Icon Books, 2015).

35 Joann S. Lublin, *Earning It: Hard-Won Lessons from Trailblazing Women at the Top of the Business World* (New York: Harper Business, 2016).

36 Lublin, *Earning It*, p. 5.

37 Jamie Doward and Gaby Bissett, 'High Fliers Have More Babies, According to Study', *The Guardian*, 25 October 2014, www.theguardian.com/lifeandstyle/2014/oct/25/women-wealth-childcare-family-babies-study.

38 Corinne Purtill and Dan Kopf, 'The reason the richest women in the US are the ones having the most kids', *Quartz*, 11 November 2017, https://qz.com/1125805/the-reason-the-richest-women-in-the-us-are-the-ones-having-the-most-kids.

39 Claire Cain Miller, 'Children Hurt Women's Earnings, but Not Men's (Even in Scandinavia)', *The New York Times*, 5 February 2018, www.nytimes.com/2018/02/05/upshot/even-in-family-friendly-scandinavia-mothers-are-paid-less.html.

40 Catherine Rottenberg's book *The Rise of Neoliberal Feminism* (New York: Oxford University Press, 2018) is worth reading for more on this topic.

41 Andrew Heywood, *Political Ideologies* (Basingstoke: Palgrave, 1998), p. 238.

42 Adriana Lopez, 'How Successful Business Women are Redefining Modern Feminism', *Forbes*, 11 August 2016, www.forbes.com/sites/adrianalopez/2016/08/11/1729/#78572aea267d.

## Chapter 2: How We Got Here

1 The 'married woman' part of this was not removed until the Finance Act 1950 (section 35). Erika Rackley and Rosemary Auchmuty, *Women's Legal Landmarks: Celebrating the History of Women and Law in the UK* (London: Bloomsbury, 2018), p. 409.

2 'Independent Taxation and Tax Penalties on Marriage', HC Deb 15 March 1988, Hansard 1803–2006, vol. 129, available at https://api.parliament.uk/historic-hansard/commons/1988/mar/15/independent-taxation-and-tax-penalties (accessed 10 February 2020).

3 Adrienne Rich, 'Compulsory Heterosexuality and Lesbian Existence', *Journal of Women's History* 15:3, autumn 2003, pp. 11–48.

4 Lady Hale, President of the Supreme Court, 'Celebrating Women's Rights', speech at Birmingham Law Society and Holdsworth Club, 29 November 2018, www.supremecourt. uk/docs/speech-181129.pdf (accessed 10 February 2020).

5 Ibid.

6 See Gabriel Pogrund, 'NHS trusts deny single women IVF treatment', *The Times*, 18 August 2019, www.thetimes.co.uk/ article/nhs-trusts-deny-single-women-ivf-treatment-gs9b7qxbt and Denis Campbell, 'NHS bosses apologise for calling single mothers a burden', *The Guardian*, 9 September 2019, www.theguardian.com/society/2019/sep/09/nhs-bosses-apologise-calling-single-mothers-burden-society.

7 'Feminist History of Philosophy', *Stanford Encyclopedia of Philosophy*, revised 9 March 2015, available at https://plato.stanford. edu/entries/feminism-femhist (accessed 10 February 2020).

8 'Illegitimacy: the shameful secret', *The Guardian*, 14 April 2007, www.theguardian.com/news/2007/apr/14/guardians pecial4.guardianspecial215.

9 Lady Hale, 'Celebrating Women's Rights' speech, 29 November 2018.

10 Ibid.

11 Richard W. Price, 'Bastardy or Illegitimacy in England', Price-Gen website, www.pricegen.com/bastardy-or-illegitimacy-in-england (accessed 10 February 2020).

12 Fiona MacRae, 'Abortion at record high with increase in older women and benefits cap effect', *The Times*, 14 June 2019, www. thetimes.co.uk/article/abortion-numbers-record-high-older-women-child-benefit-cap-v20qgp7ot.

13 Liam Collins, 'Husband's "Chattel Case" Court Victory Was Turning Point in Women's Rights', *The Independent*, 26 November 2017, www.independent.ie/opinion/columnists/husbands-chattel-case-court-victory-was-turning-point-in-womens-

rights-36353603.html. See also Henry Fielding, 'Case That Woke Us All Up to Sexual Scandal', *Sunday Independent*, 13 July 2008, www.pressreader.com/ireland/sunday-independent-ireland/20080713/282157877016294.

14  Sandra Mara, *No Job for a Woman* (Dublin: Poolbeg Press, 2008). See also 'Cork woman whose love affair became a sensational court case in 1972', *Irish Times*, 18 November 2017, www.irishtimes.com/opinion/cork-woman-whose-love-affair-became-a-sensational-court-case-in-1972-1.3294917.

15  Damian Corless, 'When a Wife Was her Man's Chattel', *Irish Independent*, 30 December 2014, www.independent.ie/life/when-a-wife-was-her-mans-chattel-30871468.html.

16  This was known as 'The Act to Confirm Certain Conveyances and Directing the Manner of Proving Deeds to be Recorded'.

17  An electronic version of the original letter is available to view on the Massachusetts Historical Society website, www.masshist.org/publications/adams-papers/view?id=AFC01d244 (accessed 10 February 2020).

18  Electronic versions of John's letters to Abigail are also available to view on the Massachusetts Historical Society website, www.masshist.org/digitaladams/archive/doc?id=L17760414ja (accessed 10 February 2020).

19  'Did Sarah Guppy design the Clifton Suspension Bridge?', Clifton Bridge website, www.cliftonbridge.org.uk/did-sarah-guppy-design-clifton-suspension-bridge (accessed 10 February 2020). See also 'Sarah Guppy: The Bridge, The Bed, The Truth', UWE Bristol website blog, 30 October 2018, https://blogs.uwe.ac.uk/engineering/sarah-guppy-the-bridge-the-bed-the-truth.

20  Lucinda Shen, 'The incredible lives of two sisters who became the first female brokers on Wall Street', *Business Insider*, 15

October 2015, www.businessinsider.com/victoria-woodhull-first-female-broker-2015-10.

21  The electronic version of the original *New York Herald* column that Woodhull wrote on 29 March 1870 is available on the Library of Congress website, https://chroniclingamerica. loc.gov/lccn/sn83030313/1870-04-02/ed-1/seq-8 (accessed 10 February 2020). And a good article describing her situation: Kayla Epstein, 'A woman who ran for president in 1872 was compared to Satan and locked up. It wasn't for her emails', *The Washington Post*, 11 September 2019, www.washingtonpost. com/history/2019/09/11/woman-who-ran-president-was-compared-satan-locked-up-it-wasnt-her-emails.

22  Danny Lewis, 'Victoria Woodhull Ran for President Before Women Had the Right to Vote', *Smithsonian Magazine*, 10 May 2016, www.smithsonianmag.com/smart-news/victoria-wood hull-ran-for-president-before-women-had-the-right-to-vote-180959038.

23  Olivia B. Waxman, '"Lucy Stone, If You Please": The Unsung Suffragist Who Fought for Women to Keep Their Names', *TIME Magazine*, 7 March 2019, https://time.com/5537834/ lucy-stone-maiden-names-womens-history.

24  Alice Stone-Blackwell, *Lucy Stone, Pioneer of Women's Rights* (Whitefish, MT: Kessinger, 2010).

25  Joelle Million, *Woman's Voice, Woman's Place: Lucy Stone and the Birth of the Women's Rights Movement* (Westport, CT: Praeger, 2003), p. 192.

26  *Loving Warriors: Selected Letters of Lucy Stone and Henry B. Blackwell, 1853 to 1893*, ed. Leslie Wheeler (New York: Doubleday, 1981), p. 110.

27  David Willetts, *The Pinch* (London: Atlantic Books, 2019), p. 40.

28  Leslie Hume, *The National Union of Women's Suffragette Societies 1897–1914* (New York: Routledge, 2016).

29  Andrew Heywood, *Political Ideologies: An Introduction* (London: Palgrave, 1998).

30  Catherine Gourley, *Flappers and the New American Woman: Perceptions of Women from 1918 through the 1920s* (Minneapolis, MN: Twenty-First Century Books, 2008).

31  Mark V. Tushnet et al., *The Oxford Handbook of the US Constitution* (Oxford: Oxford University Press, 2015), p. 525.

32  Debran Rowland, *The Boundaries of Her Body: The Troubling History of Women's Rights in America* (Naperville, IL: Sphinx Publishing, 2004), p. 55.

33  Gourley, *Flappers and the New American Woman*, p. 117.

34  Rowland, *The Boundaries of Her Body*, p. 54.

35  Ibid.

36  'The Marriage Bar', *The Spectator*, 23 August 1946, http://archive. spectator.co.uk/article/23rd-august-1946/2/the-marriage-bar.

37  Royal Commission on Equal Pay 1944–46, Cmd 6937, para. 469, available at https://archive.org/stream/royalcommission 0033426mbp/royalcommission0033426mbp_djvu.txt (accessed 10 February 2020).

38  Ibid., para. 469.

39  Ibid., para. 467.

40  More information can be found on the Union History website under 'Winning Equal Pay', www.unionhistory.info/ equalpay/display.php?irn=100273&QueryPage=%2Fequalpa y%2Findex.php (accessed 10 February 2020).

41  'Bebb v. The Law Society', Court of Appeal ruling, transcript available at https://heinonline.org/HOL/LandingPage? handle=hein.journals/canlawtt34&div=90&id=&page= (accessed 10 February 2020).

42  Judith Bourne, 'Gwyneth Bebb: The Past Explaining the Present', *The Law Society Gazette*, 29 April 2019, www.lawgazette.

co.uk/gwyneth-bebb-the-past-explaining-the-present/5070047. article.

43 'Women Making History: The Centenary', University of Oxfordwebsite,www.ox.ac.uk/about/oxford-people/women-at-oxford/centenary (accessed 23 July 2020).

44 Ibid.

45 I have used the gender-neutral pronoun 'they'. The row over the correct pronouns to describe Dr Barry is explained here: Alison Flood, 'New novel about Dr James Barry sparks row over Victorian's gender identity', *The Guardian*, 18 February 2019,www.theguardian.com/books/2019/feb/18/new-novel-about-dr-james-barry-sparks-row-over-victorians-gender-identity.

46 Michael du Preez and Jeremy Dronfield, *Dr James Barry: A Woman Ahead of Her Time* (London: Oneworld, 2016).

47 Jason Rodrigues, '30 years ago: El Vino's treatment of women drinkers ruled unlawful', *The Guardian*, 15 November 2012, www.theguardian.com/theguardian/from-the-archive-blog/2012/nov/15/el-vino-women-ban-fleet-street-1982.

48 Lady Hale, 'Celebrating Women's Rights' speech, 29 November 2018.

49 Susan J. Baserga, 'The Early Years of Coeducation at the Yale University School of Medicine', *Yale Journal of Biology and Medicine* 53:3, 1980, pp. 181–90.

50 Nancy McKeon, 'Women in the House get a restroom', *The Washington Post*, 28 July 2011, www.washingtonpost.com/life style/style/women-in-the-house-get-a-restroom/2011/07/28/gIQAFgdwfI_story.html.

51 Ibid.

52 David Pannick, 'Sex Discrimination and Pregnancy: Anatomy Is Not Destiny', *Oxford Journal of Legal Studies* 3:1, 1983, pp. 1–21.

53 'Turley v. Allders Department Store', 1980, in Sally Jane Kenney, *For Whose Protection?: Reproductive Hazards and Exclusionary Policies in the United States and Britain* (Ann Arbor, MI: University of Michigan Press, 1992).

54 Lady Hale, 'Celebrating Women's Rights' speech, 29 November 2018.

55 Alysia Montaño shared her story in a video made with *The New York Times* in May 2019.

*Chapter 3: What We Believe about Money*

1 The Pensions Advisory Service, 'Gender, Age and Pensions Savings', Behave London report, 2017, available at http://bandce.co.uk/wp-content/uploads/2017/10/16303_SSGA_TPP_Gaps_Report_2017_AW_Online_Spreads_LR.pdf (accessed 10 February 2020).

2 'Who's the Better Investor: Men or Women?', Fidelity website, 18 May 2017, www.fidelity.com/about-fidelity/individual-investing/better-investor-men-or-women.

3 Ann Marie Hibbert et al., 'Are Women More Risk-Averse Than Men?', research paper, 2009, available at www.researchgate.net/publication/228434430_ARE_WOMEN_MORE_RISK-AVERSE_THAN_MEN (accessed 10 February 2020).

4 The Pensions Advisory Service, 'Gender, Age and Pensions Savings'.

5 Yosef Bonaparte et al., 'Discrimination, Social Risk, and Portfolio Choice', UC Davis, Graduate School of Management website, 2 November 2016, https://gsm.ucdavis.edu/sites/main/files/file-attachments/discrimination_social_risk_port_choice.pdf.

6 Chris Taylor, 'Why Women Are Better Investors: Study', *Reuters*, 7 June 2017, www.reuters.com/article/us-money-investing-women/why-women-are-better-investors-study-idUSKBN18Y2D7.

7 'Are women better investors than men?', Warwick Business School website, 28 June 2018, www.wbs.ac.uk/news/are-women-better-investors-than-men.

8 Taylor, 'Why Women Are Better Investors'.

9 Patrick Collinson, 'The truth about investing: women do it better than men', *The Guardian*, 24 November 2018, www.the guardian.com/money/2018/nov/24/the-truth-about-investing-women-do-it-better-than-men.

10 'Financial advisers' gender affects their advice to clients', King's College London website, 11 March 2019, www.kcl.ac.uk/news/financial-advisers-gender-affects-their-advice-to-clients.

11 'Research on over 21,000 Companies Globally Finds Women in Corporate Leadership Can Significantly Increase Profitability', Peterson Institute for International Economics, 8 February 2016, www.piie.com/newsroom/press-releases/new-peterson-institute-research-over-21000-companies-globally-finds-women.

12 Department for Business, Energy & Industrial Strategy, 'Revealed: The worst explanations for not appointing women to FTSE company boards', Gov.uk website, 31 May 2018, www.gov.uk/government/news/revealed-the-worst-explana tions-for-not-appointing-women-to-ftse-company-boards. See also Amie Tsang, 'Here's Why British Firms Say Their Boards Lack Women. Prepare to Cringe', *The New York Times*, 31 May 2018, www.nytimes.com/2018/05/31/business/uk-women-corporate-boards-excuses.html.

13 Yoni Blumberg, 'Companies with female executives make more money – here's why', *CNBC*, 2 March 2018, www.cnbc.

com/2018/03/02/why-companies-with-female-managers-make-more-money.html.

14 Marcus Noland, Tyler Moran and Barbara Kotschwar, 'Is Gender Diversity Profitable?', research paper, February 2016, available at www.piie.com/publications/working-papers/gender-diversity-profitable-evidence-global-survey (accessed 28 November 2020).

15 'Delivering through diversity', McKinsey report, 2018, www.mckinsey.com/business-functions/organization/our-insights/delivering-through-diversity (accessed 10 January 2020).

16 Linda-Eling Lee, 'Women on Boards: Global Trends in Gender Diversity', Morgan Stanley Capital International website blog, 30 November 2015, www.msci.com/www/blog-posts/women-on-boards-global-trends/0263383649.

17 Linda-Eling Lee, 'The Tipping Point: Women on Boards and Financial Performance', Morgan Stanley Capital International website blog, 13 December 2016, www.msci.com/www/blog posts/the-tipping-point-women-on/0538249725.

18 Rupert Jones, 'Financial giant's £50m "Girl Fund" to back firms with good gender balance', *The Guardian*, 17 May 2018, www.theguardian.com/business/2018/may/17/financial-giants-50m-girl-fund-to-back-firms-with-good-gender-balance.

19 'The Alison Rose Review of Female Entrepreneurship', HM Treasury report, 2019, p. 10, available at www.gov.uk/government/publications/the-alison-rose-review-of-female-entrepreneurship (accessed 10 February 2020).

20 Ibid.

21 'Female Tech Entrepreneurs Hampered by Bias Among Male Investors, Study Finds', Caltech website, 16 November 2017,

www.caltech.edu/about/news/female-tech-entrepreneurs-hampered-bias-among-male-investors-study-finds-80420.

22 'The Alison Rose Review of Female Entrepreneurship', p. 54.
23 '80% of Newspaper Articles on the Economy Have Male Bias', Fawcett Society website, 23 November 2015, www.faw cettsociety.org.uk/news/80-of-newspaper-articles-on-the-eco nomy-have-male-bias.
24 Jim Waterson, 'Financial Times tool warns if articles quote too many men', *The Guardian*, 14 November 2018, www.the guardian.com/media/2018/nov/14/financial-times-tool-warns-if-articles-quote-too-many-men.
25 Gloria Steinem, *Revolution from Within: A Book of Self-Esteem* (London: Corgi, 1993).

*Chapter 4: The Scandal of Old-Age Poverty*

1 European Institute for Gender Equality, 'Gender Equality Index 2017', 2017 report, p. 27, available at https://eige.europa. eu/publications/gender-equality-index-2017-measuring-gender-equality-european-union-2005-2015-report (accessed 20 November 2020). For the Australian figures, see 'Australian women facing grim retirement due to gender pay gap', Industry Super-Funds website, 8 March 2018, www.industrysuper.com/media/australian-women-facing-grim-retirement-due-to-gender-pay-gap.
2 Kate Palmer, 'While a man retires with a £315,000 pension, a woman makes do with barely half that pot', *The Sunday Times,* 8 December 2019, www.thetimes.co.uk/article/while-a-man-retires-with-a-315-000-pension-a-woman-makes-do-with-barely-half-that-pot-7jw8mm3ts.

3 European Institute for Gender Equality, 'Gender Equality Index 2017'.

4 Figures from the Pensions Policy Institute: www.pensions policyinstitute.org.uk/media/3516/20200623-ppi-bn122-tax-relief-on-dc-contributions-final.pdf (accessed 26 September 2020).

5 The age limit for auto-enrolment should be raised from the state pension age (currently sixty-five) until workers actually retire from work, which is often much later. There is no reason why people should stop saving for retirement as long as they are still working, and if they are working part-time, as many people do in the years before fully retiring, they still ought to be saving.

The taxman has details of how much each person earns, so systems could be put in place to capture women who earn above the £10,000 threshold from multiple jobs, and their primary employer could be mandated to provide a pension for them. Having income from more than one job included in the conditions for auto-enrolment would mean that 60,000 more women meet the qualifying criteria.

The £10,000 level itself is an arbitrary figure – people don't start paying tax until they earn above £12,500, while National Insurance (the contribution towards a state pension) is paid on earnings above £8,632 a year. There's a good argument for lowering the threshold for auto-enrolment pensions to £8,632. People in this earning bracket will notice every penny that is deducted from their salaries, but they are also the people who are least likely to have retirement savings and need all the help they can get.

6 Steve Webb, 'My state pension is just £80.42. Is this right?', *This is Money*, 13 May 2016, www.thisismoney.co.uk/money/

pensions/article-3577195/My-state-pension-just-80-42-right-Retirement-Agony-Uncle-Steve-Webb-answers.html.

7  'Rise in death rates in older pensioners "linked with austerity measures"', University of Oxford website, 16 March 2016, www.ox.ac.uk/news/2016-03-16-rise-death-rates-older-pen sioners-%E2%80%98linked-austerity-measures%E2%80%99.

8  Maria Espadinha, 'UN Committee Urges Govt to Act on State Pension Age', *Financial Times Adviser*, 13 March 2019, www.ftadviser.com/pensions/2019/03/13/un-committee-urges-govt-to-act-on-state-pension-age.

9  'Population estimates by marital status and living arrangements, England and Wales: 2002 to 2017', Office for National Statistics website, 27 July 2018, www.ons.gov.uk/peoplepopu lationandcommunity/populationandmigration/population estimates/bulletins/populationestimatesbymaritalstatusan dliving arrangements/2002to2017.

10  'Government Should Pay into Pensions for Mothers and Carers', Social Market Foundation press release, 27 October 2019, www.smf.co.uk/press-release-government-should-pay-into-pensions-for-mothers-and-carers (accessed 19 July 2020).

11  Chetan Jethwa, 'Understanding the Gender Pensions Gap', Pensions Policy Institute paper, July 2019, pp. 2–17, www. pensionspolicyinstitute.org.uk/media/3227/20190711-under standing-the-gender-pensions-gap.pdf (accessed 20 June 2020).

12  See the Money Advice Service website: www.moneyadviceser vice.org.uk/en/articles/personal-pensions (accessed 20 October 2020). See also Citizens Advice: www.citizensadvice.org.uk/ debt-and-money/pensions/starting-a-pension/choosing-a-personal-pension (accessed 20 October 2020).

1  Kim Gittleson, 'Where are all the Women in Economics?', *BBC News*, 13 October 2017, www.bbc.co.uk/news/business-4157133.

2  According to Bruegel, an economic think tank: www.bruegel.org/2018/03/how-many-female-economist-professors-in-top-european-universities (accessed 27 June 2020).

3  Chris Wagstaff, 'Gender Balance in Asset Management', Columbia Threadneedle Asset Management investment blog, www.columbiathreadneedle.co.uk/regional-home/interme diary/market-insight/investment-blog/gender-balance-in-asset-management (accessed 27 June 2020).

4  Linda Yueh, *The Great Economists: How Their Ideas Can Help Us Today* (London: Viking, 2018), p. 6.

5  T. Forsyth and C. Johnson, 'Elinor Ostrom's Legacy: Governing the Commons and the Rational Choice Controversy', *Development and Change* 45:5, 2014, pp. 1093–1110.

6  Diane Coyle, 'Economics Has a Problem With Women', *Financial Times,* 28 August 2017, www.ft.com/content/6b3cc8be-881e-11e7-afd2-74b8ecd34d3b.

7  Claire Crawford et al., 'Why Do So Few Women Study Economics? Evidence from England', March 2018, available at www.res.org.uk/uploads/assets/uploaded/6c3fd338-88d6-47ea-bf2f302dfee7f37e.pdf (accessed 28 November 2020).

8  Alice H. Wu, 'Gendered Language on the Economics Job Market Rumors Forum', *AEA Papers and Proceedings*, 108, 2018, pp. 175–9.

9  Russell Lynch, 'Esther Duflo on winning the Nobel, poverty and the macho "locker room" culture of economics', *The Telegraph*, 10 November 2019, www.telegraph.co.uk/business/2019/11/10/esther-duflo-winning-nobel-poverty-macho-locker-room-culture.

10 Ibid.

11 Ann Mari May et al., 'Are Disagreements among Male and Female Economists Marginal at Best? A Survey of AEA Members and their Views on Economics and Economic Policy', *Contemporary Economic Policy*, 32:1, 2013, available at https://onlinelibrary.wiley.com/doi/abs/10.1111/coep.12004.

12 Ann Mari May et al., 'Mind the Gap: Differing Perspectives of Men and Women Economists May Affect Policy Outcomes', *Finance & Development*, 55:2, June 2018, available at www.imf.org/external/pubs/ft/fandd/2018/06/including-more-women-economists-influences-policy-and-research/may.htm.

13 Ann Mari May, 'Different Sight Lines', *Finance & Development*, 50:2, June 2013, available at www.imf.org/external/pubs/ft/fandd/2013/06/may.htm.

14 Phillip Inman, 'Chief economist of Bank of England admits errors in Brexit forecasting', *The Guardian*, 5 January 2017, www.theguardian.com/business/2017/jan/05/chief-economist-of-bank-of-england-admits-errors.

15 Katrine Marçal, *Who Cooked Adam Smith's Dinner?: A Story about Women and Economics* (London: Portobello Books, 2015).

16 Lynch, 'Esther Duflo on winning the Nobel'.

17 Sarah O'Connor, 'Drugs and prostitution add £10bn to UK economy', *Financial Times*, 29 May 2014, www.ft.com/content/65704ba0-e730-11e3-88be-00144feabdco.

18 'National Accounts Articles: Impact of ESA95 Changes on Current Price GDP Estimates', National Accounts Coordination report, 29 May 2014, available at https://webarchive.national archives.gov.uk/20160106064354/http://www.ons.gov.uk/ons/rel/naa1-rd/national-accounts-articles/impact-ofesa95-changes-on-current-price-gdp-estimates/index.html (accessed 10 February 2020).

19 'Women still do more household chores than men, ONS finds', *BBC News*, 10 November 2016, www.bbc.co.uk/news/uk-37941191.

20 Cassie Werber, 'The case for treating childcare like essential economic infrastructure', *Quartz*, 20 August 2020, https://qz.com/work/1894505/childcare-is-infrastructure-for-families-elizabeth-warren-says.

21 Heather Long, 'The big factor holding back the U.S. economic recovery: Child care', *The Washington Post*, 3 July 2020, www.washingtonpost.com/business/2020/07/03/big-factor-holding-back-us-economic-recovery-child-care.

22 James Plunkett, 'The Missing Million: the potential for female employment to raise living standards in low to middle income Britain', Resolution Foundation report, December 2011, p. 5, www.resolutionfoundation.org/app/uploads/2014/08/The-Missing-Million.pdf (accessed 29 November 2020).

23 'China Birth Rate Declines as Childcare Costs Deter Families', *Financial Times*, 12 March 2019, www.ft.com/content/f34bb0b0-2f8b-11e9-8744-e7016697f225.

*Chapter 6: When Governments Ignore Gender*

1 Figures from NHS England for 2012. Of the £88 million spent, £43 million was for branded Viagra, the rest for generic equivalents.

2 Rebecca Masters et al., 'Return on investment of public health interventions: a systematic review', *Journal of Epidemiology and Community Health* 71:8, 2017, pp. 827–34.

3 'First Do No Harm: The Independent Medicines and Medical Devices Safety Review', review chaired by Baroness Julia

Cumberlege, 8 July 2020, available at www.immdsreview.org.
uk/Report.html (accessed 2 November 2020).

4 Sarah Champion, 'Women have been hit hardest by austerity –
Labour would change that', LabourList website, 1 March 2017,
labourlist.org/2017/03/champion-women-have-been-hit-har
dest-by-austerity-labour-would-change-that.

5 'Estimating the gender impact of tax and benefits changes',
Parliament UK website, December 2017, p. 9. The full report is
available at https://researchbriefings.parliament.uk/Research
Briefing/Summary/SN06758#fullreport (accessed 10 February 2020).

6 Office of the High Commissioner for Human Rights, 'The
Impact of Economic Reform Policies on Women's Human
Rights', Equality and Human Rights Commission report,
March 2018, available at www.equalityhumanrights.com/sites/
default/files/consultation-response-ohchr-impact-of-austerity-
on-women-30-march-2018.pdf (accessed 10 February 2020).

7 'To ensure economic recovery for women, we need plan F',
Women's Budget Group briefing, September 2013, available at
https://wbg. org.uk/wp-content/uploads/2013/10/Plan-F_W
BG-Parties-briefing_Sept-2013_final.pdf (accessed 10 February 2020).

8 This pay freeze excluded people earning under £21,000, who
had pay increases of £250 and over: Doug Pyper et al., 'Public
sector pay', House of Commons Library, CBP 8037, 3 May 2018,
available at http://researchbriefings.files.parliament.uk/docu-
ments/CBP-8037/CBP-8037.pdf (accessed 10 February 2020).

9 Ibid.

10 'Women, Employment and Earnings', Women's Budget
Group report, October 2019, https://wbg.org.uk/wp-con
tent/uploads/2019/10/EMPLOYMENT-2019.pdf (accessed
28 November 2020).

11 'Understanding NHS financial pressures: how are they affecting patient care?', The King's Fund report, 14 March 2017, www.kingsfund.org.uk/publications/understanding-nhs-financial-pressures.

12 Dean Hochlaf et al., 'Ending the Blame Game: The Case for a New Approach to Public Health and Prevention', Institute for Public Policy Research report, June 2019, available at www.ippr.org/files/2019-06/public-health-and-prevention-june19.pdf (accessed 10 February 2020).

13 Philip Alston, 'Statement on Visit to the United Kingdom', November 2018, p. 1, available at www.ohchr.org/Docu ments/Issues/Poverty/EOM_GB_16Nov 2018.pdf (accessed 10 February 2020).

14 Nina Gill, 'The new junior doctors' contract is blatantly sexist – so why doesn't Jeremy Hunt care?', *The Telegraph*, 4 April 2016, www.telegraph.co.uk/women/life/the-new-junior-doctors-contract-is-blatantly-sexist-so-why-do.

15 Rachel Reeves, *Women of Westminster: The MPs Who Changed Politics* (London: I. B. Tauris, 2019), p. 213.

16 Alston, 'Statement on Visit to the United Kingdom'.

17 Office of the High Commissioner for Human Rights, 'The Impact of Economic Reform Policies on Women's Human Rights', p. 8.

18 Ibid.

19 Dr Helen Crawley and Rosie Dodds, *The UK Healthy Start Scheme: What Happened? What Next?* (London: First Steps Nutrition Trust, 2018), p. 27.

20 'Universal Credit and Survival Sex: sex in exchange for meeting survival needs inquiry', 2018 report, www.parliament.uk/business/committees/committees-a-z/commons-select/work-and-pensions-committee/inquiries/parliament-2017/universal-credit-survival-sex-inquiry-17-19 (accessed 10 February 2020).

21 Laura Seebohm, interview with author, pers. comm., 2019.

22 Office of the High Commissioner for Human Rights, 'The Impact of Economic Reform Policies on Women's Human Rights', p. 5.

23 Carolyn Vogler, 'Money, Power and Inequality within Marriage', *Sociological Review* 42:2, 1994, pp. 263–88.

24 'Universal Credit hands power to abusers, MPs say', *BBC News*, 1 August 2018, www.bbc.co.uk/news/uk-45029275.

25 'Social Security Experience Panels: Universal Credit Scottish Choices', Scottish Government website, 29 November 2018, www.gov.scot/publications/social-security-experience-panels-universal-credit-scottish-choices.

26 Office of the High Commissioner for Human Rights, 'The Impact of Economic Reform Policies on Women's Human Rights', p. 11.

27 'Public Sector Equality Duty', Equality and Human Rights Commission website, www.equalityhumanrights.com/en/advice-and-guidance/public-sector-equality-duty (accessed 10 February 2020).

28 Office of the High Commissioner for Human Rights, 'The Impact of Economic Reform Policies on Women's Human Rights'.

29 Also called 'gender-based budgeting' or 'gender budgeting'.

30 Zohra Khan and Lisa Kolovich, 'Do the Math: Include Women in Government Budgets', IMF Blog, 6 March 2019, https://blogs.imf.org/2019/03/06/do-the-math-include-women-in-government-budgets. See also the UN web entry on Austria here:www.un.org/ruleoflaw/blog/portfolio-items/austria-gender-budgeting (accessed 10 February 2020).

31 'What is gender budgeting?', *The Economist*, 3 March 2017, www.economist.com/the-economist-explains/2017/03/03/what- is-gender-budgeting.

32 Christine Lagarde, 'Every Woman Counts: Gender Budgeting in G7 Countries', IMF Blog, 13 May 2017, https:// blogs.imf.org/2017/05/13/every-woman-counts-gender-bud geting-in-g7-countries.

33 International Monetary Fund, 'Gender Budgeting in G7 Countries', IMF website, 13 May 2017, www.imf.org/en/ Publications/Policy-Papers/Issues/2017/05/12/pp041917gender-budgeting-in-g7-countries.

34 The White House's 2018 Budget is available at www.white house.gov/sites/whitehouse.gov/files/omb/budget/fy2018/ budget.pdf (accessed 10 February 2020).

35 Gender-responsive analysis of Trump's 2018 budget here: Quoctrung Bui and Susan Chira, 'How Trump's Budget Affects Women', *The New York Times*, 24 May 2017, www. nytimes.com/interactive/2017/05/24/upshot/how-trumps-budget-affects-women.html.

36 'Policy Basics: The Supplemental Nutrition Assistance Program (SNAP)', Center on Budget and Policy Priorities website, 25 June 2019, www.cbpp.org/research/food-assistance/policy-basics-the -supplemental-nutrition-assistance-pro gram-snap.

37 About 61 per cent of the 43 million Americans who use food stamps are women, equivalent to 26 million women: Editorial Board, 'The Problem Isn't Food Stamps, It's Poverty', *The New York Times*, 26 May 2017, www.nytimes.com/2017/05/26/ opinion/trump-budget-food-stamps-wages.html.

38 'What can SNAP buy?', Food and Nutrition Service, US Department of Agriculture website, www.fns.usda.gov/snap/ eligible-food-items (accessed 10 February 2020).

39 Seth Freed Wessler, 'Timed Out on Welfare, Many Sell Food Stamps', Type Investigations, 16 February 2010, www.type investigations.org/investigation/2010/02/16/timed-welfare-many-sell-food-stamps.

40 Bui and Chira, 'How Trump's Budget Affects Women'.

41 See more on Women's Bureau objectives at: www.dol.gov/wb/
info_about_wb/interwb.htm (accessed 28 November 2020).

42 Ibid.

43 'Women's Wealth is Rising', *The Economist*, 8 March 2018,
www.economist.com/graphic-detail/2018/03/08/womens-wealth-
is-rising.

44 See a full list of states that have ratified the convention here:
https://treaties.un.org/pages/ViewDetails.aspx?src=TR EA
T Y&mtdsg_no=IV-8&chapter=4&clang=_en (accessed 10
February 2020).

45 'A Fact Sheet on CEDAW: Treaty for the Rights of Women',
Amnesty USA website, www.amnestyusa.org/files/pdfs/
cedaw_fact_sheet.pdf (accessed 10 February 2020).

46 Ann Piccard, 'US Ratification of CEDAW – From Bad to
Worse, Law & Inequality', *Journal of Theory and Practice* 28:1,
October 2009, pp. 119–61.

47 Lin Taylor, 'Switzerland ranked as best country for women's
rights, according to the OECD', World Economic Forum
website, 13 March 2019, www.weforum.org/agenda/2019/03/
switzerland-ranked-as-best-country-for-womens-rights-oecd.

48 'A Fact Sheet on CEDAW: Treaty for the Rights of Women',
Amnesty USA.

*Chapter 7: Everyday Costs . . . That Little Bit More*

1 Emine Saner, '"Lady Doritos": a solution to a problem that
doesn't exist', *The Guardian*, 5 February 2018, www.theguard-
ian.com/lifeandstyle/shortcuts/2018/feb/05/lady-doritos-a-
solution-to-a-problem-that-doesnt-exist.

2 Murray Wardrop, 'Women spend £2,700 on bras but only
wash them six times a year', *The Telegraph*, 1 May 2009, www.

telegraph.co.uk/news/uknews/5254406/Women-spend-2700-on-brasbut-only-wash-them-six-times-a-year.html.

3  Elle Hunt, 'The truth about tights: my search for a pair to end women's hosiery hell', *The Guardian*, 17 January 2019, www.theguardian.com/fashion/2019/jan/17/truth-about-tights-search-pair-end-hosiery-hell.

4  Emily Thornhill, 'This is how much women spend on hair removal in their lifetime', *Harper's Bazaar*, 28 April 2017, www.harpersbazaar.com/uk/beauty/hair/news/a41199/women-spend-costwaxing-hair-removal-lifetime.

5  'From Cradle to Cane: The Cost of Being a Female Consumer: A Study of Gender Pricing in New York City', New York City Department of Consumer Affairs, December 2015, available at www1.nyc.gov/assets/dca/downloads/pdf/partners/Study-of-Gender-Pricing-in-NYC.pdf (accessed 10 February 2020).

6  Ibid.

7  Charlie Moore, 'Gillette charges more for women's razors than for men's – while bashing sexism in its controversial #MeToo-inspired advert', *Daily Mail*, 18 January 2019, www.dailymail.co.uk/news/article-6604583/Gillette-charges-women-men-razors.html.

8  Tanith Carey, 'Why is it so expensive to be a woman?', *Daily Mail*, 19 February 2015, www.dailymail.co.uk/femail/article-2959383/Why-expensive-woman-called-pink-tax-women-paymen-dry-cleaning-razors.html.

9  Cara Buckley, 'At the Cleaners, One Woman Seeks Gender Equality', *The New York Times*, 4 February 2009, www.nytimes.com/2009/02/05/nyregion/05cleaners.html.

10  Roz Tappenden and Linda Serck, 'Why do women pay more for a short haircut?', *BBC News*, 10 January 2020, www.bbc.co.uk/news/uk-england-50691249.

11 Details about the 'Gender-Based Pricing (Prohibition) Bill 2017–19' can be found here: https://services.parliament.uk/Bills/2017-19/genderbasedpricingprohibition.html (accessed 10 February 2020).

12 Annabelle Williams, 'Female motorists are being charged 20% more for car repairs', *City AM*, 13 August 2015, www.cityam.com/female-motorists-are-being-charged-20-more-car-repairs.

13 Meghan Busse and Ayelet Israeli, 'Repairing the Damage: The Effect of Price Expectations on Auto-Repair Price Quotes', *Journal of Marketing Research* 54:1, February 2017, pp. 75–95.

14 Li-Zhong Chen, 'Demographics, Gender and Local Knowledge – Price Discrimination in China's Car Market', *Economics Letters* 16:163, February 2018, pp. 172–4.

15 Ian Ayres and Peter Siegelman, 'Race and Gender Discrimination in Bargaining for a New Car', *The American Economic Review* 85:3, June 1995, pp. 304–21.

16 'Research on Period Poverty and Stigma', Plan International UK website, 20 December 2017, https://plan-uk.org/media-centre/plan-international-uks-research-on-period-poverty-and-stigma.

17 'End Period Poverty', Always website, https://always.com/en-us/about-us/end-period-poverty (accessed 10 February 2020).

18 Beh Lih Yi, 'Australian state provides free tampons to students to tackle taboos', *Reuters*, 12 September 2019, www.reuters.com/article/us-australia-women-health/australian-state-provides-free-tampons-to-students-to-tackle-taboos-id USKCN1VX0UR.

19 Jennifer Weiss-Wolf, *Periods Gone Public: Taking a Stand for Menstrual Equity* (New York: Arcade Publishing, 2017).

20 Bloody Good Period's website is at www.bloodygoodperiod. com/#intro (accessed 10 February 2020).

21 Anna Maria van Eijk et al., 'Menstrual Cup Use, Leakage, Acceptability, Safety and Availability: A Systematic Review and Meta-Analysis', *The Lancet* 4:8, August 2019, pp. 376–93. See also Elizabeth Peberdy et al., 'A Study into Public Awareness of the Environmental Impact of Menstrual Products and Product Choice', *Sustainability* 11:2, January 2019, pp. 1–16.

22 See details of the application for Patent No. 70,843, dated 12 November 1867, for a 'rubber sack and ring inserted in the vagina' at https://patents.google.com/patent/US70843 (accessed 10 February 2020).

23 Marion Renault, 'Menstrual cups were invented in 1867. What took them so long to gain popularity?', Popular Science website, 23 August 2019, www.popsci.com/menstrual-cups-history-period-care.

24 Van Eijk et al., 'Menstrual Cup Use'.

25 'Sanitary Product Provision for Inpatients', British Medical Association website, www.bma.org.uk/collective-voice/policy-and-research/public-and-population-health/sanitary-product-provision-for-inpatients (accessed 10 February 2020).

26 Ibid.

27 Steven Swinford, '8,000 People Get Tummy Tucks on NHS', *The Telegraph*, 28 December 2013, www.telegraph. co.uk/news/health/news/10540553/8000-people-get-tummy-tucks-on-NHS.html.

28 'France to help fund removal of breast implants', *Financial Times*, 23 December 2011, www.ft.com/content/9b2923d6-2d45-11e1-b5bf-00144feabdc0.

29 Freddie Whittaker, 'DfE seeks company for £20m contract to supply sanitary products to schools', Schools Week website,

14 June 2019, https://schoolsweek.co.uk/dfe-seeks-company-for-20m-contract-to-supply-sanitary-products-to-schools.

30  See www.periodequity.org (accessed 10 February 2020).

31  See www.taxfreeperiod.com (accessed 10 February 2020).

32  Chris Dehnel, 'Rep: Tampon Tax Elimination was "Fair" Thing to Do', Patch website, 3 July 2018, https://patch.com/connecticut/manchester/rep-tampon-tax-elimination-was-fair-thing-do. Connecticut removed the sales tax on sanitary products in 2018. North Dakota retains a tampon tax at the time of writing.

33  Emma Court, 'New York is latest state to scrap tampon tax', MarketWatch website, 12 April 2016, www.marketwatch.com/story/this-is-how-much-the-tampon-tax-costs-women-2016-03-24.

34  In 2017, President Obama said that women make better leaders: Zameena Mejia, 'Barack Obama says women make better leaders – and data shows he's right', *CNBC*, 4 December 2017, www.cnbc.com/2017/12/04/barack-obama-says-women-make-better-leaders-and-data-shows-hes-right.html.

35  When President Obama said this in 2016 the figure was forty US states. At the time of writing, thirty-five states retained tax on sanitary products.

36  Annalisa Merelli, 'The "tampon tax" in Greece just got a lot steeper', *Quartz*, 20 July 2015, https://qz.com/458404/the-tampon-tax-in-greece-just-got-a-lot-steeper.

37  Anthee Carassava, 'Greek students sell sex for food', *The Times*, 27 November 2015, www.thetimes.co.uk/article/greek-students-sell-sex-for-food-ngp6bkp79.

38  Natasha Bach, '35 States in the US Still Charge Women a Tampon Tax', *Fortune*, 11 June 2019, https://fortune.com/2019/06/11/tampon-tax-us-states.

39  Claer Barrett, 'Even women who can handle money are reluctant investors', *Financial Times*, 8 March 2018, www.ft.com/content/2e77b322-fd0c-11e7-9bfc-052cbba03425.

40  Nadine Schmidt and Sheena McKenzie, 'Tampons will no longer be taxed as luxury items, after landmark German vote', *CNN*, 8 November 2019, https://edition.cnn.com/2019/11/08/europe/tampon-tax-germany-luxury-item-grm-intl/index.html.

41  Department for Digital, Culture, Media & Sport and Office for Civil Society, 'Tampon Tax Fund application form: 2019–20 funding round', available at www.gov.uk/government/publications/tampon-tax-fund-application-form-2019-2020-funding-round (accessed 10 February 2020).

42  Gina Reiss-Wilchins, 'Kenya and Menstrual Equity: What you didn't know', *Huffington Post*, 29 March 2016, www.huffpost.com/entry/kenya-menstrual-equity-wh_b_9557270.

43  Macharia Kamau, 'Sanitary towel usage still low despite tax cuts', *Standard Media Kenya*, 9 June 2009, www.standardmedia.co.ke/business/article/1144016386/sanitary-towel-usage-still-low-despite-tax-cuts.

*Chapter 8: 'Women's Problems'*

1  Tomi-Ann Roberts et al., '"Feminine Protection": the Effects of Menstruation on Attitudes Towards Women', *Psychology of Women Quarterly* 26:2, June 2002, pp. 131–9.

2  Michael Alison Chandler, 'This woman said she was fired for leaking menstrual blood at work', *The Washington Post*, 11 September 2017, www.washingtonpost.com/local/social-issues/ga-woman-said-she-was-fired-for-leaking-during-her-period-at-work-the-aclu-is-suing-for-discrimination/2017/09/08/50fab924-8d97-11e7-8df5-c2e5cf46c1e2_story.html.

3 'Norwegian alarm system monitors length of office lavatory visits', *The Telegraph*, 31 January 2012, www.telegraph.co.uk/news/newstopics/howaboutthat/9051774/Norwegian-alarm-system-monitors-length-of-office-lavatory-visits.html. See also Ian Sparks, 'Call centre workers limited to EIGHT minutes toilet time per day . . . and risk triggering alarm if they go one second over', *Daily Mail*, 31 January 2012, www.dailymail.co.uk/news/article-2094374/Norway-centre-workers-EIGHT-minutes-toilet-time-day-monitored-alarm.html.

4 Javier Ruiz, 'La Inspección de Trabajo investiga a dos empresas que obligaban a sus empleadas a colgarse un cartel para ir al baño', *El País*, 4 October 2011, https://elpais.com/sociedad/2011/10/04/actualidad/1317679210_850215.html.

5 John Naughton, '"The goal is to automate us": welcome to the age of surveillance capitalism', *The Guardian*, 20 January 2019, www.theguardian.com/technology/2019/jan/20/shoshana-zuboff-age-of-surveillance-capitalism-google-facebook.

6 Aneri Pattani, 'In Some Countries, Women Get Days Off for Period Pain', *The New York Times*, 24 July 2017, www.nytimes.com/2017/07/24/health/period-pain-paid-time-off-policy.html.

7 'Zambia's controversial menstrual leave law', TRT World website, 30 January 2017, www.trtworld.com/life/zambian-women-can-take-menstrual-leave-but-some-say-its-not-fair-286497.

8 Christine Chen, 'Employment and employee benefits in Taiwan: overview', Thomson Reuters Practical Law, 1 January 2020, https://uk.practicallaw.thomsonreuters.com/9-633-4823?transitionType=Default&contextData=(sc.Default)&firstPage=true&bhcp=1.

9  Anna Momigliano, 'Giving Italian women "menstrual leave" may backfire on their job prospects', *The Washington Post*, 24 March 2017, www.washingtonpost.com/news/worldviews/wp/2017/03/24/giving-italian-women-menstrual-leave-may-backfire-on-their-job-prospects.

10 Camilla Long, 'Thanks, Jeremy, but we working women will give the weeping and wailing room a miss', *The Sunday Times*, 10 November 2019, www.thetimes.co.uk/article/thanks-jeremy-but-we-working-women-will-give-the-weeping-and-wailing-room-a-miss-omtwh3ct3.

11 '40% of women are taking days off. Should we have paid period leave?', *ABC News*, 8 August 2018, www.abc.net.au/triplej/programs/hack/should-we-have-paid-period-leave/10090848. HM Government, 'Gender equality at every stage: a roadmap for change', Government Equalities Office report, July 2019, available at https://assets.publishing.service.gov.uk/government/uploads/system/uploads/attachment_data/file/821889/GEO_GEEE_Strategy_Gender_Equality_Road map_Rev_1__1_.pdf (accessed 10 February 2020).

12 See 'Menopause: Symptoms', NHS website, www.nhs.uk/conditions/menopause/symptoms (accessed 10 February 2020) and HM Government, 'Menopause transition: effects on women's economic participation', Government Equalities Office report, July 2017, available at www.gov.uk/government/publications/menopause-transition-effects-on-womens-economic-participation (accessed 10 February 2020).

13 See p. 38 of 'Insuring Women's Futures', Chartered Insurance Institute report, www.cii.co.uk/media/9224351/iwf_moments thatmatter_full.pdf (accessed 10 February 2020).

14 HM Government, 'Menopause transition: effects on women's economic participation', p. 22.

15 Ibid., p. 9.

16 Ibid., p. 46.

17 'Championing diversity', North Lincolnshire Council website, www.northlincs.gov.uk/community-advice-and-support/championing-diversity (accessed 10 February 2020).

18 'Dismissal without taking account of menopause symptoms – discriminatory and unfair', Pure Employment Law website, 22 May 2012, www.pureemploymentlaw.co.uk/dismissal-without-taking-account-of-menopause-symptoms-discriminatory-and-unfair.

19 HM Government, 'Menopause transition: effects on women's economic participation', p. 12.


*Chapter 9: The Gendered Housing Crisis*

1 Sara Reis, 'A Home of Her Own: Women and Housing', Women's Budget Group, July 2019, p. 12, available at https://wbg.org.uk/analysis/reports/a-home-of-her-own-housing-and-women (accessed 13 July 2020).

2 Ibid.

3 Ibid.

4 'Over 4,000 domestic abuse arrests made since COVID-19 restrictions introduced', Metropolitan Police website, 24 April 2020, http://news.met.police.uk/news/over-4000-domestic-abuse-arrests-made-since-covid-19-restrictions-introduced-400900 (accessed 6 July 2020).

5 Stephen Little, 'New Homes Unaffordable for Eight out of Ten Families', What Mortgage website, 2 March 2017, www.whatmortgage.co.uk/news/first-time-buyers/new-homes-unaffordable-eight-10-families.

6 'A timeline of the 18 housing ministers since 1997', *Inside Housing*, 13 February 2020, www.insidehousing.co.uk/insight/

insight/a-timeline-of-the-18-housing-ministers-since-1997-
65065.

7 'Fixing Our Broken Housing Market', Ministry of Housing,
Communities & Local Government, 7 February 2017, www.
gov.uk/government/publications/fixing-our-broken-housing-
market.

8 Dawn Foster, 'Number of MP Landlords Has Risen By a
Quarter Since Last Parliament', *The Guardian*, 14 January 2016,
www.theguardian.com/housing-network/2016/jan/14/mp-
landlords-number-risen-quarter-last-parliament-housing-bill.
Liane Wimhurst, 'Theresa May earns more than £10,000 a
year from rented London flat', *inews*, 27 October 2017, https://
inews.co.uk/news/uk/theresa-may-earns-10000-year-rented-
london-flat-100100.

9 Marc da Silva, 'Which Political Party Has Been Best for
Landlords and Tenants?', *Landlord Today*, 30 August 2019,
www.landlordtoday.co.uk/breaking-news/2019/8/which-
political-party-has-been-best-for-landlords-and-tenants.

10 Anna White, 'Gender pay gap UK 2019: Women have to
save two years longer than men to buy a home', *Homes and
Property*, 5 April 2019, https://www.homesandproperty.co.uk/
property-news/gender-pay-gap-uk-2019-women-have-to-
save-two-years-longer-than-men-to-buy-a-home-a129391.
html.

11 'English Housing Survey 2015–16: First Time Buyers', Ministry of Housing, Communities and Local Government report,
13 July 2017, p. 8, www.gov.uk/government/statistics/english-
housing-survey-2015-to-2016-first-time-buyers.

12 Ibid.

13 Paul Goldsmith-Pinkham and Kelly Shue, 'The Gender Gap
in Housing Returns', Yale School of Management paper,

March 2020, p. 6, available at https://papers.ssrn.com/sol3/papers.cfm?abstract_id=3559892 (accessed 23 July 2020).

14 Ibid.

15 Ping Cheng et al., 'Do Women Pay More for Mortgages?', *The Journal of Real Estate Finance and Economics* 43:4, 2011, pp. 423–40.

16 Laurie Goodman et al., 'Women Are Better Than Men at Paying Their Mortgages', Urban Institute research report, September 2016, www.urban.org/sites/default/files/publication/84206/2000930-Women-Are-Better-Than-Men-At-Paying-Their-Mortgages.pdf (accessed 15 July 2020).

17 'Santander First Time Buyer Study', Santander website report, July 2019, p. 13, www.santander.co.uk/assets/s3fs-public/documents/santander-first-time-buyer-study.pdf (accessed 15 July 2020).

18 Ibid.

19 'Female first time buyers have bigger home ownership dreams – but confidence to buy alone remains low', Aldermore Bank website, 1 November 2019, www.aldermore.co.uk/about-us/newsroom/2019/11/female-first-time-buyers-have-bigger-home-ownership-dreams-but-confidence-to-buy-alone-remains-low.

20 Danièle Voldman, 'Gender Discrimination in Housing?', *Encyclopédie pour une histoire numérique de l'Europe*, 21 March 2018, http://ehne.fr/en/node/1232.

21 Anthony Bem, 'Removal of the expression "bon père de famille" from the French legal vocabulary', LegaVox website, 22 August 2014, www.legavox.fr/blog/maitre-anthony-bem/suppression-expression-pere-famille-vocabulaire-15730.htm.

22 This applies when tenants have an 'assured shorthold tenancy', the most common kind of rental agreement.

23 'Touch and go: how to protect private renters from retaliatory eviction in England', Citizens Advice website, 26 September 2018, www.citizensadvice.org.uk/about-us/policy/policy-research-topics/housing-policy-research/Touch-and-go.

24 Ministry of Housing, Communities & Local Government, 'Homelessness code of guidance for local authorities', updated 29 June 2020, available at www.gov.uk/guidance/homeless ness-code-of-guidance-for-local-authorities/chapter-8-priority-need (accessed 29 November 2020).

25 The Department of Social Security was replaced with the Department for Work and Pensions in 2001; however, the term 'DSS' is still used in common parlance.

26 Hannah Richardson, 'Legal victories over "No DSS" letting agents', BBC News, 27 February 2020, www.bbc.co.uk/news/education-51642316.

27 Lucie Heath, 'More than 90% of homes unaffordable for those on housing benefit, NHF reveals', Inside Housing, 7 October 2019, www.insidehousing.co.uk/news/news/more-than-90-of-homes-unaffordable-for-those-on-housing-be nefit-nhf-reveals-63593.

28 Ibid.

29 These figures originally appeared in 'Housing benefit freeze could fuel homelessness, report warns' on the Money Wise web-site (now archived). For the single room figures, see James Andrews, 'Universal Credit not even enough to cover renting a room in a shared house', The Mirror, 6 February 2020, www.mir-ror.co.uk/money/universal-credit-not-even-enough-21440838.

30 Marilyn Howard and Amy Skipp, 'Unequal, trapped and con-trolled: Women's experience of financial abuse and potential implications for Universal Credit', Women's Aid report, March 2015, www.womensaid.org.uk/financial-abuse-report (accessed 26 June 2020).

31  Jamie Grierson, 'Council funding for women's refuges cut by nearly £7m since 2010', *The Guardian*, 23 March 2018, www.theguardian.com/society/2018/mar/23/council-funding-womens-refuges-cut-since-2010-england-wales-scotland.

32  Ministry of Housing, Communities & Local Government, 'Homelessness code of guidance for local authorities'.

33  Mara Bolis and Christine Hughes, 'Women's economic empowerment and domestic violence', Oxfam report, 2015, available at https://s3.amazonaws.com/oxfam-us/www/static/media/files/Womens_Empowerment_and_Domestic_Vio lence_-_Boris__Hughes_hX7LscW.pdf (accessed 30 November 2020).

*Chapter 10: Free Carers*

1  Giselle Cory and Alfie Sterling, 'Pay and Parenthood: An Analysis of Wage Inequality Between Mums and Dads', Institute for Public Policy Research report, 2016, available at www.tuc.org.uk/sites/default/files/Pay_and_Parenthood_Touch stone_Extra_2016_LR.pdf (accessed 10 February 2020).

2  Ibid. This report was based on data from the 1970 British Cohort Study, which follows the lives of more than 17,000 people born in England, Scotland and Wales in a single week of 1970.

3  'Fathers working full-time earn 21% more than men without children', TUC website, 25 April 2016, www.tuc.org.uk/news/fathers-working-full-time-earn-21-more-men-without-children-says-tuc.

4  Ibid.

5  Ibid.

6 'Motherhood Penalty for Women and Daddy Bonus for Men', Fawcett Society website, 8 March 2016, www.fawcettsociety. org.uk/news/motherhood-penalty-for-women-and-daddy-bonus-for-men.

7 Claire Cain Miller, 'The Motherhood Penalty vs. the Fatherhood Bonus', *The New York Times*, 6 September 2014, www. nytimes.com/2014/09/07/upshot/a-child-helps-your-career-if-youre-a-man.html.

8 Michelle J. Budig, 'The Fatherhood Bonus and the Motherhood Penalty: Parenthood and the Gender Gap in Pay', Third Way website, 2 September 2014, www.thirdway.org/report/ the-fatherhood-bonus-and-the-motherhood-penalty-parent hood-and-the-gender-gap-in-pay.

9 Nancy Folbre, 'Rich Mom, Poor Mom', *The New York Times*, 25 October 2020, https://economix.blogs.nytimes.com/2010/ 10/25/rich-mom-poor-mom.

10 Jane VC, 'Jane VC Founder Survey Reveals Inequities in Tech Start Early', *Medium*, 21 March 2019, https://medium. com/janeventurecapital/jane-vc-founder-survey-reveals-inequities-in-tech-start-early-bb55a443d703.

11 Gregg McClymont, 'Call to end the "motherhood penalty" grows louder', *Financial Times Adviser*, 4 June 2019, www. ft adviser.com/pensions/2019/06/04/call-to-end-the-mother hood-penalty-grows-louder.

12 The OECD released figures which showed that England has the highest nursery costs in the world for some families. How much families pay depends on their situation because there is a tax-incentive scheme for some parents. But for the typical two-parent family who are both in work and aren't receiving benefits, they can expect to pay among the highest nursery fees of its thirty-seven member nations. For more information see: 'Childcare: Do UK parents pay the most in

the world?', *BBC News*, 13 February 2018, www.bbc.co.uk/news/uk-42966047.

13  Maya Oppenheim, 'One in four childcare providers could close as 30 hours free funding falls short', *The Independent*, 11 November 2019, www.independent.co.uk/news/uk/home-news/childcare-providers-financial-issues-30-hours-government-a9195796.html.

14  'Childcare and early years survey of parents in England, 2018', Department for Education report, 2018, p. 15, available at https://assets.publishing.service.gov.uk/government/uploads/system/uploads/attachment_data/file/766498/Childcare_and_Early_Years_Survey_of_Parents_in_England_2018.pdf (accessed 30 November 2020).

15  'Parents of disabled children and paid work', Working Families report, 2018, p. 8, available at https://workingfamilies.org.uk/wp-content/uploads/2018/07/WF-2018-Off-Balance-pages-FINAL.pdf (accessed 30 November 2020).

16  Cory and Sterling, 'Pay and Parenthood'.

17  Research from Coram Family and Childcare Trust is available here: www.familyandchildcaretrust.org/childcare-survey-2019 (accessed 30 November 2020).

18  'Women shoulder the responsibility of "unpaid work"', Office for National Statistics website, 10 November 2016, www.ons.gov.uk/employmentandlabourmarket/peopleinwork/earningsandworkinghours/articles/womenshouldertheresponsibilityofunpaidwork/2016-11-10.

19  Ibid.

20  Gemma Hartley, *Fed Up: Navigating and Redefining Emotional Labour for Good* (London: Yellow Kite Books, 2018).

21  Sharon Sassler, 'A Reversal in Predictors of Sexual Frequency and Satisfaction in Marriage', Council on Contemporary

Families website, 20 June 2016, https://contemporaryfamilies. org/sex-equalmarriages.

22 Yasemin Besen-Cassino and Dan Cassino, 'Division of House Chores and the Curious Case of Cooking: The Effects of Earning Inequality on House Chores among Dual-Earner Couples', *Rivista internazionale di studi di genere* 3:6, 2014, pp. 25–53.

23 Kenneth Matos, 'Modern Families: Same- and different-sex couples negotiating at home', Families and Work Institute report, 2015, www.familiesandwork.org/downloads/modern-families.pdf (accessed 10 February 2020).

24 Alan Manning and Barbara Petrongolo, 'The Part-Time Pay Penalty for Women in Britain', *The Economic Journal* 118, 2008, available at http://personal.lse.ac.uk/petrongo/*Manning_*Petrongolo_EJF.pdf (accessed 1 December 2020).

25 Katrin Bennhold, 'In Sweden, Men Can Have It All', *The New York Times*, 10 June 2010, www.nytimes.com/2010/06/10/world/europe/10iht-sweden.html.

26 Mark Rice-Oxley, 'MPs call for 12 weeks of paternity leave to address gender pay gap', *The Guardian*, 20 March 2018, www.theguardian.com/money/2018/mar/20/mps-call-for-12-weeks-of-paternity-leave-to-address-gender-pay-gap.

27 Akriti Manandhar, 'Should paternity leave in Nepal be extended?', *The Annapurna Express*, 6 September 2019, https://theannapurnaexpress.com/news/should-paternity-leave-in-nepal- be-extended-1876.

28 Besen-Cassino and Cassino, 'Division of House Chores and the Curious Case of Cooking'.

29 Noele Illien, 'Switzerland Votes to Approve Paternity Leave', *The New York Times*, 27 September 2020, www.nytimes.com/2020/09/27/world/europe/switzerland-paternity-leave.html.

30 Sarah Jarvis and Stephen P. Jenkins, 'Marital Splits and Income Changes: Evidence from the British Household Panel Survey', *Population Studies* 53:2, 1999, pp. 237–54.

31 Jane Croft, 'Sir Chris Hohn told to give ex-wife third of $1.5bn fortune', *Financial Times*, 12 December 2014, www.ft.com/content/3afcbe26-8221-11e4-ace7-00144feabdc0.

32 The Court of Appeal documents can be accessed here: www.bailii.org/ew/cases/EWCA/Civ/2019/2262.html (accessed 20 June 2020).

33 Ibid.

34 'Spousal maintenance landmark ruling', Winston Solicitors website,www.winstonsolicitors.co.uk/blog/spousal-maintenance-landmark-ruling.html (accessed 20 June 2020).

35 Divorce settlement figures from the UK's family courts, part of the Ministry of Justice. For the pension figures, see Chetan Jethwa, 'Understanding the Gender Pensions Gap', Pensions Policy Institute paper, July 2019, pp. 2–17, www.pensionspolicyinstitute.org.uk/media/3227/20190711-under standing-the-gender-pensions-gap.pdf (accessed 20 June 2020).

36 'Access to British justice increasingly only for the few – Law Society warns ministers', Law Society press release, 28 September 2018, www.lawsociety.org.uk/news/press-releases/access-to-british-justice-increasingly-only-for-the-few.

37 'Solicitors' guideline hourly rates', HM Courts & Tribunal Service,19April2010,www.gov.uk/guidance/solicitors-guideline-hourly-rates.

38 Amelia Hill, 'How legal aid cuts filled family courts with bewildered litigants', *The Guardian*, 26 December 2018, www.theguardian.com/law/2018/dec/26/how-legal-aid-cuts-filled-family-courts-with-bewildered-litigants.

39 'Representing yourself in Court by the Bar Council', Leeds Law Society website, April 2013, http://leedslawsociety.

org.uk/court-notice-board/litigants-in-person/representing-yourself-in-court-by-the-bar-council-april-2013 (accessed 20 June 2020).

40 Janet Allbeson, 'Government has quietly published reports on the impact of child maintenance reforms. Here's what you need to know', London School of Economics blog, 27 February 2017, https://blogs.lse.ac.uk/politicsandpolicy/dwp-surveys-child-maintenance-reforms.

*Chapter 11: Reproductive Rights*

1 Kate Bahn et al., 'Do US TRAP Laws Trap Women into Bad Jobs?', *Feminist Economics* 26:1, August 2019, pp. 44–97.

2 'Section 191.724: Discrimination based on religious beliefs or moral convictions prohibited, health plan coverage of abortion – no mandatory employee coverage of certain procedures – attorney general to enforce – sterilization defined', US Law, Justia, MO Rev Stat § 191.724 (2012), https://law.justia.com/codes/missouri/2012/titlexii/chapter191/section191724 (accessed 10 February 2020).

3 The article has been taken offline but these remarks were widely reported: Irin Carmon, 'Peggy Noonan is Wrong about Your Birth Control', *Salon*, 13 September 2012, www.salon.com/2012/09/13/peggy_noonan_is_wrong_about_your_birth_control.

4 This data is from the 2011 Harvard Center for Population and Development Studies: Simran Khosla, 'This map shows you all the places where the pill is free', Public Radio International website, 3 January 2015, www.pri.org/stories/2015-01-03/map-shows-you-all-places-where-pill-free and Zack Beauchamp, 'Here's a map of the countries where the pill is fully

subsidized (it includes Iran)', *Vox*, 30 June 2014, www.vox. com/2014/6/30/5857904/where-the-pill-is-free.

5 'How do I get birth control pills?', Planned Parenthood website, www.plannedparenthood.org/learn/birth-control/ birth-control-pill/how-do-i-get-birth-control-pills (accessed 10 February 2020).

6 'Parental leave systems', OECD report, August 2019, www. oecd.org/els/soc/PF2_1_Parental_leave_systems.pdf (accessed 10 February 2020).

7 Elizabeth Nash et al., 'Policy Trends in the States, 2017', Guttmacher Institute report, January 2018, www.guttmacher.org/ article/2018/01/policy-trends-states-2017 (accessed 10 February 2020).

8 Ibid.

9 U. D. Upadhyay et al., 'The effect of abortion on having and achieving aspirational one-year plans', *BMC Women's Health* 15:102, November 2015, pp. 1–10.

10 Bahn et al., 'Do US TRAP Laws Trap Women?'

11 US Department of Justice report, 'Attorney General Eric Holder Announces Revisions to the Uniform Crime Report's Definition of Rape', FBI website, 6 January 2012, https:// archives.fbi.gov/archives/news/pressrel/press-releases/ attorney-general-eric-holder-announces-revisions-to-the- uniform-crime-reports-definition-of-rape.

12 Rick Rojas and Alan Blinder, 'Alabama Abortion Ban is Temporarily Blocked by a Federal Judge', *The New York Times*, 29 October 2019, www.nytimes.com/2019/10/29/us/alabama- abortion-ban.html.

13 Mara Gordon and Alyson Hurt, 'Early Abortion Bans: Which States Have Passed Them?', NPR website, 5 June 2019, www. npr.org/sections/health-shots/2019/06/05/729753903/early- abortion-bans-which-states-have-passed-them.

14 'Trump is not a lawyer – Ruth Bader Ginsburg', *BBC News*, 17 December 2019, www.bbc.com/news/world-us-canada-50829474.

15 Pam Belluck, 'Planned Parenthood Refuses Federal Funds Over Abortion Restrictions', *The New York Times*, 19 August 2019, www.nytimes.com/2019/08/19/health/planned-par enthood-title-x.html. See also Compliance with Statutory Program Integrity Requirements: A Rule by the Health and Human Services Department on 03/04/2019, Federal Register, March 2019 at www.federalregister.gov/documents/2019/ 03/04/2019-03461/compliance-with-statutory-program-integrity-requirements.

16 Statistics from 'What is the Global Gag Rule?', Open Society Foundations website, www.opensocietyfoundations.org/ explainers/what-global-gag-rule (accessed 10 February 2020).

17 Liz Ford and Nadia Khomami, 'Trump administration halts money to UN population fund over abortion rules', *The Guardian*, 4 April 2017, www.theguardian.com/global-devel opment/2017/apr/04/trump-administration-un-population-fund-abortion. See also the FAQs on the United Nations Population Fund website: www.unfpa.org/frequently-asked-questions (accessed 10 February 2020).

18 'US withdraws funding for United Nations Population Fund', *BBC News*, 4 April 2017, www.bbc.co.uk/news/world-us-canada-39487617. See also 'Trump Administration Guts Funding to United Nations Population Fund', Center for Reproductive Rights website, https://reproductiverights.org/ press-room/trump-administration-guts-funding-to-united-nations-population-fund (accessed 10 February 2020).

19 Miranda Bryant, 'Global gag rule linked to abortion rise in African countries that accept US aid', *The Guardian*, 27

June 2019, www.theguardian.com/global-development/2019/jun/27/global-gag-rule-africa-abortion-study. See also Nina Brooks et al., 'USA aid policy and induced abortion in sub-Saharan Africa: an analysis of the Mexico City Policy', *The Lancet* 7:8, August 2019, pp. 1046–53.

20 Brooks et al., 'USA aid policy and induced abortion'.

21 'Prescribing Chaos in Global Health: The Global Gag Rule from 1984–2018', Center for Health and Gender Equity report, June 2018, available at www.genderhealth.org/files/uploads/change/publications/Prescribing_Chaos_in_Global_ Health_full_report.pdf (accessed 10 February 2020).

22 April Dembosky, 'March Madness Vasectomies Encourage Guys to Take One for the Team', *Kaiser Health News*, 29 March 2017, https://khn.org/news/march-madness-vasectomies-encourage-guys-to-take-one-for-the-team.

23 Henry Layte, 'Man up, guys – you're a snip away from being heroes', *The Guardian*, 24 June 2017, www.theguardian.com/lifeandstyle/2017/jun/24/man-up-guys-snip-vasectomy-women-contraception.

24 Ari Altstedter, 'A New Kind of Male Birth Control is Coming', *Bloomberg*, 29 March 2017, www.bloomberg.com/news/features/2017-03-29/a-new-kind-of-male-birth-control-is-coming.

25 Sarah Boseley, 'Number of vasectomies in England falls 64% in 10 years', *The Guardian*, 21 October 2016, www.theguardian.com/society/2016/oct/21/number-of-vasectomies-in-england-falls-64-in-10-years.

26 'How do I get a vasectomy?', Planned Parenthood website, www.plannedparenthood.org/learn/birth-control/vasectomy/how-do-i-get-vasectomy (accessed 10 February 2020).

27 'Vasectomy prices', British Pregnancy Advisory Service website, www.bpas.org/more-services-information/vasectomy/vasectomy-prices (accessed 10 February 2020).

28 Kimberly Daniels and Joyce C. Abma, 'Current Contraceptive Status Among Women Aged 15–49: United States, 2015–2017', National Center for Health Statistics, December 2018, www.cdc.gov/nchs/products/databriefs/db327.htm (accessed 10 February 2020).

29 In Britain, there were 9.8 deaths for every 100,000 live births in 2014–16, compared to 8.8 deaths in 2013–15: 'More action needed to prevent maternal deaths across the UK', Oxford University website, 1 November 2018, www.ox.ac.uk/news/2018-11-01-more-action-needed-prevent-maternal-deaths-across-uk. In Sweden, there were 4.4 deaths per 100,000 live births in 2015: Anita Slomski, 'Why do hundreds of US women die annually in childbirth?', JAMA Network website, 13 March 2019, https://jamanetwork.com/journals/jama/fullarticle/2728576.

30 Sophie Wickham et al., 'Assessing the health impact of austerity and rising poverty in the UK', Department of Public Health and Policy, University of Liverpool report, 2018, available at www.ohchr.org/Documents/Issues/EPoverty/UnitedKingdom/2018/Academics/University_of_Liverpool_Department_of_Public_Helath_and_Policy.pdf (accessed 10 February 2020).

31 'More action needed to prevent maternal deaths across the UK', Oxford University website, 1 November 2018, www.ox.ac.uk/news/2018-11-01-more-action-needed-prevent-maternal-deaths-across-uk.

32 'America's High Maternal Mortality and What Can Be Done', Center for Health Journalism website, 4 October 2017, www.centerforhealthjournalism.org/content/america%E2%80%99s-high-maternal-mortality-what-can-be-done.

33 Alison Young, 'Maternal deaths and injuries: top 10 take-aways from USA TODAY investigation of hospitals', *USA Today*, 17 December 2019, https://eu.usatoday.com/story/news/investiga tions/deadly-deliveries/2019/03/11/maternal-deaths-injuries-hospital-childbirth-investigation-findings/310 9269002.

34 Cara Heuser and Chavi Eve Karkowsky, 'Why is US Maternal Mortality So High?', *Slate*, 23 May 2017, https://slate.com/technology/2017/05/medical-error-isnt-to-blame-for-our-high-maternal-mortality-rate.html. See also Michelle H. Moniz et al., 'Population-level factors associated with maternal mortality in the United States, 1997–2012', *BMC Public Health* 18:1007, 2018, pp. 1–7.

35 Slomski, 'Why do hundreds of US women die annually in childbirth?'

36 Dennis Thompson, 'CDC: Many Maternal Deaths Months After Delivery', Web MD website, 7 May 2019, www.webmd.com/baby/news/20190507/cdc-many-maternal-deaths-months-after-delivery.

37 Slomski, 'Why do hundreds of US women die annually in childbirth?'

38 'Pregnancy-related deaths', Centers for Disease Control and Prevention website, www.cdc.gov/vitalsigns/maternal-deaths/index.html (accessed 10 February 2020).

39 Munira Z. Gunja et al., 'What is the Status of Women's Health and Health Care in the US Compared to Ten Other Countries?', The Commonwealth Fund website, 19 December 2018, www.commonwealthfund.org/publications/issue-briefs/2018/dec/womens-health-us-compared-ten-other-countries.

40 Rachel Jones, 'American women are still dying at alarming rates while giving birth', *National Geographic*, 13 December

2018,www.nationalgeographic.com/culture/2018/12/maternal-mortality-usa-health-motherhood.

*Chapter 12: The Pay Gap*

1 Claudia Patricolo, 'In Some Countries, the Emerging Europe Gender Pay Gap is Below EU Average', Emerging Europe website, 12 March 2018, https://emerging-europe.com/news/countries-emerging-europe-gender-pay-gap-eu-average.

2 Michel Christian, 'The Gender of Communism', *Encyclopédie pour une histoire numérique de l'Europe*, available at https://ehne.fr/en/article/gender-and-europe/gender-and-revolution-europe-19th-20th-centuries/gender-communism (accessed 10 February 2020).

3 An excellent book on this subject is Kristen R. Ghodsee, *Why Women Have Better Sex Under Socialism: And Other Arguments for Economic Independence* (London: Bodley Head, 2018).

4 Grant Thornton, 'Women in Business Report', 2019, available atwww.grantthornton.global/en/insights/women-in-business-2019/women-in-business-report-2019 (accessed 10 February 2020).

5 Frances Jenner, 'Chile has highest gender pay gap in OECD, fingers point at education system', *Chile Herald*, 12 September 2018, https://chileherald.com/gender-pay-gap-chile-oecd/1433.

6 'Two-thirds of gender pay gap "cannot be explained" says ONS', *Financial Times*, 17 January 2018, www.ft.com/content/f104523e-88fc-3cc5-9110-fd6dfoc00169.

7 'Research on the gender gap in New Zealand', Ministry for Women New Zealand website, https://women.govt.nz/work-skills/income/gender-pay-gap/research-evidence-gap-new-zealand (accessed 10 February 2020).

8   'Explained and unexplained share in gender wage gap', Federal Statistical Office website, www.bfs.admin.ch/bfs/en/home/statistics/catalogues-databases/graphs.assetdetail.8186855.html (accessed 10 February 2020).

9   Gabriela Inchauste et al., 'Trying to explain the gender pay gap in Europe', World Bank website blog, 3 April 2018, https://blogs.worldbank.org/developmenttalk/trying-explain-gender-pay-gap-europe.

10  Tom Schuller, *The Paula Principle: How and Why Women Work Below Their Level of Competence* (London: Scribe Publications, 2017), p. 3.

11  'The State of Wage Inequality in the Workplace', Hired.com website, https://hired.com/page/wage-inequality-report (accessed 10 February 2020).

12  Research from the Melbourne Institute found that there are significant disparities in the minimum wage and the difference is largely due to the relatively low value we place on women's work. A childcare worker with a Certificate III qualification is paid an award rate of $21.29 per hour, compared to a metal fitter with the same level of qualifications, who earns the award rate of $39.47 per hour.

13  MaryAnn Busso, 'Women Close Gender Pay Gap in Two STEM Jobs, Lag in Others', *Bloomberg*, 2 June 2017, www.bloomberg.com/graphics/2017-women-stem-jobs.

14  Ibid.

15  'ILO: Women in Europe "better educated but paid less"', *BBC News*, 5 December 2014, www.bbc.co.uk/news/business-30340870.

16  'Global wage growth lowest since 2008, while women still earning 20 per cent less than men', International Labour Organization website, 26 November 2018, www.ilo.org/moscow/news/WCMS_650551/lang--en/index.htm.

17  Jenna Johnson, 'One year out of college, women already paid less than men, report finds', *The Washington Post*, 24 October 2012, www.washingtonpost.com/local/education/one-year-out-of-college-women-already-paid-less-than-men-report-finds/2012/10/23/ece71cb0-1d3a-11e2-9cd5-b55c38388962_story.html.

18  Stephen Burd (ed.), 'Moving on Up? What a Groundbreaking Study Tells Us About Access, Success and Mobility in Higher Ed', October 2017, available at https://na-production.s3.ama zonaws.com/documents/Moving-on-Up.pdf (accessed 10 February 2020).

19  The most well-known study looked at the Boston Symphony Orchestra: see Claudia Goldin and Cecilia Rose, 'Orchestrating Impartiality: The Impact of "Blind" Auditions on Female Musicians', *American Economic Review* 90:4, September 2000, pp. 715–41. There have since been studies focused on various industries including medicine: Carol Isaac et al., 'Interventions that Affect Gender Bias in Hiring: A Systematic Review', *Academic Medicine: Journal of the Associated American Medical Colleges* 84:10, 2009, pp. 1140–6.

20  Schuller, *The Paula Principle*.

21  'Discovering the glass cliff', University of Exeter Psychology Department website, http://psychology.exeter.ac.uk/impact/theglasscliff (accessed 10 February 2020).

22  Donovan Alexander, 'Global Gender Gap Report: Women CEOs are 45% More Likely to be Fired', Interesting Engineering website, 2 December 2018, https://interestingengineering.com/global-gender-gap-report-women-ceos-are-45-more-likely-to-be-fired.

23  Elizabeth Judge, 'Women on board: help or hindrance?', *The Times*, 11 November 2003, www.thetimes.co.uk/article/women-on-board-help-or-hindrance-2c6fnqf6fng. See also Michelle

Ryan and Alexander Haslam, 'The glass cliff: women left to take charge at times of crisis', *The Times*, 12 November 2018, www.thetimes.co.uk/article/the-glass-cliff-women-taking-charge-but-at-times-of-crisis-czlvzzrns.

24 Corinne A. Moss-Racusin et al., 'Science Faculty's Subtle Gender Biases Favor Male Students', *PNAS* 109:31, October 2012, pp. 16474–9.

25 Lauren Riviera and András Tilcsik, 'Scaling Down Inequality: Ratings Scales, Gender Bias and the Architecture of Evaluation', *American Sociological Review* 84:2, March 2019, pp. 248–74.

26 Monica Biernat and Joan Williams, 'The Language of Performance Evaluations: Gender-Based Shifts in Content and Consistency of Judgment', *Social, Psychological and Personality Science* 3:2, March 2012, pp. 186–92. See also Riviera and Tilcsik, 'Scaling Down Inequality'.

27 Biernat and Williams, 'The Language of Performance Evaluations'.

28 Emilio J. Castilla, 'Gender, Race and Meritocracy in Organizational Careers', *American Journal of Sociology* 113:6, May 2008, pp. 1479–526.

29 Riviera and Tilcsik, 'Scaling Down Inequality'.

30 Juliet Eilperin, 'White House women want to be in the room where it happens', *The Washington Post*, 13 September 2016, www.washingtonpost.com/news/powerpost/wp/2016/09/13/white-house-women-are-now-in-the-room-where-it-happens.

31 'Michelle Obama: "I still have impostor syndrome"', *BBC News*, 4 December 2018, www.bbc.com/news/uk-46434147.

32 Pauline Clance and Suzanne Imes, 'The Imposter Phenomenon in High-Achieving Women: Dynamics and Therapeutic Intervention', *Psychotherapy: Theory, Research and Practice* 15:3, 1978, pp. 241–7.

33 Sheryl Nance-Nash, 'Why imposter syndrome hits women and women of colour harder', *BBC News*, 28 July 2020, www.bbc.com/worklife/article/20200724-why-imposter-syndrome-hits-women-and-women-of-colour-harder.

34 Jenna Goudreau, 'When Women Feel Like Frauds They Fuel Their Own Failures', *Forbes*, 19 October 2011, www.forbes.com/sites/jennagoudreau/2011/10/19/women-feel-like-frauds-failures-tina-fey-sheryl-sandberg/#56ee4d2530fb.

35 Caroline Henshaw, 'Female teachers plagued by "imposter syndrome"', head warns', *TES* website, 19 November 2018, www.tes.com/news/female-teachers-plagued-imposter-syndrome-head-warns.

36 As of 2004, age range 18–23: Rachel Ivie et al., 'Women's and Men's Career Choices in Astronomy and Astrophysics', *Physical Review Physics Education Research* 12, August 2016, available at www.aip.org/sites/default/files/statistics/lsags/PhysRevPhysEducRes.12.020109.pdf (accessed 10 February 2020).

37 Ibid.

38 Ibid.

39 Tara Sophia Mohr, 'Why Women Don't Apply for Jobs Unless They're 100% Qualified', *Harvard Business Review*, 25 August 2014, https://hbr.org/2014/08/why-women-dont-apply-for-jobs-unless-theyre-100-qualified.

40 The Equal Pay Act 1970 came into effect on 29 December 1975, but given that this is two days before the end of the year, for practical purposes it was in effect from 1976.

41 World Economic Forum, 'The Global Gender Gap Report 2020', available at www3.weforum.org/docs/WEF_GGGR_2020.pdf (accessed 1 October 2020)..

42 Nasser Alkalbani et al., 'Gender diversity and say-on-pay: Evidence from UK remuneration committees', *Corporate Governance* 27:5, September 2019, pp. 378–400.

43 Marc Benioff, 'How Salesforce Closed the Pay Gap Between Men and Women', *Wired*, 15 October 2019, www.wired.com/story/how-salesforce-closed-pay-gap-between-men-women.

44 Jena McGregor, 'More States Are Banning Questions about Salary History from Job Interviews', *The Washington Post*, 15 August 2019, www.washingtonpost.com/business/2019/08/15/more-states-are-banning-questions-about-salary-history-job-interviews-what-say-if-youre-asked-about-it-anyways.

45 Ibid.

46 Eva Szalay, 'Tribunal exposes gender gap in banking culture and pay', *Financial Times*, 20 September 2019, www.ft.com/content/84cf64e4-d89e-11e9-8f9b-77216ebe1f17.

47 Benioff, 'How Salesforce Closed the Pay Gap'.

Chapter 13: Beauty Standards and Social Expectations

1 Nigel Henbest, 'A woman's place is in the dome', *New Scientist*, 8 October 1988, p. 62.

2 International Astronomical Union statistics, available at www.iau.org/administration/membership/individual/distribution (accessed 20 June 2020).

3 This is the percentage of professional female astronomers who are members of the International Astronomical Union, www.iau.org/administration/membership/individual/distribution (accessed 20 November 2020).

4 'Global Gender Gap Report 2020', World Economic Forum website, 2020, p. 9, www3.weforum.org/docs/WEF_GGGR_2020.pdf (accessed 20 June 2020).

5 Michele Swers, 'Connecting Descriptive and Substantive Representation: An Analysis of Sex Differences in Cosponsorship Activity', *Legislative Studies Quarterly* 30:3, August 2005, pp. 407–33.

6 Denise Restauri, '5 Stats Prove That Female Senators Get More Done Than Men', *Forbes*, 23 February 2015, www.forbes. com/sites/deniserestauri/2015/02/23/5-stats-prove-that-female-senators-get-more-done-than-men.

7 Michael Lewis, 'Wall Street on the Tundra', *Vanity Fair*, April 2009, https://archive.vanityfair.com/article/2009/4/wall-street-on-the-tundra (accessed 28 November 2020).

8 'Brazilian congressman ordered to pay compensation after rape remark', *The Guardian*, 18 September 2015, www.the guardian. com/world/2015/sep/18/brazilian-congressman-rape-remark-compensation.

9 Lucy Osborne, '"It felt like tentacles": the women who accuse Trump of sexual misconduct', *The Guardian*, 17 September 2020, www.theguardian.com/us-news/2020/sep/17/amy-dorris-donald-trump-women-who-accuse-sexual-misconduct. See also David A. Fahrenthold, 'Trump recorded having extremely lewd conversation about women in 2005', *The Washington Post*, 7 October 2016, www.washingtonpost.com/politics/trump-recorded-having-extremely-lewd-conversation-about-women-in-2005/2016/10/07/3b9ce776-8cb4-11e6-bf8a-3d26847e eed4_story.html.

10 Erik Wemple, 'Studies agree: Media gorged on Hillary Clinton email coverage', *The Washington Post*, 25 August 2017, www.washingtonpost.com/blogs/erik-wemple/wp/2017/08/25/studies-agree-media-gorged-on-hillary-clinton-email-coverage.

11. Robert Verkaik, 'Boris Johnson's burqa remarks are no surprise – his misogyny goes far back', *The Guardian*, 10 August 2018, www.theguardian.com/commentisfree/2018/aug/10/boris-johnson-burqa-misogyny-bigotry-eton-oxford.

12 Boris Johnson, 'The male sex is to blame for the appalling proliferation of single mothers', *The Spectator*, 19 August 1995,

http://archive.spectator.co.uk/article/19th-august-1995/6/politics.

13 Jim Tankersley, 'How Sexism Follows Women From the Cradle to the Workplace', *The New York Times*, 19 August 2018, www.nytimes.com/2018/08/19/business/sexism-women-birth place-workplace.html.

14 Rachel Connor and Susan Fiske, 'Not Minding the Gap: How Hostile Sexism Encourages Choice Explanations for the Gender Income Gap', *Psychology of Women Quarterly* 43:1, 2018, pp. 22–36.

15 Andrei Cimpian and Sarah-Jane Leslie, 'Why Young Girls Don't Think They Are Smart Enough', *The New York Times*, 26 January 2017, www.nytimes.com/2017/01/26/well/family/why-young-girls-dont-think-they-are-smart-enough.html.

16 Lin Bian, Andrei Cimpian and Sarah-Jane Leslie, 'Gender stereotypes about intellectual ability emerge early and influence children's interests', *Science* 255:6323, 2017, pp. 389–91.

17 Seth Stephens-Davidowitz, 'Tell me, Google, is my son a genius?', *The New York Times*, 18 January 2014, www.nytimes. com/2014/01/19/opinion/sunday/google-tell-me-is-my-son-a-genius.html.

18 Ibid.

19 Peggy Orenstein, *Cinderella Ate My Daughter* (New York: HarperCollins, 2011).

20 'What girls say about . . . Equality for girls. Girls' Attitudes Survey 2013', Girlguiding UK website, 2013, www.girlguiding.org.uk/globalassets/docs-and-resources/research-and-campaigns/girls-attitudes-survey-2013.pdf (accessed 30 November 2020).

21 Kate Palmer, 'The morning routine: 30% spend over a week getting ready each year', YouGov website, 10 July 2012, https://today.yougov.com/topics/lifestyle/articles-reports/2012/07/10/morning-routine-30-spend-over-week-getting-ready-e.

22 Emma Halliwell et al., 'Costing the invisible: A review of the evidence examining the links between body image, aspirations, education and workplace confidence', Centre for Appearance Research, 2014, https://uwe-repository.work-tribe.com/output/806655/costing-the-invisible-a-review-of-the-evidence-examining-the-links-between-body-image-aspirations-education-and-workplace-confidence (accessed 20 June 2020).

23 Unity Blott, 'The pink tax strikes again! Girls cost £30,000 MORE to raise than boys', *Daily Mail*, 9 November 2016, www.dailymail.co.uk/femail/article-3920148/Study-finds-girls-cost-30-000-raise-boys.html.

24 Ibid.

25 Dr Linda Papadopoulos, 'Sexualisation of Young People Review', UK Home Office report, 2010, https://dera.ioe.ac.uk/10738/1/sexualisation-young-people.pdf (accessed 20 June 2020).

26 Dan Bilefsky, 'Sent Home for Not Wearing Heels, She Ignited a British Rebellion', *The New York Times*, 25 January 2017, www.nytimes.com/2017/01/25/world/europe/high-heels-british- inquiry-dress-codes-women.html.

27 House of Commons, 'High heels and workplace dress codes', Petitions Committee and Women and Equalities Committee report, 2017, available at https://publications.parliament.uk/pa/cm201617/cmselect/competitions/291/291.pdf (accessed 10 January 2020).

28 Ibid.

29 Adelina M. Broadbridge, *Research Handbook of Diversity and Careers* (Cheltenham: Edward Elgar Publishing, 2018), p. 110.

30 Ibid., p. 109.

31 Ibid., p. 110.

32 Saphora Smith, 'Iceland's Answer to Gender Equality: Compensate for Differences Between Boys, Girls', *NBC News*, 4 October 2018, www.nbcnews.com/news/world/iceland-s-answer-gender-equality-compensate-differences-between-boys-girls-n912606.

*Chapter 15: Let's Talk about Investing*

1 'Facebook Shares Outstanding 2009–2019', Macro Trends website, www.macrotrends.net/stocks/charts/FB/facebook/shares-outstanding (accessed 2 November 2020). See also Facebook's Annual Report, 2018, Form 10-K, p. 1, available at https://s21.q4cdn.com/399680738/files/doc_financials/annual_reports/2018-Annual-Report.pdf (accessed 2 November 2020).

2 At the time of writing, on 6 December 2019.

3 Leslie Picker and Anita Balakrishnan, 'Snap Soars Nearly 50% After Trading Begins', *CNBC*, 2 March 2017, www.cnbc.com/2017/03/01/snapchat-ipo-pricing.html.

4 According to Money Observer. Nina Kelly, 'Top 10 Most Popular Investment Funds: May 2020', 2 June 2020, www.moneyobserver.com/news/top-10-most-popular-investment-funds-may-2020.

# Acknowledgements

This book was a long-held dream and I'm immensely grateful to the people who became believers early on and shared their wisdom so that it could become a reality. Firstly, thanks to Alice Lutyens at Curtis Brown for believing in this project and for introducing me to my now-agent Karolina Sutton. Thank you, Karolina, for your honest feedback, which led to this book going to a ten-way auction. Many thanks to Joanna Lee and Caitlin Leydon at Curtis Brown too.

Next, the whole team at Michael Joseph, who worked so hard to bring this book to life. Thank you, Charlotte Hardman and Ariel Pakier, Lydia Cooper, Sarah Day, Emma Henderson and Ellie Hughes.

To Elisa, Ali, Pepe, Malachy, Elmo, Mum and Dad for always being there for me. Thank you, Dai, for being my friend. To Nuala O'Connell for all your support.

To my clever, talented friends who read early drafts of this book, thank you. Especially Carmen, Izzy, Jessie H, Laura, Nicola B and Jennifer Y.